God's House Is Our House

Re-imagining the Environment for Worship

Richard S. Vosko

Kenrick-Glennon

Seminary Library

Charles L. Souvay Memorial

LITURGICAL PRESS
Collegeville, Minnesota

www.litpress.org

Cover design by David Manahan, o.s.b. Cover photo: Corpus Christi University Parish Church, Toledo, Ohio, by Anne Spenny.

1   2   3   4   5   6   7   8

Library of Congress Cataloging-in-Publication Data

Vosko, Richard S.
  God's house is our house : re-imagining the environment for worship / Richard S. Vosko.
      p. cm.
  Includes bibliographical references and index.
  ISBN-13: 978-0-8146-3014-3 (pbk.)
  ISBN-10: 0-8146-3014-6 (pbk.)
    1. Catholic church buildings.   2. Liturgy and architecture.   3. Church decoration and ornament.   4. Catholic Church.   I. Title.

NA4828.V67 2006
246'.9582—dc22

                                                          2005030262

I dedicate this work to the pioneers

in the practice of liturgical art and architecture.

They have contributed to the movement

with steadfast exuberance and loyalty.

They have inspired many others

to do good work

with humility.

I am personally grateful.

✝

Adé de Bethune, 1914–2002

Frank Kacmarcik, OBL.S.B., 1920–2004

Robert Edward Rambusch, 1924–

William Schickel, 1919–

Edward Anders Sövik, 1918–

Contents

Abbreviations

BB	Book of Blessings
BLS	Built of Living Stones
CB	Ceremonial of Bishops
CCC	Catechism of the Catholic Church
CCL	Code of Canon Law
DD	*Dies Domini:* Observing and Celebrating the Day of the Lord
EACW	Environment and Art in Catholic Worship
EM	*Eucharisticum Mysterium*
GILM	General Introduction to the Lectionary for Mass
GIRM	General Instruction of the Roman Missal
HCWEOM	Holy Communion and Worship of the Eucharist Outside Mass
IRL	Inculturation and the Roman Liturgy
LA	Letter to Artists
LG	*Lumen Gentium:* Dogmatic Constitution on the Church
MCW	Music in Catholic Worship
OA	*Opera Artis:* On the Care of the Church's Historical and Artistic Heritage
OCF	Order of Christian Funerals
OP	Order of Penance
OPW	Our Place of Worship
RCIA	Rite of Christian Initiation of Adults
RDCA	Rite of Dedication of a Church and an Altar
RS	*Redemptionis Sacramentum*
SC	*Sacrosanctum Concilium:* Constitution on the Sacred Liturgy

Introduction

A Context for Change

THIS BOOK, the fruit of thirty-five years of work in the building and renovating of cathedrals, churches and chapels, is intended, first of all, for those who are becoming involved in any way in this important work. Where possible, read this book well before even the bare beginnings of organizing yourselves for the work ahead. For others, the book may serve as an update on the art and architecture reforms set in motion by the Second Vatican Council.

The creation of an appropriate Catholic place for the worship of God is a complicated task. History and geography may provide innumerable examples, but building or renovating a house of prayer is not simply a matter of architectural style, artistic choices, the correct location for ritual furnishings or the seating arrangement of the assembly. Rather, it has to do with the fundamental way in which we understand who we are and how we behave in public. There are disagreements over these issues. Different camps have arisen since Vatican II, each with its arguments. The feelings are deep and it may take generations before a common ground is realized. Unfortunately the eucharistic liturgy has become the touchstone for these disagreements. In that context the environment for worship has become the subject of intense debate. This book will address these issues. The basic principles of the Conciliar documents and post-Conciliar writings provide the foundation for this work.

- All baptized members of the Church have been called to holiness.

- The Church is the sacrament of unity.

- The baptized are obligated to participate in worship as partners and not spectators.

- Our church buildings are metaphors for this Church and must reflect these realities.

The task of building or renovating a place of worship occurs not in a vacuum but in the midst of a large mélange where the Church lives its life in any given place and time. The basilica churches of the fourth century were constructed in the aftermath of persecution. The Romanesque and Gothic buildings of thirteenth-century France were built at a feverish rate while the seventh and eighth crusades were being waged. The Renaissance of fourteenth-century Italy provided the backdrop for the artistic and architectural wonders of that age. The churches in fifteenth-century Spain were erected during the Inquisition. Churches in the new world were built while indigenous peoples were being colonized. The Protestant Reformation and the Catholic reforms provided the setting for both the iconoclasm and the Baroque flourishes of sixteenth- and seventeenth-century Germany and other parts of northern Europe. The Church cannot live in isolation from global events. The design and construction of church buildings happens within the events and critical thinking of each age.

Today at least four major concerns need to be identified. The first has to do with the global situation. As I finish this book in the winter of 2005, the planet is fragile and broken-hearted. A tsunami has just wiped out the lives and hopes of hundreds of thousands of people. Civil wars abound. Terror against innocent people is now a common weapon of states and individuals alike. Hundreds of millions of people live short lives, lacking food and health care and even potable water. HIV/AIDS takes lives in epidemic numbers. Deforestation continues. Fewer corporations monopolize the market place. The corporate culture is plagued by greed and unethical practices. Pollution and waste are destroying the very power of our planet to provide for future generations. Wealth and the planet's natural resources are enjoyed by a small percentage of earth's people.

The second concern has to do with life in the United States. The tragedy of September 11, 2001, still strangles the nation's collective spirit and has created in many a xenophobic paranoia. The middle class struggles to make ends meet while the gap widens between the rich and the poor. There is still no national health care plan, and the cost of drugs continues to climb. The citizenship is torn over the war being waged in Iraq. In the media and among politicians the tone has become mean-spirited and self-serving. Funds for the arts have dwindled while made-for-TV reality shows mesmerize households every evening. Testing scores in the nation's public school systems are below par when compared to other countries. The infrastructures of once great urban centers are decaying while exurban developments are depleting the nation's farmlands and taxing highway systems.

Restlessness in religion is the third concern. The search for the sacred appears to be in a state of restive change. A new and fiery evangelistic form of fundamentalism challenges mainstream religions. Islam is growing in the Western world. Enormous Christian churches are empty on Sunday. New sects offer alternative avenues to spiritual growth blending Eastern mysticism and twelve-step self-improvement programs. Older church members cling loyally to revered rituals while youths search for a more hip-hop venue that speaks to their lifestyles. In North America the ordination of an openly gay bishop in the Episcopal Church created divisions in the worldwide Anglican communion, which has in turn challenged relations with other Christian denominations. The Jewish population continues to decrease because of intermarriage. New state laws providing legal status to same-sex partners have altered the traditional definitions of marriage and family. Issues dealing with birth control, capital punishment, abortion, cloning and stem cell research have polarized citizens in both Church and country. In brief, the strong biblical and traditional foundations of old-world religions are being rocked.

The fourth concern is the state of the Catholic Church itself. The pedophile scandal in North America is leaving a mark on everything the Church does. The laity appear to have lost trust in the bishops. Lay organizations like Call to Action and Voice of the Faithful are demanding more participation in the governance of the Church.[1] The September 12, 2004, *Boston Globe* newspaper reported that in discussing the United State sex-abuse scandal with bishops from New England, Pope John Paul II encouraged them to be more open to the needs of parishioners in the wake of a "crisis of confidence in the church's leadership." The bishops themselves seem to differ on important matters. This was obvious when some stated they would deny Communion to church members (particularly civil servants) who do not publicly uphold the moral teachings of the Church. Catholics in the United States can be polarized on just about any significant issue dealing with their lives.

As the membership of the Catholic Church increases annually, the percentage of those attending church dwindles. The number of lay leaders increases, but vocations to the priesthood, brotherhood and sisterhood are in decline. The remnant ordained pastorate claims to be

[1] Read, for example, Peter Steinfels, *A People Adrift: The Crisis of the Roman Catholic Church in America* (New York: Simon & Shuster, 2003) and Stephen J. Pope, ed., *Common Calling: The Laity and Governance of the Catholic Church* (Washington, DC: Georgetown University Press, 2004).

happy while showing symptoms of demoralization. Shifting populations are altering the Catholic landscape. In larger metropolitan centers the closing or merging of parishes is met with strong opposition. Meanwhile, in the suburbs, especially in temperate regions of the country, churches are being built with megachurch proportions. New immigration paths are also changing the face of the Church. Once solidly Eastern and Western European in its makeup, a new diversity is taking hold as more people migrate from Asia, the Pacific Islands, Mexico, Central and South America and the Caribbean.

On the liturgical front some church authorities and laity clearly wish to return to a pre-Conciliar mode. Language, music and ministerial roles during Mass appear to be the first targets for such a restorative effort. Proof for this is found especially in the proposed retranslations of liturgical and biblical texts and the renewed emphasis on the preeminent role of the priest during the celebration of Mass. While many responsible faith communities, scholars and bishops continue to work for the adaptation of the rites that would celebrate the diversity of the Church, others seem interested in "restoring" the liturgy to a prescribed homogeneous form to be used by all, defining unity as uniformity.

In the midst of all these perplexing observations, this *is* a book about the environment for worship and how we can re-imagine what characterizes and defines our places for public and private prayer. I hope my insights will enable the reader to think anew about sacred space. During the past thirty-five years, while working with hundreds of congregations, most of them Catholic, I have learned two valuable lessons. First, no one of us knows more than all of us. We can and desperately need to learn from one another. Dialogue works. Second, the construction or renovation of a church building always benefits when all work in awareness of the larger regional, national and global situations. Without this, we divorce ourselves from any sense of stewardship.

I begin this book by presenting a framework for going about building or renovating a place of worship. This process could be used as a guide for any project. Then the book is divided into three parts.

In Part One, "Building Blocks," I will explore various areas that shape our beliefs. Unexplored misunderstandings about religion, worship, art and architecture will make for an emotional and hostile atmosphere throughout a church building or renovation project. These issues are not always directly architecturally or artistically related. They must be addressed before embarking on a project.

In Part Two, "Building Plans," I will present a conceptual program describing the spaces and appointments that comprise a place of worship. These ideas for re-imagining a worship environment are founded on principles that have served us well in the past. For example, I believe that the architectural setting for worship must always accommodate processions. The building itself must feature elements of verticality, color and illumination. The choice of materials and their textures should be harmonized to present a space that is extraordinary to the senses. However, a worthy worship place does not begin with an architectural or artistic idea but a liturgical one. Thus the building must first serve the worship of the assembly and foster its engagement. This is a real challenge in older church buildings. How the site and the building are laid out, then, will be the main thrust of the second section.

In Part Three, "Further Planning," I will review those areas that require more attention and the cooperation of anyone involved in a church building or renovation project. The stewardship factor is troubling in an age where more and more people have neither adequate nutrition nor decent housing. The creation of environments for worship that are ecologically sound has become an urgent issue. The size of church buildings is another concern. They will have to be much larger to accommodate the growing population of worshipers at a time when there are fewer persons authorized to preside over a eucharistic liturgy. But is the megachurch phenomenon a healthy trend? At the end there is a glossary, resources and an index to facilitate your work.

Why write or read a book on church art and architecture when so many urgent issues press in upon us? There is an old saying, *lex orandi, lex credendi,* how we pray determines what we believe. I believe that *where* we pray shapes *how* we pray and so not only proclaims what we believe but also how we live. In this way there is a vital connection between our church buildings and our lives and deeds as religious people.

This book is written from a Catholic perspective about Catholic places of worship, but through my work with other Christians and with various communities within the Jewish faith, I know that we hold many things in common with regard to the creation of buildings to house our worship. I hope this work will serve others in the ecumenical and interfaith community and that it will advance our work together.

I am grateful to the following persons who have helped me think through and write this book. Gabe Huck served as the primary editor and helped me craft a more readable manuscript. His liturgical acumen made his contributions all the more valuable. Good friends and professional colleagues James Bacik, Bill Beard, Larry Cowper, Eileen

Crowley, Dennis Fleischer, Walter Kroner, Maggie McInnis and Fred Moleck read different sections and gave me straightforward critiques. I am indebted to the staff at Liturgical Press whose enthusiasm and hard work have helped to produce this work—Ann Blattner, Susan Hogan/Albach, Stephanie Lancour, Brother David Manahan, O.S.B., Colleen Stiller, Mark Twomey, and Mark Warzecha. I could not have written this book if it were not for the encouragement and support of Janet Walton.

I also thank those to whom I dedicate this work. The late Ade dé Bethune and the late Frank Kacmarcik, along with Robert E. Rambusch, Edward A. Sövik and William Schickel all have been courageous and talented pioneers in liturgical art and architecture dating back to the 1940s. Their work is a solid foundation for all of us.

Finally, because I often recommend that congregations allot a portion of their project budget to construct a Habitat for Humanity home I will donate all royalties I receive from the sale of this book to Habitat for Humanity, Albany, New York.

Overview

Processing a Project

THERE ARE many ways to go about building or renovating a place of worship. In some instances, where the pastor works alone with the architect, there is no real process. In others, there may be a modest one where the pastor invites a few people to participate in the planning. And, in other cases, an elaborate process includes the entire congregation. No matter what approach, every project must follow some steps that are laid out in an organized fashion. In my judgment it would be difficult to build or renovate a church without a process. Yet most projects in North America take place without one. It is for this reason that I begin this book by outlining steps that may be taken to assure the successful completion of a project.

Some professionals use the word "process" as a noun. It is a systematic methodology employed to carry out the project. It will identify the goals and objectives and who is responsible for reaching certain milestones. It will also establish step-by-step ways to develop and monitor plans, the budget and the timetable. I prefer to use the word as a verb. In this sense it has more to do with managing experiences, information, stories of faith, imagination and designs in addition to organizing the project in an efficient and developmental way. When all the members of the congregation, and not just the committees are involved, the end result will be a more complete reflection of the faith community.

A project that includes very few people ignores the baptismal dignity of the rest of the congregation. If there is any truth to the axiom, "We are formed by what we form," it is imperative that the whole assembly be involved in shaping its house of prayer. This is why I contend that God's house is our house. The dedication of the building becomes a time for the re-dedication of the whole Church— the people of the community. This is the only way the building can be understood as a metaphor for that congregation and not just a template copied out of some architectural history book. If the church building is to be a resonator of the community, then there is a responsibility to review what the Church is in the modern world. What does it believe? What is its vision? What is its mission? Not to ask these questions could result in a building that does not reflect the local church. The topics I raise in Part One of this book are the ones the community must wrestle with before they even begin to think about designs.

Here is a brief overview of the steps that have proven successful in many projects.[1] It can be adapted for a small chapel in a religious community or for a large cathedral. Although some of these steps can occur simultaneously, the overall organization is sequential.

STEP 1: OBTAINING DIOCESAN APPROVAL

In the Catholic Church the bishop is responsible for the liturgical life of the diocese. He also oversees the ongoing development of the local church. In this sense the work of every parish and organization must serve the common good and vision of the whole diocese. Some dioceses have established long-term plans for building and property development. Many dioceses have set a limit on how much money may be spent before permission is given to begin a project. This is why contacting the proper personnel is important. It is also a time to review local policies and guidelines, find out if consultative services are available and learn if the bishop has any particular concerns or requirements.[2] Other denominations may have similar guidelines.

STEP 2: PREPARING A SCOPE OF WORK

Before the congregation hires an architect it should have a clear understanding of what it wants to do in the project. This will facilitate the selection of the best architect and other professionals for the job. Also, it is important to test the economical climate of the community. It makes good sense to find out if there will be financial support later on.

---

[1] Much of the information presented here is employed by the Architecture and Building Commission in the Diocese of Albany.

[2] Note here that Catholic bishops have the right to mandate a liturgical practice in their respective dioceses that may not be the norm in the neighboring diocese or even throughout the rest of the country.

A project committee should be organized to prepare this scope of work.

Committee Organization. The primary mission of this committee is to ascertain the needs of the congregation and assure the members that their input is important and that they will be kept informed in a transparent way. A liturgical design consultant (see below) can be very helpful in organizing and guiding this committee. Different tasks can be carried out by various subcommittees: e.g., prayer and worship, acoustics and musical instruments, art and furnishings, architect selection, construction, data gathering, finances, hospitality and logistics, communications and publicity. Inviting women and men with knowledge in these areas has its advantages. However, the insights, wisdom and memories from crones, sages and elders in the congregation should not be overlooked. Nor should the input from teenagers be neglected. The idea is to involve more people from the congregation in doing less work.

Each subcommittee is given a number of reasonable things to accomplish within a realistic timeframe. For example, the prayer and worship team would identify the devotional practices that are popular in the congregation. At the same time the art and furnishings committee would document what works of art are important to the people as well as their artistic value. The musical instruments group might begin its task by evaluating the style of music used during worship as well as the instruments and space required.

Local customs, pastoral instructions and current ritual books can be used to guide these activities. In a renovation project the objective is to document what could be done to the church to improve public worship. In a new church project the report will state what is expected from the community as it prepares to worship in a new building. This committee is obliged to include members from the assembly in determining what is best for their church. Part Two and Part Three of this book can serve as a basis for all of this work.

Some committees spend a lot of time worrying about details. Some even try to design the building. The professionals hired for the project will tend to these issues later in the process. The subcommittees bring their reports and recommendations to the core committee, which presents them to the pastor who is ultimately responsible for the welfare of the congregation. This system is apropos for a hierarchical style of governance. In more congregational-style churches where a board of directors makes all major decisions and where the pastor does not have unilateral authority, other models would be appropriate.

Project Catechesis. Before asking for input from the congregation, it is important to provide a catechetical opportunity for all members early in the process. There may be aspects of the project that are unknown to the congregation. For example, some may wonder why the project is even necessary. A liturgical design consultant usually conducts this educational component. This is the time to deal with the topics I raise in Part One of this book that have to do with the identity, purpose and worship practices of the local faith community.

This is also the time for the liturgical design consultant to conduct a series of illustrated lectures that deal graphically with the history of the Christian place of worship, the spaces that are essential in any church building and the role of art and music in the worship environment. These topics are addressed later in this book and can be helpful to the congregation in understanding the nature and purpose of a church building.

The education sessions could be supplemented with handouts at weekend liturgies to assure that all members of the congregation have access to the same information. These sessions could also be video recorded for the convenience of those who cannot leave their residences.

Congregation Input. The primary work of the subcommittees is to collect information from the congregation and make recommendations. In addition to the research of the subcommittees, at least four questions should be asked of all participants at the educational sessions. (1) What one thing about Catholic church buildings pleases you most of all today? (2) What one thing about Catholic church buildings bothers you most of all today? (3) What one thing is absolutely essential for you personally in your church building? (4) If you have very young children, what one thing is absolutely essential for your family?

The participants are invited to talk about the questions in small groups so they can learn from one another. Each group presents a summary to the entire gathering at the conclusion of the session. All participants are asked to return their written answers to the data subcommittee. The compilation of the answers to these questions alone would provide a fairly accurate picture of the needs and expectations of the entire congregation. The advantage of asking the questions during the catechetical phase is that the participants may have learned something new or thought about something in ways they never imagined before. The youth of the congregation should not be excluded from the process. Various exercises could be scheduled to give all ages the chance to discuss their place of worship.

Liturgical prayer should provide the structure for this entire catechetical phase. For example, each teaching opportunity and group discussion could take place before, after or during the celebration of the Liturgy of the Hours. The end result of this period of catechesis could be a document that states the vision or mission of the community, which should then be reflected in the church building.

Scope of Work Document. The end product of this step is the scope of work document that will be sent to each of the architects invited to submit proposals. This document will include data about the congregation (e.g., a budget for the project, sacramental statistics, demographic studies, site possibilities and constraints and programmatic requirements pertaining to the worship environment). It will also describe what is expected from the architects (e.g., economic analysis, site evaluation, existing conditions studies). A liturgical program that specifically addresses the worship space components of the project should be included in this scope of work package. Written by the liturgical designer, it should contain the owner's needs and expectations regarding the worship environment, applicable church teachings and the consultant's recommendations. This "foundation" document could be quite specific and will complement other information and ideas collected as the process moves forward.

STEP 3: ASSEMBLING THE PROFESSIONAL DESIGN TEAM

A church project can involve many specialists. They include the following:

- Liturgical design consultant
- Architect
- Acoustical consultant
- Lighting consultant
- Landscape architect
- Decorative paint studio
- Organ builder
- Fund-raising company

Artists are also part of the design team. Ideally, they should be identified in time to include them in decisions pertaining to the architectural settings for their art. I will discuss the role of artists more fully later in this book. There are also different project delivery methods, which I will describe at the end of this step. Here, I will discuss the liturgical designer and the architect.

The Liturgical Design Consultant. A liturgical design consultant is frequently the first professional retained for a project. It is important to find someone who understands all aspects of building and renovating and can provide clear and unambiguous direction throughout the process. That person should be able to do a number of things for you including:

- Organize and work with your committees

- Provide catechesis for the entire congregation

- Develop a liturgical and artistic program

- Prepare conceptual sketches

- Guide the design, fabrication and installation of all art, furnishings and appointments

Experience is essential if this person is to establish credibility with other professionals on the design team. At a minimum this consultant should have expertise in liturgy, art and architecture. Experience in organizational development is also helpful. It is not too much to expect a *liturgical* design consultant to have an advanced degree in one or all of these areas. Would you ever hire an architect who had no formal training in architecture?

The Architect. The liturgical design consultant can be instrumental in helping the congregation put together the professional design team. This selection process begins with a list of architects and others to be considered. Some dioceses can provide names of architects that have worked in the region before. Caution should prevail when considering architects that may have done a lot of church work but have not continued their own formation in the field of religious architecture.

Each firm on the list is presented with the scope-of-work statement and a request for a proposal. Interested firms will decide whether to pursue the project. If so, they may visit the site and review all of the information gathered so far. Their reply should include their proposal and a copy of the contract that the congregation is expected to sign. A firm is selected based on the interview and the quality of the proposal. The contract should be negotiated before the signing takes place.

What can be expected from an architect who designs church buildings? Edward A. Sövik once offered these criteria for architects. They could be used in searching for other professionals.

- Not mere competence but extraordinary ability

- The capacity for excellent design appropriate to the Christian faith

- The ability to actualize truth and poetry in structure; not merely to solve problems

- The ability to produce work with spiritual qualities:

  - Integrity (no deceit or affectations)

  - Hospitality and humanity (not presumptuous, dominating, harsh or ostentatious)

  - Beauty (which leads to wonder and is appropriate to God's presence)

- Good technical skills as well as artistic skills

- Good administrative skills

- The ability to be open, responsive and articulate

- Intelligence, literacy and scholarship (worship, theology and spirituality)

- Experience and commitment to the social good more than personal advantage

Not every architect can live up to such expectations. Creating a place for the worship of God will demand that even the most experienced design professionals start from scratch and go through some sort of growth and learning process—a transformation. Although this expectation is laudable it must not be overlooked that the construction of religious buildings is a big business,[3] and professionals have to decide if a project is worth their time.

Sometimes the best architect for the project is not a local one. It would not be unusual to hire an architect with impressive credentials from outside the community. When this happens it is best to add a

[3] Religious building projects accounted for nine billion dollars worth of business according to the 2000 United States Census Report. This is not much compared to the defense budget or what is spent on diets and cosmetics. However, it is a large amount considering it is raised through private donations.

local firm to the team to handle day-to-day concerns (e.g., working with contractors, addressing local code issues).

Some architects advertise as "liturgical" architects. If the liturgical expertise is there, it could be an advantage. However, it could present a conflict of interests when the architect is biased on certain issues. For instance, who will advise a congregation in the most objective way when an aspect of the architectural plan is called into question for liturgical reasons?

Although there are different approaches to architectural services the important thing to remember is that the architect as well as all other design professionals must be willing to participate in the pilgrimage of the community every step of the way. Their role is to be good listeners and good guides. In the end the church building should never be considered the architect's showcase but the work of the community. The selection process will help the congregation determine which candidate is best suited for the job.

Project Delivery Methods. Designing a place of worship is one thing. Getting it built is another. There are different acceptable delivery systems that can be used in building a new church or renovating an older one.

a. The Design-Bid-Build is the most traditional method. It begins with an architect who prepares all of the architectural drawings and documents, which are then put out to bid to general contractors (GC). The GC selected is then responsible for building the church according to design specifications.

b. The Construction Manager method is gaining popularity in church projects. The architect and construction manager (CM) are hired at the same time. The CM prepares bid packages and supervises the work of individual trade contractors who sign a contract directly with the congregation.

c. The Contract Manager method is a variation on the previous one. In this case the congregation hires the Contract Manager who then hires an architect and all of the subcontractors who sign a contract directly with the congregation.

d. The Design-Build method has at least two variations. In one, an architect is the manager of the firm, which is also a construction company. In the other, a construction company is the manager and the architect is an employee. In both cases the firm is responsible for the design and construction of the church.

The advantages and disadvantages of each method should be examined carefully to assure the one selected for a particular project is appropriate.

STEP 4:
DEVELOPING A FEASIBILITY STUDY AND MASTER PLAN

Once the architect is selected the first task is to embark on a feasibility study, which will have several parts to it. The end product of this study will be a master plan for the project.

Needs and Constraints. In this part the professionals retrieve as much information pertaining to the project as possible. This would include the liturgical program, the demographic data and the sacramental statistics presented earlier in the scope of work. All needs, ideas and constraints are identified at this time. Certain issues are pursued: What are the site possibilities? Are there any restrictions governing the property or existing building? Is the church on a local or the national historic register, or a potential candidate for such designation? What are the urgent priorities? What is the level of enthusiasm in the congregation? Where is the money coming from to carry out this project? In the case of an older church building that should be stabilized, this phase would include an existing-conditions report.

Studying Alternatives. This part examines various conceptual alternatives that might satisfy the needs and expectations of the congregation. These studies will help everyone work toward an agreement on what is the preferred alternative. If, for example, the congregation has outgrown its church building the alternatives may include: adding on to the present church, razing it and building a new one on the same site, moving to a new site and constructing a church there.

If a decision was made earlier to build a new church the alternatives would include: possible sites, the location of the church on the site, traffic patterns. The preferred alternative also represents the start of a master plan.

Preferred Alternative. After the committee agrees on a preferred alternative and how it fits into a master plan, it is developed into a schematic design so that it can be presented to the diocese and the congregation along with approximate cost estimates. Which presentation is made first will depend on diocesan policies. The diocese will also want to know how the project will be paid for. In other denominations an outside agency can be helpful in reviewing the conceptual plans and estimated costs. They might even be able to assist in funding the project in some way.[4] The architect and the liturgical designer should assist the committee in explaining the preferred alternative. The members of the congregation should be given ample time to see the plan and ask questions pertaining to the project.

Search for Consensus. Assuming that the diocese approves the preferred plan a process should be in place to see if the congregation has reached consensus regarding the preferred plan. Mitigated consensus is a reasonable goal because it is highly unlikely that there will be complete agreement on every aspect of a church building or renovation project. Those who are not part of the emerging consensus should be given enough time to explain why they do not agree. It is not advisable to take a vote in the congregation in order to make a decision. When a group votes on something, there will always be winners and losers, which only creates deeper feelings of division. The members of the congregation should also be apprised from the outset that not everyone will be completely satisfied with the church.

Master Plan Development. Once consensus has been reached and the diocese approves the plan and budget, the design team finalizes the master plan, which becomes a stand-alone document. This master plan clearly identifies what is the first phase of the project and details the cost estimates. If the money is already available, the schematic design can be immediately developed. If the money is not yet raised, the master plan and the schematic drawings of the first phase can be used to give everyone an idea of what the place could look like.

STEP 5: RAISING FUNDS

Because the fiscal waters were tested at the start of the project, the stage is now set for the major capital campaign. Sometimes the diocesan comptroller or development officer will recommend or determine how much a congregation can spend on a project. Some dioceses still lend money to its constituents. Otherwise, the local congregation is left on its own to finance the project. Permission to break ground or proceed with a renovation is usually not given by a diocese until a certain amount of money is already on hand. This percentage varies from diocese to diocese.

---

[4] Founded in 1880, the Episcopal Church Building Fund (http://www.ecbf.org/) provides a variety of services: planning processes, workshops, consultations and loans.

The finance subcommittee can now announce to the congregation how money will be raised. It is most important at this time to explain the raison d'être for the plan in a way that energizes the entire congregation. Choose a person who can best speak with vision and enthusiasm. It is essential that the reason for the project be perceived as the collective vision of the congregation. If the catechetical aspects of the project were successful, the congregation will now see the plan as something of its own making—one that truly reflects who they are, what they believe and how they worship. Conventional wisdom suggests that if they feel ownership, they will help to pay for it.

This is also the time to recognize the lead donors. Some projects start off with a generous gift from one or two donors that encourages others to join the cause. Banks and other local institutions often will provide some financial support for religious buildings because of their architectural presence and the congregation's service to the community.[5] Plans should also be made for the ongoing fiscal management of the space—a never-ending project. For example, I usually suggest that the estimated operating budget for the first year be included in the project budget. The whole campaign should be conducted in the spirit of good stewardship, which is discussed in Part Three of this book.

STEP 6: DEVELOPING THE DESIGNS

Based on the success of the fund-raising campaign, the architects begin to develop that part of the master plan that the congregation can afford to build at this time. During this phase the architects work closely with engineers and consultants to prepare more detailed drawings. This is when careful attention is paid to the lighting and acoustical plans. Also, final decisions are made regarding materials, finishes, architectural ornamentation, decorative painting and other specializations, e.g., the incorporation of glass art.

As plans become more detailed and comprehensive the costs will change. Therefore during this phase it is also a good time to review the budget, continue the capital campaign and keep the congregation informed about the progress being made. Some dioceses ask for a review of plans at the completion of the design development phase.

[5] Consider the questions asked most frequently by someone moving into town because of a new job. What is the cost of housing? What is the crime rate? How good is the school system? And, where is the nearest place of worship?

I will discuss in more detail the process of finding and working with artists in Part Three. The integration of art and architecture is important. The art program developed during the liturgical programming phase will identify the pieces that need to be commissioned. The locations for all art, furnishings and appointments should be incorporated into the schematic plans mentioned above. The liturgical designer and architect should be able to pinpoint these places with the help of the arts-and-furnishings committee. However, the best approach is to have the artist who will actually be doing the piece involved in the design details of the setting, including the choice of materials, color and light.

This means that, ideally, the selection of artists should occur in the early stages of the process when other professionals are being hired. If the money is not available to establish a full contract, most artists are willing to prepare a sketch or a maquette along with a cost estimate for a fixed fee that would be applied to the account. That model then could be used in presenting memorial opportunities for the congregation. The important thing is to involve the artists in the design of the settings that will eventually house or frame their works of art.

STEP 8: PREPARING RITUALS

As the drawings are being developed attention should shift back to the involvement of the congregation in preparing the church or the site for the work that will soon begin. In the case of a new church the groundbreaking liturgy should be an event that is more engaging than merely watching dignitaries turn over the sod. Consider inviting the whole congregation to walk the site, pray over it and claim it for the worship of God. Again, the process suggests that this holy ground is an extension and reflection of the people of God. It does not become blessed or sacred simply because a bishop sprinkles water on it. Rather, the whole assembly blesses God for the gift of the earth. The human response is to care for that land in the best way possible. I will discuss environmental and ecological issues in the final part of this book.

In the case of renovating or departing an existing church, a "leave-taking" liturgy will be important. Over time churches become vessels of personal and communal experiences of God. Most often the memories connected with sacramental celebrations are foremost in the minds of the members. This is why closing a church can be so traumatic for some. When moving from an old church to a new one, it is essential to transfer significant images, books and relics. These belong to the heritage of the community. There is theological impoverishment when only the reserved sacrament is transferred while the sacred Scriptures are not.

Committee work at this time would include liturgical planning and rehearsals. The publicity-and-communications team would see to the promotion of the events. The financial campaign could be given a boost as people begin to see something happening. More catechesis can help newcomers catch the spirit.

STEP 9: PREPARING CONSTRUCTION DOCUMENTS

During this phase the working drawings or construction documents and the project manual are completed. There are frequent professional design-team meetings to monitor the schedule and the work being done. A review of code issues should take place especially if there is a chance that changes were made since the inception of the project. A final diocesan review of plans may be required.

STEP 10: NEGOTIATING BIDS

Many dioceses are closely involved in the bidding process and may have applicable policies. Typically the project is advertised and bids are received and reviewed. A selective bidding process is when certain firms are invited to submit their interest. In some cases the bid is negotiated with a contractor who may have an outstanding reputation in the diocese or the region or who has done work for the congregation already. When the congregation uses a construction manager, contract manager or design-build method of delivery, there will be no bidding process. However, every caution should be taken regarding the credentials of the subcontractors and all others working on the project. It is wise to agree on a guaranteed maximum price in every case.

STEP 11: CONSTRUCTING THE CHURCH

Once the contract is awarded, the entire design team should meet with the builders to review everybody's responsibilities. The general contractor or construction manager is responsible for completing the project according to design specifications. That person prepares a schedule and conducts weekly meetings with various subcontractors and the congregation's representative. During this time it is important for the liturgical design consultant to monitor the work of artists and artisans. The timely delivery and installation of all art, furnishings and appointments should be coordinated by the construction manager or general contractor.

STEP 12: DEDICATING AND CARING FOR THE CHURCH

The liturgy planning team in the parish should prepare for the dedication or re-dedication of the church. It is important to know with assurance that the project will be turned over to the owner and that a certificate of occupancy will be issued by a certain date and *before* a dedication date is set. All consultants should gather for a review of the building either before or just after the dedication.

Liturgical planning sessions and rehearsals are held at this time. Collaboration between the bishop's office and the parish planners regarding the dedication ritual is important. Care should be taken to use the event as a time for the re-dedication of the faith community.

PART ONE
Building Blocks

In any church building or renovation project certain theoretical foundations must be recognized and appreciated. One objective is to identify and understand issues that will affect the project. Another is to clarify the areas of agreement and disagreement. The establishment of a common ground early in a process can alleviate misunderstandings later on. These conversations should occur before specific planning programs or drawings are developed. Difficult as it may be to take the time, planning committees should discuss these issues at their first meetings.

I summarize these foundations in Part One in order to create a platform for examining other issues later in this book. I will identify each factor here and present the practical applications in Part Two. This brief overview of the following fundamental factors is not intended to be all-inclusive.

- Memory

- Imagination and Creativity

- Catechesis

- Scriptural Foundations

- Christian Writings

- Early Church History

- Early Church Architecture

- Later Movements in Church Architecture

- Theology

- Liturgy

- The Language of Sacred Space

- Beauty and Aesthetics in Church Design

- Proxemics

- The Place of the Assembly

Chapter 1

Memory

MEMORY is an important component of a worship space. Without it there can be no connection with the history or traditions of a religious group. Words are used to articulate what is remembered. In the *Dedication of a Church and an Altar*[1] expressions like beacon, bride, holy city, vineyard and spouse are used as metaphors for the church. The building is understood as an extension and reflection of the people who gather there. It balances and gives life to both the traditions and the visions of the community. It is not a museum of relics that revere only the past. It is not a mere container for ritual objects, gestures or even people. Instead it is a resonator of the community. It energizes the assembly gathered to enact the narrative that sustains it. This narrative is a story that the faithful believe even though it cannot be fully understood or explained. It is a story about us. In the Christian tradition the paschal event is that story.

I have memories from my childhood that have affected my thinking about art and architecture in a post-Vatican II Church. I grew up in the 1940s and '50s in a mill town along the Mohawk River in upstate New York. Founded in the eighteenth century by Dutch settlers, Amsterdam became an important industrial city because of its location in the river valley. Like many residents, my parents worked in the Mohawk Carpet Mills—the largest rug manufacturer in the world. My mother was a weaver and my father was a night watchman. Neither one had a high school diploma. Both left home as teenagers to earn money to help their parents.

My siblings and I attended the neighborhood Catholic school. Saint Stanislaus was a Polish parish in a city that had seven Catholic

---

[1] *Dedication of a Church and an Altar,* Sacred Congregation for Worship and the Discipline of the Sacraments, May 29, 1977.

churches. At that time at least fourteen priests served a population of twenty-five thousand people. Neither of my parents was Polish, but this school was the closest to where we lived. My father's family was Slovak. My mother's family belonged to the Ukrainian Greek Catholic Church, but we attended their church, Saint Nicholas, only for weddings and funerals. My childhood memory of that church is filled with incantations, incense and mysterious processions through the elaborate iconostasis.

Saint Stanislaus parish was started in 1894 to serve the growing number of Polish immigrants who lived in the valley and worked on farms and in stone quarries. Like many Eastern Europeans they settled together in neighborhoods, which quickly took on the character of their homeland. They cherished their close-knit friendships and families but were often suspicious of other nationalities and races. Their language, art, music, dances, folktales and recipes affirmed and sustained their identity in the American melting pot. They spent their hard-earned money to build a church as a place to worship God and as a visual and tangible connection to their roots.

My most vivid recollections of that church begin when I was an altar boy. It was quite a responsibility then. First, you had to learn by heart the Latin responses to the priest's prayers. Endless rehearsals conducted by the Felician Sisters guaranteed that the ceremonies of the Mass would be carried out with respect and precision. The church and school were only four blocks from where we lived. The rows of apartment houses and shops along the neighborhood streets were friendly companions during my pre-dawn walks to serve the early Mass. The aroma of fresh bread and buns from the corner bakery eventually got mixed up with the scent of incense and burning candles.

The focal point in the ornate church was the lily white, gold-gilded high altar into which were nestled brightly colored statues of Saints Michael and Stanislaus. Tall angels holding a dozen lights each were perched on pedestals to the left and right of the *reredos*. We switched them on at the Sanctus. Six tall candles and fresh flowers were interspersed between these statues and flanked the shiny tabernacle located in the center. Mindful of the watchful eyes of the sisters who filled the first row of pews, we servers raced to see who would finish lighting the candles first.

Before Mass parishioners carried out their private devotions beneath the ornately painted ceiling that looked like a heavenly picture gallery. Some followed the Stations of the Cross; others knelt before one of the many statues; still others were crouched in their seats fingering their rosary beads. The blowers of the pipe organ in the choir loft seemed to cough and wheeze, creak and rumble just as I yanked the tiny sacristy bell to signal the start of Mass. The elderly organist chanted back and forth with the priest who almost always wore black vestments. We began by kneeling on the bottom of three steps leading up to the altar. A coterie of smiling angels painted high in the vaulted ceiling of the apse stared down at us as we prayed under our breaths, "Introibo ad altare Dei. Ad Deum qui laetificat juventutem meam." Everyone knelt through the entire twenty-to-twenty-five-minute liturgy but no one else in the church uttered a word. Some received communion. Fifteen years later I was ordained a priest on this very same spot.

Human bodies have a way of remembering things that are not often clear in the mind. That is why people who grow up Catholic have liturgy in their bones. Some may leave the Church, but few shake the memory out of their bodies. Catholic life embraced more than the commandments. It was still in my youth a culture, a way of life, which provided a comfortable framework for morality, education, worship and even athletics. But it was the liturgy and the church buildings that gave the Church much of its unique identity and lifestyle.

I share this glimpse into my past because one of the main roles of a church building is that of a *storyteller*. This is one of the deep-seeded reasons why churches are so important in the lives of people and why there is so much angst when a church is remodeled, merged or closed. These buildings stimulate our memories and imaginations. I am sure my fond recollections are similar to yours no matter where you grew up. For the parishioners of Saint Stanislaus in Amsterdam the church has always been a sacred place that resonated with their stories of faith. The biblical and sometimes fictional narratives depicted in the iconography on the walls, the ceilings and in the stained glass some-how came alive in the personal piety and public prayers of the people in the pews. And even though the imagery was not always directly related to a person's own story, a connection was made and hope was sustained. In this church favors were requested and received, babies were baptized, confessions were heard, Communion was shared, lovers married and the Church said farewell to the deceased. Fifty years ago liturgical customs enacted in novenas, forty hours devotions, Corpus Christi processions and benedictions framed the celebration of the Eucharist and sustained the Old World traditions of the community.

What took place in these churches prior to the current liturgical reforms was profound. At those sunrise Masses, the laity and the sisters, the priest and the two of us altar boys were somehow subliminally

5

wrapped up in the act of repetitive ritual making in a building that literally and figuratively embraced us with familiar words, art, architecture, music, incantations, smells, gestures and postures. Somehow we were involved in the liturgy together and the church building was like a blanket on a chilly night, a cozy and comfortable wrap. And then, of course, it all changed.

The bishops at Vatican II overwhelmingly approved the Constitution on the Sacred Liturgy[2] by a vote of 2,147 to 4. It altered the liturgical practice of the Church almost overnight. The language in the document surprised many: the notion that liturgical celebrations are not private functions but the work of the whole Church (26), the call for a radical adaptation of the rites (40), the required participation of all the faithful who are no longer to be considered silent spectators (48). These were a few of the teachings that would jar old habits and customs.

The implementation of conciliar reforms in the United States came at a time when the sociological and political climate of the country was also in the midst of change. Protests on campuses and in public streets, mistrust of authority figures, political assassinations and an unwanted conflict in Viet Nam contributed to the restlessness even while the council was going on. The exodus from cities to suburbs began the slow disintegration of intimate neighborhoods like the one I grew up in. The Eisenhower Highway Act of the 1950s built highways bypassing urban centers. Sidewalks became a rarity in warren-like suburban housing developments. Longer commutes to and from work changed behavior patterns in the family. More households saw both parents going off to work as the children boarded school busses. Day care centers and sprawling malls provided services to the new communities. The stress was greater for households with single parents. Gradually the nuclear and extended family system that provided a sense of security and familiarity was largely lost.

The scene in church was also different. New churches were being built in the suburbs while some older downtown churches were beginning to look empty and worn. The liturgical experience was significantly changed. New music, the vernacular, and sermons calling for social consciousness rocked the quiet Catholic sensitivities of the congregation. Little time was left for the already busy churchgoers to pray privately near the image of a favorite saint—if one could be found. No wonder why the liturgical life of the church still appears disjointed. It is!

[2] Constitution on the Sacred Liturgy, December 4, 1963.

Although sociologists differ on this, many believe that this untimely coupling of events (Vatican II and the restlessness of the 1960s in the U.S.) led to a perfect storm, the remnants of which still linger today. The current polarization that exists in society also exists in the Church. Some Catholics still object to the reforms. Many of these people, clergy and laity alike, were not even alive when the council took place. It is obvious that while a great deal of attention has been given to the many changes in the liturgy, the actual transformation of the Church itself, the baptized community, prompted by the reforms has been slow to develop. People disagree over exactly what story should be told in their church buildings and how liturgy should be enacted. It is this unsettling atmosphere that greets any congregation planning to build or renovate a place of worship.

Vatican II redefined the Church and everything it does including education, personnel, governance and worship. The bishops at the Council did not act irresponsibly in authorizing such a major reform, but how could they have known that it would take three to four generations before the concepts of the council could be brought into reality?

Some people now consider the council as an unfortunate blip on the screen of church history. Although it would be difficult to negate or turn back the tide in areas like revelation, ecumenism or the role of the Church in the modern world, there is a concerted effort underway to "restore" the liturgy to a pre-Vatican II practice. Pope John Paul II was clearly not among these restorationists. He reminded the Church: "With the passing of years, the Council documents lost nothing of their value or brilliance. They need to be read correctly, to be widely known and taken to heart as important and normative texts of the Magisterium, with the Church's Tradition."[3]

The restorationist movement ignores the fact that the pre-conciliar liturgy had serious problems (what else could have prompted the ever-conservative bishops toward such reforms?). That liturgy was basically unrecognizable when compared to the liturgical practice of the early Church. My boyhood experience is a good example. The same glorious solemn "high" Mass of Christmas Eve, which seemed to take forever, was "said" in fifteen to eighteen minutes by the athletic and handsome young priest who usually had the 6:00 A.M. Saturday "low" Mass in the sisters' convent chapel.

The understanding of the Mass and all other sacraments at that time was summed up in the dictum *ex opere operato,* meaning that the effectiveness of the liturgy occurred because the priest simply did it. It

---

[3] *Novo Millenio Ineunte,* Pope John Paul II, January 6, 2001, 57.

did not matter whether or not it was done with reverence, or if the people understood the language, or if there was no homily, or if few people took Communion, or that there was no music at the "low" Masses.

In any age there will be abuses. The rites are done by human beings. I remember one cleric saying, "Isn't liturgy supposed to take care of itself?" The Mass today often does lack the reverence, rhythm, silence and *joie de vivre* that should accompany any serious ritual making. However, the correction should not be legislative but catechetical. Yet in the present moment, concern about how the liturgy should be celebrated has become an authority issue. Uniformity is sometimes promoted as if it were the same as unity or led to unity. Imagine some distant office prescribing all the hymns, homilies and artwork to be used in churches. Imagine someone from another culture choreographing every procession, gesture and posture. Imagine a requirement that every church building look the same inside and out.

I raise these issues that, at first glance, have nothing to do with art and architecture because power, authority and clericalism are factors that will affect any liturgical practice and, therefore, the environment for worship. The intent of this book is to focus on how a place of worship is affected by many elements. Churches are different today because the liturgical rites are different. The rituals have been reformed because the Church has been reformed. There is no doubt that over the past forty years the quality of liturgical practice has been uneven and that there is tremendous room for improvement. However, this legitimate hope for a more reverent and relevant liturgical life should not become a time to undo all of the good work that has been accomplished in understanding the liturgy as the public prayer of the entire assembly.

Similarly, there is no doubt that the quality of church art and architecture has also been uneven. Church buildings tell the stories of the local church and how it is connected to a larger body of history, scripture and tradition. Our memories are important here. The ongoing work of creating faith communities, which are distinct but not separate from the whole Church, is far from over. The designs for the church buildings that house these worshiping communities are also in a state of transition. It is too early to turn back. Vaclav Havel once remarked: "Today many things indicate that we are going through a transitional period where it seems that something is on the way out and something else is painfully being born. It is as if something were crumbling, decaying and exhausting itself, while something else, still indistinct, is rising from the rubble."[4]

[4] Address of Vaclav Havel, Liberty Medal Ceremony, Philadelphia, July 4, 1994.

Chapter 2

Imagination and Creativity

THE *9/11 REPORT* of the National Commission on Terrorist Attacks Upon the United States indicated that a lack of imagination was one of the reasons why the country was not better prepared for the tragedies of September 11, 2001. The commission concluded, "Imagination is not a gift usually associated with bureaucracies."[1] It is widely recognized that imagination is a very important part of the Catholic culture. Indeed without it Catholic people would have difficulty grasping stories about a God who becomes human, suffers and dies. It would be hard to adhere to stories of bodily resurrection and ascension to a heavenly place. It would be incomprehensible to postulate life after death, angels, a virgin Mother who intercedes for us along with a vast array of saints and blessed ones. The stories that come to life in the glass, bronze, wood and stone found in churches and cathedrals would make no sense without lively human imagination.

Imagination is indeed important to a Catholic way of thinking about life, death and eternal life. It is also important in the creation of worship spaces. But what is it? How does one become creative or imaginative? And, in the end, when a major religion like the Catholic Church places so much stock in imagination, is it possible that the teachings of the Church will make any sense to those without it? Andrew Greeley claims that the Catholic imagination is central and meaningful to us. His writings suggest that a collection of religious stories or myths is more central and attractive to Catholic people than any complicated doctrine.[2] While their own lives are presumably

---

[1] *The 9/11 Report,* The National Commission on Terrorist Attacks Upon the United States (New York: Saint Martin Paperbacks, 2004) 492.

[2] See, for example, Andrew Greeley, *The Catholic Imagination* (Los Angeles: University of California Press, 2000).

based on the teachings behind the stories, they come to church to hear the stories over and over again. Keeping stories alive is important to the longevity of any institution, including the family.

Memory fuels the imagination in any work of creativity. With family stories, the narrative has to be remembered in order for it to be passed on to another generation. Maxine Greene suggests that our life experiences provide "only a partial view of things."[3] She continues, "This is where the imagination enters in, as the felt possibility of looking beyond the boundary where the backyard ends or the road narrows, diminishing out of sight. . . . Consciousness, I suggest, is in part defined by the way it always reaches beyond itself toward a fullness and a completeness that can never be attained."[4] I have fond memories of my childhood church, but they provide me with only a narrow view. My imagination now helps me look beyond the restrictions of my memory and that imagination enables me to see things in new ways—without forgetting my past.

The way to remember the paschal event, the story embraced by the Church, is to do it over and over again using the imagination. The enactment of a ritual is not just the mindless repetition of various ceremonial actions or words. Instead it can be the playground for the imagination. Just look around any church and sense how it plays with your imagination. The place for enacting the paschal memorial is a building that reflects the narrative. Stories or narratives are essential ingredients in church art and architecture. In order for the stories to be effective they have to be remembered and lived out. The Catholic imagination has room for stories in each successive age or generation.

How can the imagination affect the design of a place of worship? Is there a way to capture the collective imagination of an entire congregation? The Church has never espoused one style of art or architecture, yet there is what many call the "Catholic look." Until recently this meant that one could experience, albeit in different styles, similarities in any Catholic church. There was the sanctuary lamp that indicated where the tabernacle was. There was the crucifix. There were the statues and stained glass windows. And, there was the smell of candles and incense that seemed embedded into the woodwork. Still today, these elements loom large in many people's memories of what a Catholic church should look like. How is the Catholic imagination needed now in the design of church buildings?

[3] Maxine Greene, *Releasing the Imagination* (San Francisco: Jossey-Bass, 1995) 26.
[4] Ibid.

Consider two new but very different Catholic places of worship. When Cardinal Roger Mahony and the church of Los Angeles envisioned a new Cathedral of Our Lady of the Angels, they worked with the time-honored images of pilgrimage and light (fig. 1). The architect Rafael Moneo responded with a respectful reference to the mission-style churches of the Southwest. His plan is a contemporary reflection on a previous style of architecture. The massive concrete forms are reminiscent of simple adobe churches. The use of alabaster instead of glass allows abundant light to bathe the space just like the fenestration in the renowned Saint Francis Assisi Church in Taos, New Mexico (fig. 2). Moneo had to imagine these connections and then contemplate

Fig. 1 *Cathedral of Our Lady of the Angels, Los Angeles, CA.*
Architect, Rafael Moneo and Leo A. Daly.
Photograph by Julius Schulman and David Glomb.

Fig. 2 *Saint Francis Assisi, Taos, NM.*

11

how to design a place to embody them. This allusion is lost on some critics who claim the cathedral does not look like a Catholic church. Perhaps they are relying only on their memories of their childhood churches.

Architect Richard Meier's new church in Rome, on the other hand, does not emulate a previous style of architecture. It could be considered even more metaphorical than the Los Angeles cathedral. Dio Padre Misericordioso is unlike any other building in the working-class neighborhood of Tor Tre Teste outside of Rome (fig. 3). The church has three convex shells that soar like billowing sails (reminders of a ship) on the outside. From the inside, Michael Crosbie writes, "one senses the release of a spirit that expands the space, filling it like the Pentecostal wind."[5] Is this connection a neo-literalistic statement wrapped in modern skin? Did not earlier builders design churches to look like crosses or the Body of Christ? Or, did Meier, like Moneo, create something new? Why do new churches have to replicate older models? Why do they have to resemble the utilitarian structures in strip malls? Where is the imagination?

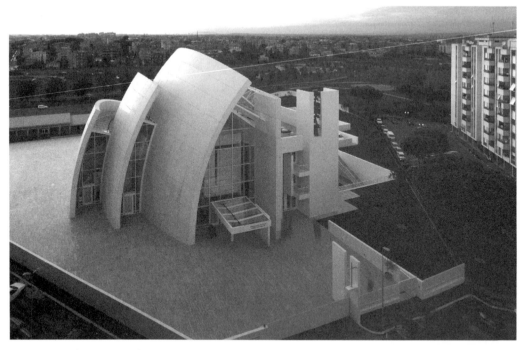

Fig. 3 *Dio Padre Misericordioso, Tor Tre Teste, Italy.*
Architect, Richard Meier. Photograph: Alan Karchmer/Esto.

[5] Michael Crosbie, "Meier in Rome," in *Faith & Form*, vol. XXXVII, no. 2 (2004) 7–8.

Often imagination and creativity within a community context are initially perceived as subjective and self-serving. Only later comes the public perception that the fruits of the exercise are, in the end, for the common good. So there are concerns today that imagination and creativity are partly responsible for the demise of beautiful places of worship in the traditional sense of the term. John Paul II cited this concern when he wrote, "It must be lamented that, especially in the years following the post-conciliar liturgical reform, as a result of a misguided sense of creativity and adaptation there have been a number of abuses which have been a source of suffering for many."[6]

How are we to resolve problems, especially those affecting the common good, in an imaginative way? I once attended an exposition on creativity and imagination that changed my understanding of the Catholic religion and worship environments.[7] It described those things that imaginative people held in common. Creative people challenge assumptions, recognize patterns, see things in new ways, make connections, take risks, take advantage of chance and construct networks. I will take each one of these items and use them as ways of re-imagining the environment for worship.

Challenging Assumptions. When Francisco José de Goya y Lucientes painted the cupola in Igelsia de San Antonio de la Florida in Madrid, he challenged the assumptions of the art world and the Church. In painting the Miracle of Saint Anthony of Padua (1798) "he took the usual Baroque layout—heaven and angels above, Earth and people below—and stood it on its head. Here, the cupola is the zone of Earth and people, and the angels in the pendentives and the intrados of the arches are holding it all up."[8] In effect, Goya altered the understanding of heaven and earth. In the typical hierarchy found in other great domes, Christ is at the apex and the saints and angels are depicted in concentric circles below, and all of these images appear to be staring down at the onlookers. The characters in Goya's dome are interacting with each other, and the visitor cannot help but be caught up in the imaginative conversations taking place. Unwittingly, Goya suggested in his work that real people make up the communion of saints.

---

[6] *Ecclesia De Eucharistia,* Pope John Paul II, April 17, 2003, 52.

[7] *Creativity: The Human Resource* was researched and designed by The Burdick Group with the cooperation of the California Academy of Sciences through a grant from the Chevron Family of Companies. Consultant: Dr. Frank Barron, University of California, Santa Cruz.

[8] Robert Hughes, *Goya* (New York: Alfred A. Knopf, 2003) 212.

If people accept things the way they are, everything will stay the same and no advancement would be possible. A good teacher can stimulate young minds to explore and imagine all the possibilities. Why cannot pastoral leaders and designers do this? How can we challenge the assumption that in order to be "appropriate" the church building has to look like something out of a history book?

Here are some assumptions about church buildings. Can they be challenged? Are there others that could be listed?

- A certain architectural style is more appropriate for Catholic churches than others.

- The clergy must have a place that is distinct from the rest of the worshiping assembly because they are different.

- The baptismal font should be placed near the altar so everyone can "see" the baptism.

- Cry rooms are the only way to satisfy the needs of restless children and their parents or guardians.

Recognizing Patterns. When Gregor Mendel crossbred peas, he observed patterns that helped develop new perceptions about heredity. Similarly, observations of the sky have lead to an understanding of the known universe. Freud noticed patterns of human behavior in trying to understand the human psyche. Recognizing patterns is the ability to perceive significant similarities or differences in ideas or events.

Here are some patterns of behavior occurring in church art and architecture. They are already affecting the design of church buildings. Are there others that could be listed?

- The movement of the Church from urban neighborhoods to suburban developments.

- The return of images of saints to the worship environment.

- The increase of the seating capacity of churches to two thousand and even more.

- The diminishing number of priests available to preside at eucharistic liturgies.

What do these patterns of behavior suggest to church leaders, designers and artists about the environment for worship in the future?

Seeing in New Ways. How often do we look at, hear, touch or smell something in the same way? Some studies suggest that great numbers of humans do not notice things in their immediate environments. Upon seeing the Pantheon in Rome, Filippo Brunelleschi knew he could build the dome for the Santa Maria del Fiore in Florence. His "real stroke of genius was in creating a kind of circular skeleton over which the external octagonal structure of the dome took shape."[9] Creative people use their imaginations to perceive things in new ways. Jazz musicians play around familiar melody lines to give new interpretations to old tunes. To see things in new ways is to take what is commonplace and transform the idea into something else.

Musical composers and design consultants are helping the Church see new ways of singing liturgical music and arranging churches for worship. Language experts, poets and writers have attempted to breathe new life into ritual and biblical texts. Dancers have helped presiders with their body language and posture during liturgy. Drama teachers have assisted readers in proclaiming the Word of God. Visual artists have transformed gloomy churches into vibrant, colorful places.

Here are some new ways of seeing things. Are there others that could be listed?

- A sculpture of an animated Mary helping Jesus learn to walk instead of a statue of Mary holding a statue of Jesus.

- Bold, geometric, colorful art glass windows without figurative drawings.

- Large baptismal fonts with an abundant quantity of living, moving water.

- Nurseries designed to meet the needs of pre-verbal infants and toddlers.

- Flexible spaces to accommodate more than one liturgical or non-liturgical activity.

When the imagination is nourished by but freed from imitation of previous solutions, creative solutions are possible.

Making Connections. Edward Jenner noticed that milkmaids who were exposed to the disease of cowpox never contracted smallpox. From this he developed a vaccination to prevent smallpox. Making connections is the ability to merge ideas, objects or events that seem to be unrelated. The end result is a brand new idea. Once the Ford Foundation gave Paolo Soleri a grant for solving the problems connected

---

[9] Ross King, *Brunelleschi's Dome* (New York: Walker & Company, 2000) 103.

with traffic, pollution and the ever-growing population in the greater New York City metropolitan region. He studied beehives and then designed a vertical city that contained layers of public and private spaces to accommodate millions of people.

Here are a few ideas, some better than others, that have appeared in church design because of connections made with other ideas. Can you identify others?

- Larger gathering spaces based on the concept of atriums in shopping malls and performing-arts venues.

- Covered drop-off areas based on similar provisions at hotels and mortuaries.

- Better acoustical systems based on concert hall technology.

- The incorporation of digital media equipment for the projection of images during liturgy.

- New seating plans based on athletic arenas and theatres designed for better sightlines and acoustics, which in turn engage the participants in the activity in more rewarding ways.

Taking Risks, Using Chance and Constructing Networks. The four components mentioned above can be achieved only if creative people using their imaginations are also willing to take risks. This is no easy task. New ideas are quickly dismissed if they challenge customary practices. Church authorities try to discern how to organize, operate and guide a religion that reaches into every corner of the planet and has over a billion members.[10] Every idea or notion that comes up has so many ramifications. What might work in one country might be a disaster in another. Further, what might be an issue in one region might be a small concern or no concern at all in another.

Nevertheless, is it not possible that a Church could be universal and indigenous at the same time? Is it not possible that the Church could function both as a hierarchical and as a collegial network? There is no reason why a shift in the governance of the Church could not lead to more fruitful participation by everyone in all aspects of Church life.

Shifts in understanding the governance of the Church would have an impact on the design of churches and cathedrals. Instead of separating clergy and laity as if they belonged to different classes, the place

---

[10] With sixty-three million members, the Catholic Church in the United States makes up only 5% of the world's Catholic population.

of worship would celebrate the strength of the whole membership. Instead of presiding from a "clergy only" location, the ordained minister of the Church would take a place among the people as servant of the servants of God.

Imagination is key to advancement and progress in any organization. The Church is a large organization. Could it be that the development of the Church in the future will depend on how well creative thinkers (and all of us) use the imagination? Will pastors, committees, artists and architects become more willing to take risks and challenge assumptions? Could creative actions like constructing networks serve the Church in a better way? These are some questions that should be addressed in the process of building and renovating places of worship. In the end the church building will undoubtedly be a more realistic reflection of the faith community it houses.

Chapter 3

Catechesis

ASK AT LEAST two questions in conversations about liturgy, art and architecture: "Where did you learn that?" and "Do you know if it is true?" Much confusion about what constitutes an appropriate place of worship is, ironically, caused by an abundance of information, fact and fiction, available to anyone with a computer. The Internet provides access to thousands of sources using the word "catholic." How many of these represent the best scholarship on any issue?

Opinions abound in the secular world of art and architecture. Architecture and art for religious buildings cannot escape similar criticism and commentary. Everyone has an idea about what a place of worship should look like. The debate has become so contentious that it has polarized some faith communities. So, how does a congregation find out what is required in its church? What and who decides the location of the altar table and the tabernacle, the seating arrangement and the architectural style of the building itself? What room is there for imagination, creativity, diversity and inculturation?

One way to pursue a building project is to base everything on the official or legislative requirements for the construction and adornment of a church. The end result could be a typical place of worship that may honor the requirements of the law but will not necessarily reflect the character or personality of the local congregation. None of the Church's directives provide details about the architectural style, the finishes or the ornamentation of a church building. Nor do instructions describe what the art should look like or who should make it. That makes sense. Decisions are ideally based on the culture and location of the congregation and not on isolated prescriptions. We need to know the instructions and to know what their rightful role is in the process. The bibliography at the end of this book and the process outlined in the first chapter can be helpful to anyone involved in the task of building or renovating a church.

Another way to begin a church building or renovation project is to consider it an opportunity for catechesis and the spiritual renewal of the entire community. Church buildings are all about the people of the Church. That is where these spaces ultimately acquire their symbolic strength—from the lives and stories of the faithful. The building will possess little objective worth if it does not resonate with the people who will be using it.[1] One role of the building is to play back those stories and re-energize the assembly in doing so. The paschal event—the life, passion, death and resurrection of Jesus Christ—is *the* Christian narrative that is memorialized during eucharistic rites. The worship space must enable the proper enactment of these rites and so draw the faith community more fully into the embrace of the paschal event through the use of a verbal and non-verbal symbol system. The space resonates with the very narrative that is embodied in the gathered assembly. Literally, the people are wrapped in an environment that tells the same story they are celebrating. The manner in which a parish community embraces and identifies with the paschal event will be important to the design of a church. There will be differences based on the local culture of the congregation.

The congregation misses an opportunity for transformation when they or the leadership are content to follow generic rules or revere stories of faith generated in the past that may or may not have something to do with their own lives. A church building could be compared to a homily. Poor homilies have nothing to do with the lives of the parishioners while good ones are crafted in light of the experiences of the community. Thus, before plans are made, church members should be invited to take a look at how their own stories of faith can shape the church building. In turn, the new or renovated place of worship will begin to reshape the community. Only in this sense can the church building be understood as a metaphor for the Church.

The catechumenate process is a good model for a church building or renovation project. The initiatory rituals begin with a time of inquiry when the candidate gathers information about the Catholic faith. A period of separation occurs when the person decides to leave

---

[1] Admittedly, one could engage here in an age-old discussion about the objective value of a work of art that is not dependent upon the subjective interpretation of the one who interacts with the art. That is, can a church be objectively beautiful and not appreciated by the congregation? Similarly, is it possible that a church that satisfies the minimum requirements of the law not be useful liturgically to a congregation? In the case of a church the discussion is exacerbated because it must serve an entire congregation. Subjectivity is difficult to gauge in these situations, and not everyone will get their way.

the security of the past in order to be shaped by new experiences. The next step is an ordeal. It is a slow incubation and learning process when previously unknown resources begin to shape the person anew. This is a time of both adventure and tension where the old understanding struggles with the new information. The next stage is one of re-entry where the transformation of the person is publicly acknowledged and celebrated. The final stage really never ends. It is about the ongoing formation that all Christians are called to.

A true conversion experience is a slow maturing process whereby a person enters a deeper dimension of life. The course of action must first begin with a willingness to be shaped by the experience at hand and not fight it. There has to be a trust that whatever happens will somehow be a good thing. Conversion will not occur if a person stubbornly clings to the old life and does not want to move forward. The journey is informed by personal experiences of God and community, sustenance from families and friends and the steady guidance of the Spirit God.

The task of building or renovating a place of worship will be fraught with anxiety and tension if it is allowed to be a time of partisan politics where one agenda is argued against another. Although a healthy process will allow differences of opinions to be aired and resolved, the best place to begin is to engage the entire congregation in an experience similar to that of a catechumen. In this process the members of the faith community are invited to inquire more about the meaning of church building. They then separate themselves from preconceived notions of what the church should look like. Next they enter into a time of learning and discernment whereby their experiences of God and community help to form the church building. In the end, the dedication of the place will be a public acknowledgment and celebration of the conversion that the congregation experienced now reflected in art and architecture. Over time, the building will begin to reshape the congregation that had a hand in shaping it.

Chapter 4

Scriptural Foundations

THE BIBLE does not present designs for churches—at least not those of our own time. The Bible begins in a garden and ends in a city. There is not a temple, church or cathedral in either place. There are references throughout to places where God meets with humans. These include gardens, mountaintops, deserts, riverbanks and tents. Manifestations of God are found in floods, rainbows, war, fire, manna and stone as well as in female and male imagery. There are detailed directions for the construction of the tabernacle (Exod 25ff.) and Solomon's temple (1 Kgs 5ff.), but these could hardly be considered as plans for a place of worship today.

In the New Testament we learn that early Christians celebrated the "breaking of the bread" in their homes. The biblical texts provide no description of exactly how these houses may have been arranged for such gatherings.[1] The architectural style of these places would have been indigenous to the region. Powerful metaphorical language is used in Scripture to understand the Church as the Body of Christ, living stones and temples of sacrifice. The early Church is also characterized by acts of charity, hospitality, tenacity and courage. These images should not be overlooked today in identifying or defining the local faith community. The final book in the Bible dramatically envisions a heavenly liturgy in a new city of Jerusalem. These texts in Revelation are occasionally used to promote an ornamental and triumphal style of church architecture. Yet no one really knows what such a place might look like. And even with the best imaginations at work the notion of a heavenly place will surely be different for people living in Calcutta, São Paulo, Florence or Camden, New Jersey.

---

[1] Acts 2:46; Rom 16:3-5; 1 Cor 16:19; Col 4:15; and Philemon 3.

The Bible may not be a source for building plans, but it is a marvelous narration of the encounters between human beings ever on a journey and a God who never really leaves them alone. If we come to the building or renovation work as people of the Bible, we come knowing that places of worship are first of all about people's journeys and their communal relationship with God and so with one another. The Bible's stories are full of the human tensions between death and life, sickness and health, poverty and power, sin and reconciliation, good and evil, justice and peace. A church is a place for the enactment of our various rituals that mark these encounters between God and humans throughout the life cycle.

A building to house such a church is a link between vibrant present and our past. It is not a house of nostalgia. A church is not a museum that treasures relics from bygone periods of ecclesiastical history. Some writers suggest that today most people visiting the great religious buildings in the European Union are tourists.[2] They go there to admire the art and architecture. During worship these places are almost empty. Have these magnificent church buildings become romantic storybooks? Are they curious attractions that say nothing about the living Church today? A building to house the Church is to be a holy place that blends the ancestral diary with a contemporary one. It is to link the past with the present and the future.

In the Exodus story the people must press onward into the sometimes uncomfortable and unfamiliar depths of the mysteries and epiphanies of God. Along the way tents provided shelter. The tabernacle (tent) was a visible reminder that God was also on the journey. The New Testament Scriptures point out that it is the pilgrimage and work of a faith community that generates the need for shelter. The earliest understanding of a Christian church building implies that it is a meeting house—a place of camaraderie, education and worship. In fact, the earliest Christian tradition clearly held that the Church does not build temples to honor God. That is what the civic religions did. Thus, a significant ingredient in the building of every church is this narrative that says the faithful journey of the congregation is what matters—not a landmark of a building. Opinions will vary regarding the design and decoration of our spiritual oases, but everyone should know that we humans are the ones who need the shelter, not God.

---

[2] T. T. Reid, "Hollow Halls in Europe's Churches: Attendance by Christians Dwindles as Number of Faithful Decreases," in the *Washington Post,* May 6, 2001, A1.

The Scriptures should be a constant presence during the catechetical phase of the project. In our revered texts there is wisdom for the design of a church. It tells how the people of God are on a never-ending journey where the unexpected is commonplace and where the destination just might be found in the delights and travails of the journey itself. The scriptural foundations for a church building suggest that spaces set aside for the worship of God are also places of refuge where human beings can find sustenance in one another and so encounter the mercy of God. In this sense the church is more like a meeting place that houses the work of the people (liturgy) rather than a shrine that focuses on the deity only. This understanding of a church building and the liturgy that takes place there will greatly enhance our obligation to bless and thank the God of all creation who dwells also in the midst of the Church.

Chapter 5

Christian Writings

THE EARLY CHRISTIAN writers do not provide specific plans for constructing places for the worship of God. But these texts do provide insights on how the church members grew in their understanding of themselves and how they wrestled with the internal and external controversies of their time. Sometimes these writers describe the evolving liturgical practices of the early Church. The *Didache*, Justin Martyr and Hippolytus, for example, give us three vivid accounts of how initiatory and eucharistic rituals were carried out. The Syrian document *Didascalia Apostolorum* portrays a large community but offers minimal information about the building, that is, that presbyters were at the eastern end of the room around the bishop's chair and that the laity filled in the rest of the eastern part.

Eusebius does provide a very early description of a Christian church—the cathedral at Tyre, an ancient Phoenician city (in present day Lebanon). His enthusiastic writings from the early fourth century help the reader understand the exuberant feelings that filled the Church after the Diocletian persecution. The reconstruction of church buildings destroyed by the enemies of Christianity reflected a newfound religious freedom. Eusebius saw abundant symbolic meaning in the lavish design of the cathedral.[1] One could argue that this basilican style also served as a blueprint for other early fourth-century churches, e.g., at Aquileia in Northeastern Italy and Orléansville in North Africa.[2]

---

[1] G. A. Williamson, *Eusebius: The History of the Church from Christ to Constantine* (New York: Penguin Books, 1965) 393–94.

[2] Richard Krautheimer, *Early Christian and Byzantine Architecture* (New York: Penguin Books, 1965) 43.

Other writers like Minucius Felix and Origen wrote that they required no temples for worship, that their hearts were the altars. Tertullian called the church the house of God, that is, the place where the Body of Christ gathered. Ambrose described his basilica saying that the temple is in the form of a cross. Chrysostom wrote that it is not the church building that makes the people holy. Rather it is the people who make the building holy. Likewise, Christian mystics also do not provide plans for building churches. However, their journeys can also provide significant foundations for building up the local community.

Early Christians were intent on distinguishing their Church from other religious practices of the time. This is one of the reasons why they did not worship in temple-like places. It is also the reason why the Church was persecuted—they refused to honor the gods of the empire. Christians, even in the face of persecution, continued to gather together for solidarity, safety and the worship of God with their evolving rituals of Scripture, intercession, psalmody, thanksgiving and sharing in Holy Communion. Homes and other edifices like homes were the obvious settings for this.

The innumerable sources that followed the early Christian writers provide more information about emerging doctrines, philosophical treatises and theological foundations for the practice of the faith. A huge and powerful institution, rivaling any government, emerged from a very small, persecuted band of people who believed in Jesus as the Messiah. The history of the Christian place of worship, from the simple, intimate house church to the enormous, triumphant basilica, mirrors this evolution.

Chapter 6

Early Church History

TO TRACE the evolution of the place of worship throughout the entire history of the Church would be to map out how the social, political and theological events of each age shaped the identity of the Church, its style of governance and its liturgical practice. This history is another important building block when planning a place for worship. The purpose of studying history is not to emulate a particular period but to see how various forces shaped the teachings, rituals and worship places of the Church in the past. We know this will be true of our time also, but we can approach our work with greater care when we have some understanding of the past.

For now, here is a single example of how the times influence the way Christians constructed their meeting places. I believe that the Edict of Milan was the key turning point in the life of the early Christian community. The growth of the Christian church was rapid in its foundation years. Despite (or maybe because of) persecutions, by the early fourth century Christianity was a common religious practice throughout the Roman Empire. Constantine I defeated Maxentius in the Battle at the Milvian Bridge on October 28, 312, and so won outright control of the empire. According to legend he was victorious because of the intervention of the Christian God signaled by the words in the night sky: "In this sign you will conquer." Constantine then returned the favor. His Edict of Milan in 313 allowed the public practice of alternative religions like Christianity, something that he had already done in Britain and Gaul. Many believed he did so out of political motivation rather than any spiritual affinity with the Christian Church. Later in the fourth century Theodosius established Christianity as the official religion of the empire.

In hindsight, the Edict of Milan was a "good news/bad news" event. It helped to establish a unique relationship between the Church and the state. Christianity had endured persecutions and suspicions for nearly three hundred years. Now the emperor guaranteed protection for Christians and used the cross as a banner for the empire. The cost for this safeguard, however, was the unwavering allegiance of church leaders, the bishops, to state government.

As the emperor and his advisors became key players in the polity of the Church (calling councils, naming bishops), the Church itself was slowly taking on the trappings of imperialism. Images of Christ illustrate this shift. Earlier depictions show Jesus as a shepherd. After the edict, however, he was painted as a king, a ruler and a judge, reflecting how the emperor took on the identity of a surrogate Christ. Bishops at that time worked with municipal administrators and enjoyed a privileged rank that would further solidify the clerical caste system in the Church. The new status of Christianity affected everything the Church did including how and where it worshiped. The places of Christian worship began to take on a form that reflected the Church's new identity and power in society.

The study of history can be helpful in many ways. For one, we realize that a congregation building or renovating a church today should establish its own identity not only in the context of the universal Church but also within the various communities where these Christians live. Then it will be ready to shape a space that resonates with that image. Will the shape and style of the church's building reflect the presence of a faithful people doing good work in their neighborhood and beyond? The most beautiful church building in the world would be an empty shell without the presence of a hard-working, faith-filled congregation.

Chapter 7

Early Church Architecture

IS A PARTICULAR architectural style more appropriate than another for Catholic worship? The history of the Christian place of worship is a study in diversity. The evolution of church architecture in various regions of the world was shaped by and gave shape to the social-political-liturgical evolution of the Church in each age. While it is not the intent of this work to examine each and every style of church architecture, a cursory review may be helpful to develop an appreciation for the many architectural forms used to house Christian worship over the last two thousand years.

The history of the Christian place of worship begins in the house. Archeological discoveries and scholarly commentaries provide us with examples of the early house-churches dating to the third and fourth centuries.[1] These were usually the residences of wealthier members of the Church. One well-known example was found in Dura-Europus, a caravan town in Mesopotamia on the Euphrates River. It contained a courtyard, a large meeting room and a baptistery, complete with a font under a canopy. Baptismal images were found on the wall. Another example is the villa at Lullingstone, near Kent, England. In the fourth century rooms in this building were converted for Christian use. Excavations show Christian paintings on the walls including the *labarum* (XP), the sign that Constantine presumably saw in the sky. The church at the Red Sea port Al'Aqabah, Jordan, dates to the late third–early fourth century and will most likely provide more insights about the early house-churches as archeological studies continue there.[2]

---

[1] See Richard Krautheimer, ibid. and L. Michael White, *The Social Origins of Christian Architecture,* vols. I and II (Valley Forge, PA: Trinity Press, 1990 and 1997).

[2] See http://www.chass.ncsu.edu/history/rapweb/home.htm.

According to the historian Eusebius, the Christian community, growing even before the Edict of Milan, had to construct larger gathering places. These were known as assembly halls. Examples in Rome include the early fourth-century church beneath San Crisogono and San Sebastiano planned in a modest architectural style. Thus the evolutionary path of the Christian setting for worship began with the house-church or villa and then the assembly hall. After the Peace of Constantine, Christian buildings both reflected and, perhaps, even gave shape to the various architectural forms of the period. The basilican style, adapted for use by the Christians, was later modified based on regional tastes and liturgical appropriateness. Already in the fourth century there was an eagerness to promote Christianity through construction of buildings for meeting and worship, especially at places of pilgrimage and martyrdom.

This desire marks the beginning of a "building boom" in what was slowly emerging as the Holy Roman Empire. The projects undertaken include the first Saint Peter in Rome (313), the Cathedral in Aquileia (313–319), the Cathedral at Tyre (reconstructed in 316–318), the Cathedral in Orléansville (324), the Cathedral in Trier (326), the Basilica and Anastasis in Jerusalem (335) and Hagia Sophia, Constantinople (360). Many of these edifices had two things in common. (1) They were constructed in the architectural style of the basilica with some modifications. (2) The liturgical plan appears to reflect a more formal arrangement for liturgy where the clergy and laity were separate. The location of the altar table varies depending on the region.

As the Church grew and became more powerful, it influenced emerging cultures, diverse ideologies, political rhetoric, educational institutions and the work of artistic guilds. The philosophical, theological, architectural and artistic productivity stimulated by the Church and endowed by its resourceful members comprised some of the most important contributions to the development of Western culture. Throughout the history of the Church, wealthy patrons of the arts, including members of the hierarchy, commissioned important artists and artisans for artistic and architectural projects.

Architectural styles are diverse and represent each period of church history. They include the Basilican, the Byzantine, the Carolingian, the Romanesque, the Gothic, the Renaissance (a return to classical ideals), the Baroque, the Rococo, the colonial, the neo-Gothic, the modern and post-modern. Tucked within these major movements are endless regional nuances that also contributed to the shape of religious buildings, e.g., tenth-century Anglo–Saxon churches in Britain, eleventh-century Stave churches in Norway, twelfth-century monastic churches and thirteenth-century Gothic structures with their own subsequent French, English, High and Late variations.

In times of transition a certain comfort may be found in returning to something familiar from the past, to bring back architectural styles and liturgical patterns that seem to have "worked" in a previous age. But, this is a false comfort. The study of history does not relieve us of our responsibilities to be creative in our own times. That study becomes a resource for us when it brings enthusiasm for understanding of our own situation. As the playwright Tony Kushner wrote in *Angels in America*, "In this world there is a painful progress; longing for what we have left behind and dreaming ahead."[3]

---

[3] Tony Kushner, *Angels in America* (New York: Theatre Communications Group, 1995) 275.

Chapter 8

Later Movements in Church Architecture

CHURCHES TODAY also manifest a remarkable diversity. One could trace the evolution of architecture by studying places of worship. Our churches also tell something about the liturgical and devotional practices of each age and place. And here we also observe that the basic arrangement of space for eucharistic liturgy in the Roman Church did not change much for sixteen hundred years—until now. Even though the public worship of the Church has always been in a state of constant but usually very slow evolution, from the fourth century to the twentieth century the formal components of the Mass dominated by the clergy remained basically the same in Catholic churches. The style of the architecture and ornamentation evolved, but the general understanding of what people did in the space did not.

The great builders, artists and patrons of the Church worked hard and very creatively to provide spectacular settings for the worship of God in the context of the liturgical norms of their own time. The list of important artists and builders in the annals of Christianity is long and impressive. Fillipo Brunelleschi, Donato Bramante and Michelangelo Buonarroti provided inspiration for major religious buildings during the Renaissance from the fourteenth to the sixteenth centuries. Great builders like Andrea Palladio, Christopher Wren, A. W. Pugin, Ralph Adam Cram and Patrick Keeley were instrumental in reviving the Classical and Gothic forms from the sixteenth to the twentieth centuries. In every project the direction for the designs would come from the clergy and wealthy patrons. It was taken for granted that a church building should be planned to house the liturgy as it was celebrated at the time. Pugin himself wrote that the design should fit the purpose of the building and that it should be obvious to all.[1]

In the twentieth century emerging liturgical reforms in the Roman Church added to the evolving mixture of art, architecture, Church, patron. Dom Prosper Louis Guéranger (1805–1875) was among the pioneers who brought new energy into monastic prayer and stimulated interest in changing the liturgy to give the assembly a more active role. At the turn of the twentieth century, Pope Pius X altered the discipline governing Holy Communion and urged reforms in music and liturgy. In 1932, Pius XI encouraged openness to new styles of art and architecture. Pius XII, in his 1947 letter on architecture, sculpture and painting, wrote: "Modern art should be given free scope in the due and reverent service of the church and sacred rites."[2] The revitalization of Holy Week in the early 1950s also set the stage for the liturgical reforms that would come as a result of Vatican II called by John XXIII (1962–1965).

A combination of burgeoning liturgical reforms, the development of building technologies and the utilization of new materials set the stage for a modern rebirth in church architecture. Conversations focusing on how the arts were giving expression to patterns of new sociological developments coincided with discussions about how to involve the laity in the celebration of the liturgy. New movements were emerging in art and architectural communities. They were most diverse and not without their critics. For example, the Beaux Arts movement (1885–1920) in France, which merged Roman and Greek forms with Renaissance ideals, was highly criticized as too ostentatious by some modernists. The Arts and Crafts Movement of late nineteenth-century England and later in the United States applied standards of fine art to furnishings and interiors. The Bauhaus School (1919–1933) founded by Walter Gropius in Germany wanted to harmonize technology, architecture and crafts.

The movement toward liturgical reform in the Church and the transitions that were taking place in the world of art and architecture led to some very different places for worship. In 1922, Johannes van

[1] A. G. Pugin, "Contrast; of a Parallel between the Noble Edifices of the Fourteenth and Fifteenth Centuries and Similar Building of the Present Day; Shewing the Present Decay of Waste," Salisbury, 1836, in Edwin Heathcote and Iona Spens, *Church Builders* (New York: John Wiley, 1997) 9.

[2] For a commentary on these papal letters, see Karl Borromaeus Frank *Fundamental Questions on Ecclesiastical Art,* trans. Sister M. Margretta Nathe, O.S.B. (Collegeville: Liturgical Press, 1962).

Acken wrote a booklet entitled *Christ-focused Ecclesiastical Art* in response to Pius X's liturgical reforms. Acken called for a very different church plan that would center on Christ symbolized in the altar table. This focus would reject the Tridentine formularies calling for a directional seating plan that drew attention to the place of the clergy or the thresholds to the beyond.[3] The long naves facing the sanctuary where the clergy presided were replaced by a Christo-centric plan where all of the worshipers would sit in concentric circles facing the altar in their midst. Architects like Otto Bartning, Dominikus Böhm, Auguste Perret and Rudolf Schwarz responded to this idea with new church plans. The centralized plan is not new to the Christian tradition. San Stefano Rotondo in Rome (468–483) is a round building 210 feet in diameter (fig. 4). In 1547, Michelangelo favored a centralized plan for Saint Peter's Basilica similar to the one Bramante proposed earlier (fig. 5).

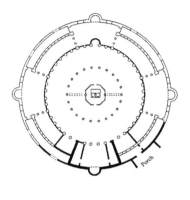

Fig. 4 Plan. *San Stefano Rotundo, Rome.*

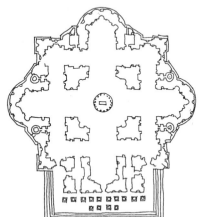

Fig. 5 Plan. *Saint Peter's Basilica, Rome.*
After Etiene Dupérac's sketch of Michelangelo's plan.

[3] Albert Gerhards, "Spaces for Active Participation," in *Europäisher Kirchenbau 1950–2000 European Church Architecture,* Herausgegeben von / Edited by Wolfgang Jean Stock (New York: Prestel Verlong, 2002) 17–18.

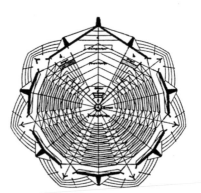

Fig. 6 Plan. *Sternkirche project, Berlin.*
Architect, Otto Bartning.

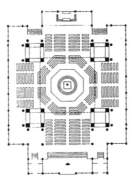

Fig. 7 Plan. *Saint Joseph Church, Le Havre, France.*
Architect, August Perret.

In 1922 Bartning created the Sternkirche (on paper only), which illustrated a centralized altar in a star-shaped building (fig. 6). In 1923, Böhm designed a circular church that challenged the rectangular rooms long used for worship. Perret built Notre Dame du Raincy in 1923 out of reinforced concrete. Devoid of columns the space was open and celebrated the sense of a communal gathering. In 1959 he would design Saint Joseph in Le Havre where the altar was exactly in the center of the church[4] (fig. 7). In 1935, architect J. H. Langtry Langton built the Church of the First Martyrs in Bradford, England, with an octagonal plan and a centralized altar table. Eric Gill wrote, "The altar is right in the middle and the result is very remarkable. The sacrifice is offered not only for the people but by and in the midst of them."[5]

[4] Edwin Heathcote and Iona Spens, op. cit., 25.
[5] *Letters of Eric Gill* (Ed. Walter Shewring). Jonathan Cape, 1947, 351, in Peter Hammond, *Liturgy and Church Architecture* (New York: Columbia University Press, 1961) 69.

In 1928 theologian and liturgical scholar Romano Guardini collaborated with Rudolf Schwarz in the renovation of the chapel at Schloss Rothenfels am Maim, the center for Catholic youth in Germany. Guardini was the chaplain at the time. Frédéric Debuyst called this renovation "an astonishing anticipation of our advances of today."[6] Debuyst, for many decades an important teacher and critic of modern church buildings, wrote: "The important point indeed in a new church is not to arrange as well as possible a set of impersonal objects (the altar, the pulpit, the baptismal font, etc.), but to give form and shape to a living, praying, offering community."[7]

In 1947 Schwarz[8] continued his exploration of church designs that summoned the assembly to be participants and not spectators. One of his church plans (fig. 8) was an exact circle with the altar in the middle (he called it Holy Intimacy); another was a traditional layout with the altar at one end of a long nave (Holy Journey); and still another (fig. 9) allowed an opening to the heavens (Holy Departure). This variety reflected some of the tensions regarding the theology of sacred space. Should the church represent Christ facing the congregation or should it symbolize Christ in the midst of the assembly?[9] The conversation

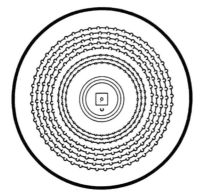

Fig. 8 *Holy Intimacy.* Rudolf Schwarz.

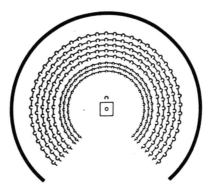

Fig. 9 *Holy Departure.* Rudolf Schwarz.

[6] Frédéric Debuyst, *Modern Architecture and Christian Celebration* (Richmond, VA: John Knox Press, 1968) 60.

[7] Ibid., 59.

[8] Rudolf Schwarz, *The Church Incarnate the Sacred Function of Christian Architecture,* trans. Cynthia Harris (Chicago: Henry Regnery, 1958).

[9] Gerhards, ibid.

that is going on today regarding the arrangement of the assembly during worship is nothing new.

Other significant churches of that time include Notre Dame du Haut (Ronchamp, 1950–1954) by Le Corbusier in a style that is often described as expressionist modern and the Chapelle du Rosaire (Vence, 1951) by Henri Matisse, an inspirational marriage of architecture and color. Instrumental in both of these churches was Dominican priest Marie-Alain Couturier (1897–1954) who fostered, often with great difficulty, the importance of contemporary art and architecture in the creation of inspiring places of worship. In 1955, Emil Steffman designed Saint Laurentius in Munich, a church with the assembly seated on three sides of the table. This masonry structure is decorated sparsely and is devoid of iconography. Gottfried Böhm designed the pilgrimage church at Neviges, Germany, in 1972 incorporating a sinewy pathway leading to a massive concrete edifice with large colorful stained glass windows and an altar table that stands freely in a vast open space surrounded by the assembly.

Such modernist architectural expression was slow to catch on in the United States. The prolific church builder Patrick Keeley (1816–1896) designed hundreds of churches in the Gothic style. James Renwick Jr. (1818–1895) built the present Saint Patrick's Cathedral (New York City, 1858–1879) in the Gothic Revival style. Ralph Adam Cram (1863–1942), a foremost exponent of the French and English Gothic styles, constructed many churches. Architects Christopher Heinz and George LaFarge started the Cathedral of Saint John the Divine in New York in 1892 in an eclectic style—the interior is a mixture of Romanesque and Gothic with Byzantine flourishes.[10] These magnificent places of worship are good examples of my earlier premise that nineteenth- and twentieth-century immigrants to this country were most interested in maintaining a sense of identity while they assimilated to a new society.

At the turn of the twentieth century, church buildings in the United States slowly began to reflect the excitement surrounding the modern period. Frank Lloyd Wright's Unity Temple (1907) in Chicago, Bernard Maybeck's First Church of Christ Science (1912) in Berkeley and Eliel Saarinen's First Christian Church (1942) in Columbus, Indiana, all echo a departure from the traditional Gothic and Romanesque styles.

---

[10] One hundred and thirteen years later the cathedral is still not finished. But, according to one docent, "We are on schedule!"

Coincidently or not, the liturgical movement in Europe and the church buildings constructed there in the 1940s and 1950s reflected a more communal sense of worship that would eventually fuel similar movements in North America. We see this in the publication of *Orate Fratres* (eventually *Worship*) magazine in 1926, the founding of The Liturgical Arts Society in 1928 and the Catholic College Art Association in 1937 (eventually the Catholic Art Association), and in the annual Liturgical Weeks (the first one was in 1940). These were the primary movers educating American Catholics about the worship of God as the work of the people. Architects, artists and the first generation of liturgical consultants began to connect the liturgical movement to the creation of worship places. Among those consultants were Adé de Bethune, Robert E. Rambusch, Frank Kacmarcik, Edward A. Sövik and William Schickel.

In 1957, Cleveland architect Richard Fleischman, aware of the intent of the liturgical reforms and the movements taking place in France and Germany, designed Saint Martin de Porres in a centralized plan with the altar in the center (fig. 10). Louis Kahn's First Unitarian Church (Rochester, 1959) depicts the architect's preference for organic materials like brick, exposed wood and poured concrete. Marcel Breuer, a student of the Bauhaus school, designed one of the first great modern worship edifices built in North America, Saint John the Baptist Abbey Church (Collegeville, Minnesota), dedicated in 1961 (fig. 11). Brother

Fig. 10 *Saint Martin de Porres, Cleveland, OH.* Architect, Richard Fleischman.

Fig. 11 *Saint John's, Collegeville, MN.* Architect, Marcel Breuer. Consultant, Frank Kacmarcik.

Fig. 12 *Saint Louis Priory, Saint Louis, MO.* Architect, Gyo Obata with Pier Luigi Nervi. Consultant, William Schickel. Photography by J. Philip Horrigan.

Frank Kacmarcik was the consultant. Gyo Obata with Pier Luigi Nervi designed The Priory Chapel (Saint Louis) in 1962. It has a centralized plan with the altar in the midst of the space. Emil Frei designed the windows and William Schickel was the consultant for the interior (fig. 12). These pre-Council churches were evidence that the spirit of liturgical reform was now gradually affecting the way in which people in the United States would think about the arrangement of their churches.

The modern and international styles of the mid-twentieth century grew under the influence of people like Walter Gropius, Mies van der Rohe, Charles Edouard Jeanneret (Le Cobusier), Breuer, Eero Saarinen and Kahn. Their schools of thought would emphasize function over form, breaking away from the more ornamental traditions of previous ages. More recently architects like Oscar Niemeyer, Raphael Moneo, Ricardo Ligoretto and Mario Botta would become part of the family of architects who have designed major ecclesiastical buildings in a style reminiscent of the modern movement. Although frequently criticized as ignoring the Catholic genre, the cathedrals they designed (in Brasilia, Los Angeles, Managua and Evry, respectively) are bold examples of the imagination at work. These examples are not to discount the liturgical advancements and accompanying architectural statements that were being made in local communities across the country. In many ways, it was these grass root places that gave birth to the liturgical movement in the United States.

This précis of recent architectural history is by no means complete. A larger perspective emerges when one looks at the history of architecture for worship as it evolved in Eastern Europe, the Middle East, South Asia, East Asia, Africa, and the rest of the Americas along the same course of history. I hope, however, that it is evident that there are ideological tensions between the new and the old in every age. The evolution of a new movement is almost always countered by a reaction (e.g., the post-Modern reaction to Modernism). This is normal whenever paradigms shift.

Such a paradigm shift appears to be the situation today in the world of church architecture. Different schools of thought debate the opportunities and problems resulting from developments in the areas of liturgy and architecture. On one hand, Vatican II affirmed a liturgical reform that necessitated redesigning the interiors of church buildings. One could say that the principle of form following function could be applied in this era. Some would contend even that it does not matter what the exterior looks like as long as the interior accommodates the participation envisioned by the Council. On the other hand, critics of the direction set by the Council suggest that both the exterior and the interior should inspire reverence and pious devotion. This fundamental disagreement has been around for a long time and will not soon go away.

The story of architecture and art is astounding and overwhelming, like trying to visit Florence, Italy, on a day trip! Given the breadth and diversity of this incredibly enormous body of work, it would difficult to argue for any single architectural form or artistic style as more suitable for worship than another. It is clear that the church buildings are distinguished by how they reflect the cultural, political, sociological and artistic environment of its place and time. We can understand why the Catholic religion has never endorsed one building type over another. This itself is a strong, common-sense indication that architectural and artistic diversity can embrace the liturgical practices of each ensuing age.

Chapter 9

Theology

ARE THE STANDARD theologies of sacred space no longer adequate for understanding the purpose and design of a church building in the modern world? Are there emerging theologies that can provide fresh direction? Will these, in turn, affect the study of ecclesiology, which addresses the nature, constitution, function and membership of the Church? Will they also contribute to our understanding of worship?

Liberation theology, for example, arose out of the experiences of oppressed people living in Latin American countries. Pastoral leaders like Oscar Romero and Dom Helder Cámara; educators like Paolo Freire; and theologians like Ivone Gebara, Gustavo Gutiérrez and Leonardo Boff responded to the need for justice and espoused a critical consciousness in the classroom, the *favelas* and the Church. This theology was an attempt not to break away from tradition but to adapt it to a compelling situation that actually threatened people's lives. The actions and writings of these theologians and bishops collectively triggered a whole new perspective on Christian living in countries where poverty and oppression were the rule and the Church's voice often silent.

In a similar way feminist theology rose out of the experiences of women who have been oppressed by male dominated societies, businesses, churches and households. Feminist or womanist[1] theologians like Joan Chittister, Rosemary Reuther, Diana Hayes and Elizabeth Johnson are less interested in breaking away from the founding institutions and more concerned about giving voice to their issues. The objective is Church practice that gives equal status to all members. Church officials have frequently misunderstood feminism and womanism to be thorns in the side of the Body of Christ rather than a movement

---

[1] Alice Walker once described a womanist as an African American feminist or a feminist of color.

that serves to inform the Church on matters pertaining to justice for women in all areas of church life. Is there something in these two theological movements that speak to us about our places of worship?

The theological discourse of the twentieth century provides us with two main currents worthy of attention. What follows is clearly an oversimplification, but it can still serve our purposes here. The writings of Karl Rahner and Hans Urs von Balthasar have attracted both passionate and curious followers. John Allen wrote, "If the Rahnerians held the upper hand for the twenty years (after the Council), the Balthasarians dominate today, at least in terms of official Church teaching and policy."[2]

In rather simple terms, von Balthasar's theology is iconic. He describes his worldview using aesthetic examples. In doing so he eschews a conventional systematic approach and submits that the revelation of God is always by way of a surprise, something that no one can control or predict. God can never be fully grasped and will always remain transcendent to the human experience. The discovery of God is like walking through an art gallery to view the work of a famous artist. Then all of a sudden something is noticed in the art that was not previously known to the viewer and a new revelation about the artist, the art and life itself occurs. In this example, the personal interaction with the work of art does not in any way alter the essence of the work or exhaust its content. No matter how much a person experiences the presence of God and no matter how varied those encounters might be in one's life, the essence of God cannot be altered or exhausted.

Thus, von Balthasar believes that it is not possible to completely grasp the totality of God who always remains elusive. In this iconic world God is beauty and does not have to be perceived or noticed by an observer in order to be beauty objectively speaking. (Some theorists question whether the essence of that which is beautiful is dependent upon the subjective recognition of that object as beautiful.) For von Balthasar that which is beauty on earth exists to provide a glimpse of God who is beauty.

In von Balthasar's world the sacraments are vehicles for the journey toward heaven and the complete experience of God. Necessarily and objectively, the rites have to be formal and prescribed. Anything that would make them too subjective or vulnerable to human interpretation would diminish or eradicate the innate power of the sacramental

---

[2] John Allen, "A View From Rome," vol. 3, no. 14, November 28, 2003.

ritual. Such manipulation could deprive the sacrament of its ability to transport someone beyond the present reality to a liminal state, a taste of the heavenly banquet. Thus the eucharistic liturgy—the music, language, art and architecture employed in its enactment—must be as beautiful, pure and untainted as possible in order for it to serve as an appropriate avenue to the holy One. The focus of the liturgy therefore is not on the actions of the assembly or any one minister but on God to whom the worship is directed. This could be called a vertical dimension of worship.

Rahner, on the other hand, takes a theological position that stresses the Incarnation, the God who, by becoming human, transformed humanity. In doing so God who is not limited by space or time can be experienced freely in the deeper dimensions of reality. God is immanent. Right here. Right now. For Rahner, God is discovered not only in the travails of everyday life but also in the grace-filled celebrations of the sacraments.

The eucharistic liturgy is the ritual activity wherein a person can engage fully in the presence of the incarnate God. While Jesus Christ is the high priest presiding over the sacrificial meal, the people of God, who make up the Body of Christ, are invited to embrace this paschal event as their own mystery. Thus to speak of liturgy is to speak of the God who is present in the very body of the Church at worship. In this theology of immanent presence there is no linear map for getting to God. It is existential and evolutionary at the same time. God is here now but the actual encounter with God is always evolving—expanding and contracting—like the universe. During the eucharistic liturgy the Rahner school suggests that the experience of God in the midst of the assembly is acknowledged in prayers, songs, movement, color and light that sustain the liturgical action of the congregation. The prayer is not addressed to a God who is remote as much as it celebrates the presence of God in the midst of the Church. This may be referred to as a horizontal approach to worship. Humans do aspire to the fulfillment of God's plan in Rahner's thinking, but they also figure in the outcome of that plan. There is always a covenant relationship.

With von Balthasar the setting for the eucharistic liturgy could be understood as a rectilinear box with God at the top, the laity at the bottom and the clergy in the middle (fig. 13). Here the liturgy is understood as a foretaste of the celebration of a heavenly banquet in a new holy city.[3] The worship of God is the responsibility of the clergy who

---

[3] See the Constitution on the Sacred Liturgy, no. 8.

mediate between God and the congregation. Spatially, the worshipers are seated together in a linear arrangement (at the bottom of the box) facing the altar area from which the clergy preside (in the middle of the box). At the far end of this sanctuary (the top of the box) one might find the tabernacle—the holy of holies—where the sacrament is reserved.

In Rahner's school the act of worship is not linear (laity > clergy > God) and could suggest a very different design for a church building. The same could be said of the liberation and feminist theologies. It is a more inclusive place that focuses on the liturgical action of the assembly and not just on the clergy. The spatial setting must be beautiful and pleasing to all the senses but arranged in a way to indicate that the ritual action is one of engagement by all participants. No one in the room is a spectator. The altar belongs to everyone and is not located at one end of the building. Instead it is located in the midst of the gathered assembly (fig. 14). In this plan a circle replaces the rectangular box, and there are no reserved areas that distinguish people according to sex, age, ability or ecclesiastical rank. All members of the assembly, including the clergy, stand, sit and kneel during worship as one Body of Christ.

This centralized plan for a church building offers an alternative theological perspective, another way of understanding an ancient eucharistic theology that speaks about the grace in which we stand (Rom 5:2). Augustine said in his work on the Trinity: "Why should we go running around the heights of heaven and the depths of the earth looking for him who is with us if only we should wish to be with him?"[4] Annie Dillard put it in another way. "Beauty and grace are performed whether or not we will or sense them. The least we can do is try to be there."[5] To paraphrase Dillard, Christ is that grace and is "constantly present in the Church especially during the liturgy."[6] All we have to do is become aware of it and be present to it.

The theological study of God and God's relationship with the Church can offer many perspectives. We can learn from each one of them when thinking about our worship environments. Perhaps the liberation and feminist schools can teach us that church buildings are places that are "evocative, honest and connected to our everyday lives, all its heartaches, terrors, accomplishments; as well as what we yearn

[4] Edmund Hill, ed. and trans., *Augustine: The Trinity*, The Works of Saint Augustine I/5 (Brooklyn: New City Press, 1991) 253.

[5] Annie Dillard, *Pilgrim at Tinker Creek* (New York: Harper, 1974) 8.

[6] Constitution on the Sacred Liturgy, no. 7.

to know and be."[7] It is also possible that Rahner's approach is clearly more in line with the tenets found in the Constitution on the Sacred Liturgy and that von Balthasar adds a dimension of beauty that cannot be overlooked. It is important, when building or renovating a church to understand that these theological conversations have been going on for a long time and will most likely continue to shed light on our understanding of our relationship to God and one another.

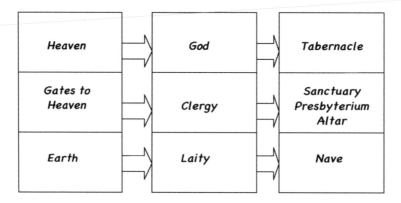

Fig. 13 *Rectilinear plan graphic.*

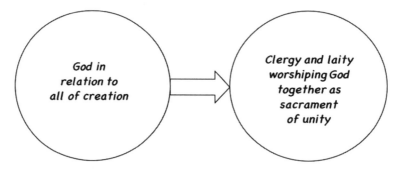

Fig. 14 *Centralized plan graphic.*

[7] Janet Walton, *Feminist Liturgy: A Matter of Justice,* in American Essays in Liturgy (Collegeville: Liturgical Press, 2000) 36.

Chapter 10

Liturgy

THE DESIGN of the interior and exterior of a church is a concern for congregations in any faith tradition. The "success" of the church building or renovation for the life of the community begins not with taste in art and architecture but with questions like these: (1) What model of Church will the building embody? (2) What notion of "full, conscious and active participation" by all the baptized will the building encourage and even demand? (3) What role will the building play in the life of the neighborhood community?

Winning architectural prizes will not matter if the place does not call forth the celebration of the liturgy as envisioned by Vatican II. So, before any plans are made it is important for the congregation to understand not only the theological and ecclesiological implications discussed earlier, but also the liturgical factors.

A pastoral and scholarly understanding of liturgical tradition contributed significantly to the modern reforms. The wisdom of the bishops and their advisors at the Council, the resourcefulness of educators and writers, and the creativity of pastoral leaders over the past fifty years have made some beginning (based on so much good work that went before) at reshaping the worship life in the Church and guiding the reformation of the ritual books. The Constitution on the Sacred Liturgy was the first major document to come from the Council. Its call to "full, conscious and active participation in liturgical celebrations, which is demanded by the very nature of the liturgy"[1] has become the mantra of liturgists, pastoral leaders and congregations desirous of engaging the whole Church in the paschal event. Pope John Paul II reaffirmed this teaching when he wrote that the faithful "must realize that, because of their common priesthood received in baptism, 'they participate in the offering of the Eucharist.'"[2]

---

[1] Constitution on the Sacred Liturgy, no. 14.
[2] *Dies Domini*, Pope John Paul II, May 31, 1998, 51.

Some bishops have published instructions to foster a renewed emphasis on the "right and duty" of all baptized people to participate fully in the Eucharist. Two pastoral letters are noteworthy for their clarity. In his pastoral on the liturgy, Our Communion Our Peace Our Promise, Cardinal Joseph Bernardin wrote about the gathering place for the assembly as it relates to the liturgical event.

> This building called a "church" is a kind of living room of the family of God—it is *our* room when we assemble as the Church. Here we are at home.
>
> Its style differs from parish to parish. Its architecture and decoration may be in one tradition or another. What matters most is that the room allows us all to gather closely, see one another's faces, be truly present to one another. The common focus is the holy table and near it the chair of the presider and stand where the scriptures are read. But liturgy is not a performance, and we are no audience. Liturgy is an activity, and the room itself should help this happen.[3]

In his pastoral, Gather Faithfully Together, Cardinal Roger Mahony indicated that more work needs to be done in this area. "It seems to me that only now are we getting glimpses of the wondrous experience when a parish lives by that full, conscious and active participation in the liturgy by all the faithful. Only in some parishes have we seen the sustained effort from well-prepared leaders to work over many years toward a Sunday Liturgy that is for the people of that parish the nourishment they need."[4] Mahony's letter also addressed some of the tensions that exist in the liturgical renewal. "We do not choose between solemnity and festivity, between reverence and community. The vertical and horizontal dimensions of liturgy must be held together to work for us." On the issue of unity and diversity he wrote, "On Sunday we gather in one Lord, one faith, one baptism. Yet, we are many. When we gather, it is also to witness to the universality of our faith, evident in the many parts that make up the one Body. We celebrate the diverse experiences, cultures, and charisms that assemble around the one table."[5]

---

[3] Our Communion Our Peace Our Promise (Chicago: Liturgy Training Publications, 1984) 7.

[4] Gather Faithfully Together: Guide For Sunday Mass (Chicago: Liturgy Training Publications, 1997) 6.

[5] Ibid., 8–9. See the video guide for this pastoral letter also available from Liturgy Training Publications.

46

We are not free to disregard Vatican II. The notion of participation expressed at the Council and in these pastoral letters is normative. Those responsible for shaping a place for worship should have a thorough grasp of what is to happen in the space, namely the liturgy of the Church.

Chapter 11

The Language of Sacred Space

RELIGIOUS LANGUAGE in the Western world is often based on dualities. Consider some words that are commonplace in the Catholic Church: "immanent" and "transcendent," "vertical" and "horizontal," "laity" and "hierarchy," "heaven" and "earth," "human" and "divine." A problem can occur when we consider these terms as opposites only and not as different aspects often found in the same realities. The language of duality can be a useful way of teaching. Religions use words like "good" and "evil" to help people develop a sense of moral responsibility. The language of duality works best as an expression of wholistic relationships.

The concept of synergy can be helpful here. Synergy is a mutually advantageous conjunction of distinct elements. The word "parent" has no meaning at all without the word "child" and vice versa. "Father" and "son," "mother" and "daughter" get their meanings by what distinguishes them from one another. Do we understand that that is true of the sets of words mentioned above? Are the words "human" and "divine" perceived as opposites and separated from one another? If "human" and "divine" were thought of as relational words then maybe God could be considered more in the midst of the Church and the faithful would be considered standing in the gracious presence of God. Likewise the faith community would not consider the paschal event as something outside its experience but something that it embraces as its own.

The same would be true of the words "sacred" and "profane." Is a church building or work of art sacred? Is it possible for an architect to design spaces or for an artist to create works of art that are "automatically" sacred? Or do these places and objects *become* sacred because of the relational experience a person or group has in a space or in the presence of an icon. Built environments or crafted objects become sacred only when they are experienced in a particular situation. In rituals of dedication we bless and thank God for the gift of land or a building. Churches and ritual objects will acquire sacredness over time just like the materials bronze and copper acquire a patina.

Most cultures have and continue to use up-and-down, here-and-there language to describe the search for the holy or the sacred. Mountains and skies are the dwelling places of gods, saints and angels while the world and the underworld remain the domain of all others. Some research even suggests that this insatiable craving for the wholly other or transcendent is in the very genes of all human beings.[1] So much conversation about church buildings is based on the language of dualities and inevitably tensions will arise: Is God immanent or transcendent? Is the church building sacred or profane? Worship is often explained as either "vertical" or "horizontal."

These tensions can be healthy when they lead us beyond dualities. What if the presence of God were not understood in terms of opposites but relationships? What if the presence of God were not limited to one place or another (heaven or earth)? What if the act of worshiping God took on a more relational meaning that demanded an assembly be fully present, fully involved? What if any place of assembly for liturgy would be considered a sacred place not because of architectural style or atmosphere but precisely because of the presence of the organic, living and breathing Body of Christ, the Church, as it gathers there for worship?

It is often said that the church building is a metaphor for the Church. The Gothic church was often thought of as a perfect expression of scholastic thinking. The vertical stature of the building, the illumination through the windows and the harmonization of architectural forms resonated with the scholastic *Summa*. The high Gothic cathedral sought to embody the whole of Christian knowledge—theological, moral, natural and historical—with everything in its place.[2] The processional style of the long and narrow buildings suggested that the threshold leading to the eternal city is through the sanctuary. The place for the congregation is in the long nave from where they view the

---

[1] See Dean Hamer, *The God Gene: How Faith Is Hardwired into Our Genes* (New York: Doubleday, 2004). Hamer writes that the feeling of transcendence is part of human nature.

[2] Edwin Panofsky, *Gothic Architecture and Scholasticism* (New York: Penguin, 1951) 43–45.

gates of heaven, the ornate backdrops for the Mass and the reserved sacrament. The clergy who dispense the graces to get to heaven preside from this area like sentinels protecting the sacred space. This model of church design, for all its majesty and beauty, does not embody much of the vision that has become central for us now through the documents of Vatican II and through the work of so many who have labored to build up the Church and to serve the needs of the world in these recent generations.

Can our work in building and in renovating churches look beyond the dualities? Does a concentric circle model reflect relationships between heaven and earth, between people and God, between the hierarchy and laity? In the words of Ken Wilber, it "converts disjointed fragments into networks of mutual interaction."[3] So the New Jerusalem in the Christo-centric church plan is not depicted as a remote destination but as a journey that is taking place here and now. It is not a city in the sky but a communal society here on earth working very hard for justice.

---

[3] Ken Wilber, *The Essential Ken Wilber* (Boston: Shambala, 1998) 56.

Chapter 12

Beauty and Aesthetics in Church Design

THERE ARE STUDIES in theological aesthetics that address the relationship of beauty to God.[1] Is there such a thing as a "Catholic" aesthetic when it comes to building or renovating churches? Although the words "aesthetic" and "beauty" do not mean the same thing there is a connection. Aesthetics means to perceive with the senses. Learning how to perceive is important in knowing how to distinguish one thing from another.[2] One could say that the ability to judge the beauty of a place of worship depends on how perceptive someone is. And, while everyone agrees that a place of worship should be beautiful, it is more difficult to agree on the definition of beauty. Are there any principles or standards that could be applied when designing a church to assure that it will be beautiful?

Looking at Church Buildings. When someone evaluates a building in terms of aesthetics many factors have to be taken into consideration. Kelly Knauer in her "Seven Ways of Looking at a Building"[3] provides possible insights for those approaching the design or renovation of a

[1] See, for example, Alex Garcia-Rivera, *Community of the Beautiful: A Theology of Aesthetics* (Collegeville: Liturgical Press, 1999) and Frank Burch Brown, *Good Taste, Bad Taste, and Christian Taste: Aesthetics in Religious Life* (New York: Oxford University Press, 2000).

[2] See Rudolf Arnheim, *Art and Visual Perception* (Los Angeles: University of California Press, 1954) and Mihaly Csikszentmihaly and Rick E. Robinson, *The Art of Seeing: An Interpretation of the Aesthetic Encounter* (Malibu, CA: J. Paul Getty Trust, 1990).

[3] Kelly Knauer, "Seven Ways of Looking at a Building," in *Great Buildings of the World* (New York: Time Books, 2004).

church. In this collection of great buildings the editors used seven "prisms" in making their selections. Each choice was perceived: as a witness to history, as an object of beauty, as exemplar of style, as an artifact of technology, as an emblem of a culture, as the work of an architect, as a repository of social values. Based on these criteria, buildings are important when they are storytellers, exhilarating to behold, good examples of a particular architectural style and building technology, representative of certain cultures, the work of inspired architects and reflections of distinct social value systems.

Can the same be said about churches? We acknowledge that they must first be designed for the liturgical work of the assembly. But is there more? Can you learn something about the history of the faith community in the building? Is the church a place that fills your spirit and makes you feel good to be there? Does the architecture say something about your culture? Was the latest technology used in the project to save energy or to protect the environment? Did the architect design the church to be a unique servant in the community? How well does the church reflect values based on the Gospels?

Past master builders have also presented criteria for judging the worth of a building. Marcus Vitruvius Pollio, a first-century architect and engineer, gave very detailed instructions for designing and constructing buildings.[4] He wrote that all buildings must be designed with reference to durability, convenience and beauty. John Ruskin, the great British art critic of the Victorian Age, distinguished between architecture and mere building.[5] A pre-Raphaelite at heart, he showed a dislike for classical works and advanced the Gothic style. In this work he depicted how sacrifice, truth, power, beauty, life, memory and obedience are vital aspects of the work of architecture. He would later become one of the founders of the British arts and crafts movement.

Thus, in order to be considered a worthy work of architecture the place that houses the community in its worship of God has to be designed with many attributes. How does one go about designing a church so that it will be pleasing to all the senses? Are there any time-honored principles of design that should be followed when planning a church building?

---

[4] Vitruvius, *The Ten Books on Architecture,* trans. Morris Hickey Morgan (New York: Dover Press, 1960).

[5] John Ruskin, *The Seven Lamps of Architecture* (New York: Dover, 1989).

Designing Church Buildings. It has often been said that any building will be pleasing if it is designed with proper proportions and a fitting scale. The Greek philosopher Pythagoras believed that mathematics could inform the creation of structures in a harmonious way and would provide inspiration for the human spirit. Robert Lawlor writes: "The implicit goal of this education was to enable the mind to become a channel through which the 'earth' (the level of manifested form) could receive the abstract, cosmic life of the heavens."[6]

Many great cathedrals and churches have been constructed according to a system of mathematical proportions. Robert Barren in writing about the many characteristics of a Gothic building discusses sacred geometry and how "any one thing can be related to any other in a mathematical fashion, much as any point on a Cartesian scale can be related numerically to any other." He then describes how numbers, often used in the Scriptures (e.g., the number 12), intrigued Christian writers and occur repeatedly in the composition of Notre-Dame de Paris.[7]

One popular geometrical premise for the construction of great cathedrals was the body of Jesus Christ with outstretched arms (fig. 15). The mathematician Luca Pacioli wrote about how the proportions of the human body, also referred to as the cosmic man, reveal the secrets of nature.[8] The human body also offers a good way of appreciating the

Fig. 15 *Human body in a church plan.*
After Francesco Di Giorgio.

[6] Robert Lawlor, *Sacred Geometry* (London: Thames and Hudson, 1982) 6.

[7] Robert Barren, *Heaven in Stone and Glass: Experiencing the Spirituality of the Great Cathedrals* (New York: Crossroad Publishing, 2000) 104–06.

[8] See Anthony Lawlor, *The Temple in the House: Finding the Sacred in Everyday Architecture* (New York: G. P. Putnam & Sons, 1994) 105.

Golden Proportion equation, which can be mathematically complicated. Leonardo da Vinci drew the human figure within a circle and a square delineating the relationships between the parts of the body in proper proportions (fig. 16). Anthony Lawlor wrote "these proportional relationships were called the golden proportion because they not only united the diversity with the body but also appeared to bring coherence to numerous structures in nature."[9]

We need not look very far to discover that these harmonies are all around us. The Italian mathematician Leonardo Fibonacci noticed recurring mathematical patterns in nature. Snowflakes, pine cones, sunflowers, seashells all have perfect proportions. No wonder that builders of religious structures, in seeking designs that would integrate the human experience with the divine, used such proportions in their work. British stone circles, Egyptian pyramids, Japanese pagodas, Hopi kivas, Greek temples, Buddhist stupas and Christian cathedrals all encompass in some way "the archetypal harmonies of the circle, square and golden proportion."[10]

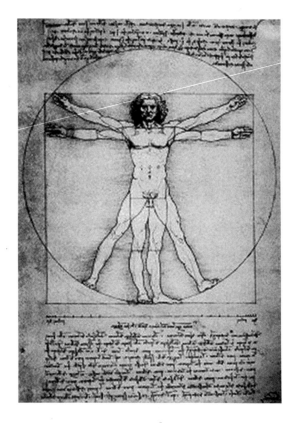

Fig. 16 *Vitruvian Man.* After Leonardo Da Vinci.

[9] Ibid., 108.
[10] Ibid.

The mandala, where the circle and square intersect, is another important shape used to symbolize unity where there is diversity and to show how multiplicity can become one (fig. 17). A Christian adaptation of the mandala could be interpreted in this way. God is present everywhere and cannot be kept separate from creation.[11] The circle represents that which is infinite. The square represents the finite including earth and the Church. The spokes of the wheel in the mandala represent the many journeys of the pilgrim Church. Like aisles in a church building they all lead to the center where the altar table, the symbol of Jesus Christ, is located. The presence of the altar serves as the *axis mundi* gathering the earth and the heavens together. The incarnate God, Jesus Christ, is present in the midst of the church and serves as the way to the truth and the light. In this sense, the centralized plan for a church—in which the entire assembly, clergy and laity, is arranged around the altar table—is a perfectly harmonized expression of the sacrament of unity gathered to worship the God that is in its midst.

The classic circle and square arrangement could again be an important configuration in the design of beautiful and theologically metaphorical places of worship.

Fig. 17 *Mandala Mahakala Gonpo-Magpo Chakra.*
Simplified. After A. T. Mann.

[11] I am not espousing a neo-Pantheism, which would posit that all reality is essentially divine, i.e., that there is no distinction between the creator and the creation.

Chapter 13

Proxemics

THUS FAR I have been discussing various factors that will affect the design of a worship environment. Decisions made on these matters will shape those who frequent the building. Minds, hearts and spirits are shaped by our building. There are additional areas where the decisions of planners will have an impact on those who gather for liturgy. Lighting, acoustics, temperature, glare and seating are among the elements that can affect people no matter how good the homilist or choir is that day. If an assembly wants to create a space for liturgy that fosters full, active, conscious participation, it is clear that some decisions about these matters are going to work better than others.[1]

The three environmental factors discussed below are part of a body of work called "proxemics."[2] This is the study of how people relate to other people and objects in certain spatial settings. What contribution can proxemics make to the design of churches when full and active participation is the goal?

Territoriality. Have you ever noticed that many worshipers like to sit on the perimeter of a congregational space, at the end of a pew or in the last row? They do so for different reasons. Some adults do not want to get too close to the clergy who represent authority or, even, in the minds of some, the divinity. Others would rather not sit close to other worshipers. Some people suffer from claustrophobia and need to sit near exits and away from crowded areas.

---

[1] J. H. Burgess, *Human Factors in Built Environment* (Newtonville, MA: Environmental Design and Research Center, 1981) and R. D. Huchingson, *New Horizons for Human Factors in Design* (New York: McGraw-Hill, 1981).

[2] E. T. Hall, *Handbook for Proxemic Research* (Washington, DC: Society for the Anthropology of Visual Communication, 1974).

Human beings like other creatures tend to establish physical boundaries. We do this to give meaning to our space and to create a sense of comfort, familiarity and ownership.[3] This is also why some people prefer to sit in the same seats or same area of a church every time. When someone encroaches on our personal space we tend to become defensive and protective.[4]

In Catholic churches there is a definitive "pecking order" to distinguish the clergy from the laity, the ordained from the non-ordained. Usually these two groups sit and function in different spaces. Within each space there may be further seating privileges. This pecking order creates psychological and social walls or barriers that take form in such things as titles, attire, language, railings, chancels and sanctuaries in church buildings. The same thing happens in classrooms and courts of law.

For us, the entire assembly is referred to as a sacrament of unity. Shouldn't we create seating areas that do not distinguish some people from others?[5] Settings where the clergy and laity are seated together would manifest the unity of the assembly gathered for worship. The concentric circle mentioned in earlier chapters would be the perfect setting for a congregation seeking to eliminate divisions during worship.

Spatial Arrangements. There are obviously various ways in which people can arrange themselves or be arranged by the furniture at any sort of assembly. "Sociofugal" is the name given to seating arrangements[6] where the gathered people are expected to focus on one or a few persons or objects in one part of the room. These are typically long rectilinear plans with rows of seats moving out from the focus point (fig. 18). This arrangement fosters no interaction among those in attendance; by its very nature, this plan discourages involvement in the action witnessed. Cinemas and other theaters, most concert halls, and older lecture halls are usually arranged in this fashion. All of the attention is either on the movie, the performing artist or the teacher. There

[3] N. Ashcraft. *People Space: The Making and Breaking of Human Boundaries* (Garden City, NY: Anchor Books, 1976) and P. M. Insel and H. C. Lindgren, *Too Close for Comfort: The Psychology of Crowding* (Englewood Cliffs, NJ: Prentice-Hall, 1978).

[4] I continue to maintain that, early in the liturgical reform, some worshipers balked at sharing a sign of peace for no other reason than it was an invasion of their personal space.

[5] See Galatians 3, "Neither male nor female, Jew or Greek, slave or free, all are created equal in the eyes of God."

[6] H. Osmond, "The Relationship Between Architect and Psychiatrist," in C. Goshen, editor, *Psychiatric Architecture*, American Psychiatric Association, 1959.

are times when such undivided attention on something is obviously advantageous. In watching a film, the best seating plan is comprised of linear rows of seats oriented toward the screen.

Catholic worship is not like a theatre or a lecture hall. The liturgy demands active, conscious participation. Every worshiper has a responsibility to engage fully with the liturgical event. The sociofugal seating plan does not work for our liturgy. This is true even in smaller churches, but when churches are constructed to house very large assemblies such an elongated seating plan will inevitably move some worshipers too far away from the liturgical actions.

A better worship environment for liturgy is one that fosters the full participation of every person present. Such an arrangement of any assembly is called a "sociopetal" plan[7] (fig. 19). It can and most often does create the kind of worship setting where the participation of the whole congregation is expected. The assembly, including the clergy, engages in the ritual activities together, each according to different offices and ministries. This approach to the assembly space simply recognizes that the work to be done here is done by all. Decisions flow from this.

Many of us grew up thinking of churches as long, narrow edifices that have immovable, straight rows of seats grouped together so that congregations can face the platform from which the clergy conduct

Altar

Fig. 18 *Sociofugal plan.*

Altar

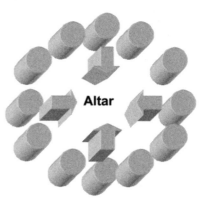

Fig. 19 *Sociopetal plan.*

[7] Ibid.

the worship services. In most Catholic churches the building is still divided into a nave where the laity sit and a sanctuary (also know as a presbyterium or chancel) from which the clergy preside. We have been learning since the Council and even before that this arrangement discourages and often makes impossible the participation expected of every member of the assembly. Such plans also convey quite a different notion of the church from those favored by the Council.

Sight Lines. Here is another good reason for a sociopetal seating plan. The growth of church membership coupled with fewer priests to preside at liturgy has prompted the construction of larger church buildings. This is a concern that I will treat later in the book. I have observed that in a church that seats one thousand people in long straight rows, the last row could be as much as 150 feet away from the altar table, depending on the width of the building. Sight lines in such a long church would be considered undesirable in any other public space, even a space where a sociofugal plan is desired (e.g., a concert hall, theatre or sports arena). A centered or sociopetal seating plan for one thousand to fifteen hundred allows every person to be within a radius where the distance from the altar would not exceed seventy feet. The sight lines in this setting would draw the assembly into the liturgical event and would be more conducive to active participation.

Chapter 14

The Place of the Assembly

THE CHURCH, clergy and laity, bonded by baptism, is called the Body of Christ, the people of God, the sacrament of unity. This is to be especially apparent when the Church gathers for liturgy. In this chapter I will review the transformation that has occurred in the liturgical practice of the Church because of the renewed emphasis on the assembly during all sacramental celebrations. I will then continue the path begun in earlier chapters by examining ways of arranging the whole space that are more expressive of the Church in the modern world.

Studies in sociology and archeology help us realize that the table fellowship practiced in the Greco-Roman culture may have influenced the meal customs of Jews and then Christians in the first decades of the Common Era.[1] Similarly, various ecclesiological, liturgical, social and political factors had an impact on the design of churches.[2] The places where Christians celebrated the Eucharist went through a gradual transition from the intimate domestic settings of the early Church to the large, formal assembly halls and basilicas. This shift was accompanied by changes in the ritual practices at the liturgy.

The eventual clericalization of the liturgy established barriers between the laity and the hierarchy in terms of language, ceremony, liturgical roles, clothing and seating. As different ministries, once shared by baptized members of the Church, became the sole responsibility of the clerics the altar table was moved from the midst of the congregation to beneath the triumphant arch and eventually against the back wall.[3]

---

[1] Dennis E. Smith, *From Symposium to Eucharist: The Banquet in the Early Christian World* (Minneapolis: Fortress Press, 2003) and Dennis E. Smith and Hal E. Taussig, *Many Tables: The Eucharist in the New Testament and Liturgy Today* (Eugene, OR: Wipf & Stock, 2001).

[2] L. Michael White, *The Social Origins of Christian Architecture*, op. cit.

[3] Louis Bouyer, *Liturgy and Architecture*, op. cit.

After the Reformation, the practice of preaching to vast crowds led to the installation of extended rows of pew benches aimed at towering pulpits. Due to the privatization of the liturgy by the clergy, devotions to Mary and the saints became increasingly popular for the laity (even while the Mass was being celebrated). The adoration of the sacrament became more important to the laity than the actual enactment of the Eucharist. The practice of indulgences and stipends further compromised the understanding of the nature of the liturgy.

The Catholic Church countered the Reformation in the sixteenth century with legislation to end liturgical abuses. It then settled into four hundred years with little development in worship. This does not mean that the Church was free of tensions. Certainly movements like Jansenism and Gallicanism created plenty of stress. Church buildings themselves were going through architectural and artistic changes as regional nuances flourished. This period provided some of the most diverse and handsomely crafted houses of prayer. Nevertheless, the interior arrangement of space was basically unaltered for hundreds of years. The nave was the place for the congregation and the sanctuary was reserved for the clergy. In some areas, a highly ornate and often opaque rood screen further divided these spaces. Eventually a communion rail would replace the screen as a divider.

In the mid-nineteenth century, reformers began to raise questions on the nature of the Eucharist and the participation of the assembly. One hundred years later Vatican II would give credence to the research and scholarship amassed in the fields of archeology, biblical studies, history and liturgy, which collectively affected the understanding of how a Church in the modern world governs itself and gathers for prayer. Today, the liturgical movement is also being informed by women's studies and inculturation. The Church, which has a reputation for moving slowly from age to age, is being challenged more than ever before to respond to the issues affecting the global community.

The current liturgical reforms are not modeled after the worship practices of the sixteenth century or even the late Middle Ages. Instead, the instructions now call for a richer and simpler ritual life. The focus is on the participation of the assembly, vernacular language, different ministries, indigenous hymnody, primary symbols, and accessible, interactive worship environments. Indeed the modern liturgical movement draws on many disciplines and attempts to understand and work with vital cultural factors. It continues to study the worship patterns of the early Christian Church as well as those which followed. Above all the renewal of the liturgy springs from a recognition of the Church itself, of the rights and the duties of all baptized persons. The

Eucharist and all sacramental rites are thus always the work of the assembled Church. This is the most fundamental and compelling reason for parishes to create church buildings that resonate with this ideal, places that allow and expect and celebrate the full, conscious and active participation of all the baptized assembly.

The liturgical reforms are seen at present most clearly in such things as ministerial roles, biblical texts, ritual books and hymnals. This has happened in a relatively short period of time, albeit not without much hard work and difficulty. And while most new churches in North America have been designed to reflect at least a limited acceptance of the reformed liturgy, the transformation of older worship environments has been slow.

No doubt older artistic and architectural treasures are an important part of the heritage of the civic and ecclesial community and should be preserved. But there is no reason why these places cannot appropriately be adapted to the ritual requirements of the Church today. It takes imagination and courage, but we have examples now to show that older churches and cathedrals can accommodate the reforms without destroying their architectural beauty. Of course, we also have examples where "renewal" has meant no more than installing a new altar table that "faces the people" while leaving everything else the same. Other churches have been redecorated at great cost without any significant changes in their ability to house the renewed liturgy. Sometimes the artistic elements of the church have been made more important than the enactment of the rituals.

Most of the cathedrals in the world, which are the models for all other churches,[4] have not been reformed since Vatican II. This has contributed to the confusion and frustration in this time of transition. Although legislative and instructional manuals are helpful, they cannot provide a real example of an environment for worship. An appropriately designed and reordered cathedral building can.

As long as the Church remains polarized on many issues affecting its life and liturgy, we will not agree on how the space of the assembly should be arranged. Yet the challenge of the Council seems clear: How can the place of worship be created so that it does not limit or constrain the participation of the assembly during the liturgy?

The design of a church building is now to be based on relationships and not divisions. There is no reason why the concept of a clergy in the service of the Church could not be expressed in the liturgy and its space. The responsibilities that the clergy have in our worship can

[4] *Ceremonial of Bishops* (Collegeville: Liturgical Press, 1989) 46.

never honestly be expressed in terms of power and authority. Instead, the tone of voice, gracious manners, the content of homilies, the body language, the seating preference, and the overall "presidential" style of bishops and priests during the liturgy are expressions of leadership and of service.

Are there, then, models for designing church buildings where all parts architecturally resonate with the ecclesiological and gripping notion of the sacrament of unity? In the period following the council, three types of floor plans emerged in building or renovating churches. The fan shape, the semi-circular and the horseshoe arrangements became popular ways to implement the liturgical norms. Recently, the choral or monastic plan has also been used (figs. 20, 21, 22, 23, 24, 25 and 26).

Some are concerned about being able to see the face of the presider in these sociopetal seating plans. Even if some of the assembly is behind the priest during the Eucharistic Prayer, the presider should proclaim it in such a way that all worshipers are drawn into the prayer, which is rightfully theirs. While it may be important for some to observe the Eucharist elements at this time, seeing the face of the priest is no more important than seeing the faces of everyone else in the assembly. Some presiders have begun to stand away from the altar during the Eucharistic Prayer to make it possible for others to see the table in circular plans.

Fig. 20 *Saint Peter's Church, Boerne, TX.*
Architects, Davis & Rexrode Architects, Inc.
Photograph by Larry Pearlstone.

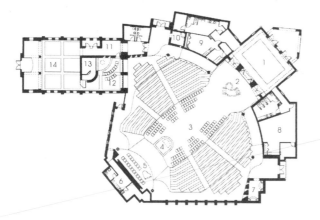

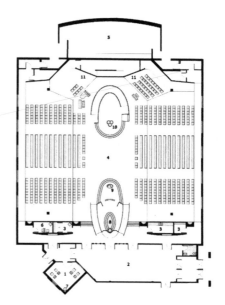

Fig. 21 Plan. *Saint Peter's Church, Boerne, TX.*
Architects, Davis & Rexrode Architects, Inc.

Fig. 22 Plan. *Corpus Christi Church, Ushers, NY.*
Architect, James Hundt.

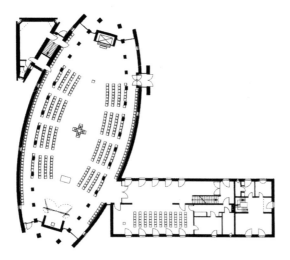

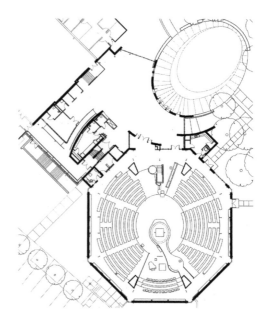

Fig. 23 Plan. *Saint Christopher Church, Westerland, Sylt.*
Architect, Dieter G. Baumewerd.

Fig. 24 Plan.
Saint Rose of Lima Church, Gaithersburg, MD.
Architect, The Kerns Group.
Consultant, John Buscemi.

64

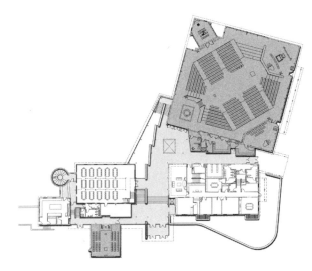

Fig. 25 Plan. *Saint Francis de Sales, Morgantown, WV.*
Architect, Rafferty Rafferty Tollefson. Consultant, James Moudry.

Fig. 26 *Saint Francis de Sales, Morgantown, WV.*
Architect, Rafferty Rafferty Tollefson.
Consultant, James Moudry.
Photography by Steve Bergerson.

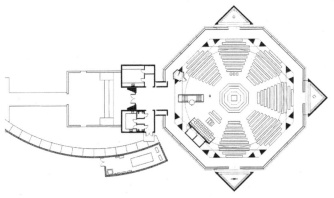

Fig. 27 Plan. *Saint Jean Vianney, Baton Rouge, LA.*
Architect, Trahan Architects.
Consultant, Marchita Mauck.

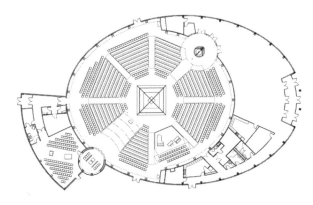

Fig. 28 Plan. *Saint Theresa, Tuckerton, NJ.*
Architect, Phil Kunz, R. A.
Consultant, Richard Vosko.

65

I have already indicated that the truly centralized plan (where the entire assembly including the clergy gather around the altar table) is not new in the Church. A centrally planned building may be square, polygonal or circular. In my opinion, this plan resonates best with the vision of the liturgy enunciated by the Constitution on the Sacred Liturgy. By its very nature the circle symbolizes and fosters unity in the Body of Christ. It is also an archetype of the relationship between heaven and earth, God and creation. The circle is a natural form with no beginning or ending. It embraces the energy and prayers of the entire community. Within the sacred circle the wholistic experience of the union of God and creatures is apparent in time. There is no separation. God and heaven are no longer depicted as elusive rewards for good works on earth. Instead they are perceived and celebrated as distinct but not separated parts of the whole entity (figs. 27, 28, 29, 30 and 31).

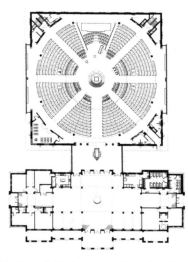

Fig. 29 Plan. *Saint Bede Church, Williamsburg, VA.*
Architect, The Kerns Group.
Consultant, Richard Vosko.

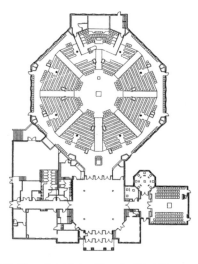

Fig. 30 Plan. *Saint John Church, West Chester, OH.*
Architect, John Ruetschle Associates.
Consultant, Richard Vosko.

Fig. 31 *Saint John Church, West Chester, OH.*
Architect, John Ruetschle Associates.
Consultant, Richard Vosko.

The centralized layout of a church based on concentric circles can be an excellent model for the design of church buildings today. There is vigor in this form that celebrates equity and solidarity. The circle can embrace and empower those within. The circular plan invites participation and discourages spectatorship as the studies in proxemics point out. There is no audience or stage. Dualistic notions of God and creation, heaven and earth, clergy and laity, are gone and relational notions are suggested. The sense of mystery or sacredness is not to be found in some distant place or ideal but in the deeper dimensions of the gathering where the worshipers enjoin themselves to the sacrifice of the redeemer God. And, there is no beginning or end to the circle, making it a perfect expression of the sacrament of unity, the Church, the Body of Christ. The mystery of the incarnate God is found in the circle, a shape so organic and indigenous to the human experience that it has been incorporated in the domes, windows and floors of the world's great religious buildings.

The behavior of the assembly during worship can be affected by the plan itself. Standing in a circle, all know they are vital to what is being done here. The Church is encountered as the body of believers, face to face. The words "vertical" and "horizontal" are important in this issue. Because they are dualistic terms they can imply that worship is to be one thing or the other. Yet worship must be both horizontal and vertical. Can a church space be designed in such a way that we are simultaneously drawn into both dimensions? I believe the style of liturgical celebration, the interior design and the artwork in the church as well as the shape of the building are essential factors in achieving this.

The key principle to observe is that a church or cathedral is primarily a place set aside for the worship of God. The seating plan should honor this function. "The most powerful experience of the sacred is found in the celebration and the persons celebrating, that is, it is found in the action of the assembly: the living words, the living gestures, the living sacrifice, the living meal."[5]

[5] *Environment and Art for Catholic Worship* (Washington, DC: United States Conference of Catholic Bishops, 1978) no. 29.

Part Two

Building Plans

A church should be a pleasant place to be in and should function well as we celebrate the Church's rituals. This section reviews the spaces and objects that ought to be considered in building or renovating. Because of the diversity of the Church, it should be kept in mind that these are generic concepts and are brought into our experience within the practice of the local community.

My examples draw upon the Catholic experience yet my hope is that other liturgical traditions will find these contributions helpful to their own situations. The references to a parish or congregation embrace also projects undertaken by religious communities.

This section is not intended to be a commentary on existing policies or instructions published by one entity or another. Therefore there are no cross-references to such manuals within the text. The reader is encouraged to access such documents for more information. The topics include:

- The Church Gathers

- The Church Baptizes

- The Church Celebrates the Eucharist

- Music Ministry, Instruments and Acoustics

- The Role of Art in Worship

- Light and Color and Glass

- Chapels

- Memorial Places

- Auxiliary Rooms

Chapter 15

The Church Gathers

THE ENVIRONMENT for worship begins on the outside of the church building—in parking lots, along sidewalks, in gardens and plazas. The entire site, whether a small plot on a city street or a vast field in the suburbs, is hallowed ground because of the many sacred journeys that have occurred or will occur there. The site as well as the building should be inviting and hospitable, key characteristics of the assembly. Everyone should feel welcomed! The following elements are important to the gathering of the community.

Pathways. The pathways leading to places of worship are images and reminders that Christians are ever on a spiritual journey, always on the way.[1] The ubiquitous automobile and dangerous neighborhoods have compromised the notion of such a pilgrimage. To counter hectic lifestyles and routine distractions, walkways from parking areas become important as a respite for worshipers as they move toward the church. Not always the shortest distance between two points, such pathways transport people from our individual lives to our assembly as the Body of Christ. In non-urban settings, the challenge is to keep cars as far away from the church as possible. In the city, well-lighted, barrier-free and landscaped sidewalks can contribute to a pleasant and safe experience. Civic governments are often cooperative in closing off a street for major church events or changing traffic rules on weekends.

There should be one major barrier-free access to the main commons (gathering place) of the church so all persons can have the same gathering experience. Multiple entries discourage this. If possible, a covered entry near the handicapped parking area would provide protection

---

[1] Christopher V. Stroik, "Path, Portal, Path," in the *Meeting House Essays* (Chicago: Liturgy Training Publications, no. 10, 1999).

from the elements and would accommodate physically challenged and elderly worshipers, bridal parties and funeral processions. Although it does not have to be constructed over the main entrance to the building, this *porte cochere* should provide direct access to the commons.

Signage. Ideally, a church building should not require a sign to identify it. Nevertheless we live in a time when signs are everywhere. One simple and conspicuous sign should be sufficient to identify the building and the community. Clear but discreet signage can direct pedestrians and vehicular traffic. The use of neon or fluorescent lamps or light emitting diode (LED) technology to illuminate the signs could create a gaudy and commercial appearance. All signs should be designed in a consistent way out of materials that honor the environment, the architectural style and the materials of the buildings. Local ordinances will apply in every case. Schedules and announcements could be placed on a kiosk near the main door or inside the building. All signs could be written in the two or three major languages widely used in the community. Braille should be used where appropriate.

Landscaping. A comprehensive landscaping plan for the church grounds is important, especially in an urban setting where the buildings may be surrounded by concrete. A garden-like environment, even if very small, creates a softer connection between the roads, streets and the actual church complex. The retention of trees wherever possible helps even in the parking areas. The plan should also consider landscaped islands and walkways that would connect the car parking with the main entrance to the church.

Berms, islands, perennial and annual flower gardens, new trees and shrubs are not frills. The landscaping should take into consideration natural resources including water, soil types and sunlight. For example, in arid regions a xeriscaping plan would incorporate slow growing, drought tolerant plants. Where space is available, a landscape plan could also include a water garden (e.g., a pond), which might serve as a retention basin. Ecological and safety issues should be taken into consideration wherever water is used.

Lighting. All walkways and outdoor spaces on the church grounds should be adequately lighted for safety and security. The lighting system could also highlight the church, outdoor works of art and seasonal displays (e.g., the crèche or a cross). The church itself is a symbolic beacon to the world. At times it may be desirable to light the building from inside and out. The aesthetic illumination of the exterior should be clear and decisive. The shadows should run in the same direction. The color-rendering properties of the lamps should honor the materiality of the building. The reflectance value of the materials should also be noted. High intensity discharge lamps are suitable for these purposes.

The Plaza. The main purpose of a plaza in front of a church is to foster the gathering of large numbers of people (fig. 32). Such spaces are often found outside churches that are unencumbered by vehicular traffic. The immense *zócalo* in front of the Metropolitan cathedral in Mexico City or the plaza at the new cathedral in Los Angeles are similar to the outer precincts of the Jewish temple and the area surrounding the Ka'bah in Mecca. These are places for people to mingle and meditate. In San Antonio the parishioners use the streets and public main plaza in front of San Fernando Cathedral to enact their Holy Week dramas. The plaza in front of Grace Cathedral in San Francisco encompasses a labyrinth where pilgrims can walk in search of peace and harmony. The church serves its own members and the larger community when it creates significant public exterior space where people can be alone or in small groups or sometimes in large assemblies. This can be an important way of being present to the larger world.

As the celebratory and liturgical entry to the church, the plaza is a place for the blessing of candles, palms and fire, as well as other preparatory rituals (e.g., at weddings and funerals). A permanent hearth, perhaps inscribed with a cross, could be located at the center of

Fig. 32 *Plaza.*
Blessed Sacrament, Warren, OH.
Architect, Richard Fleischman.
Consultant, Richard Vosko.

73

Fig. 33 *Outdoor Art.*
Brasilia Cathedral, Brasilia, Brazil.
Architect, Oscar Niemeyer.

the plaza to mark a place for lighting the Easter fire. The color of the stone used in the hearth should complement the building and the surrounding pavement. The location of the plaza should take advantage of the winter sun and protect itself from strong winds. In southern regions a plaza needs protection from the summer sun.

The plaza is really an outdoor room that provides a processional link from the streets and parking areas to the main entrance and commons. The pavement in this plaza could incorporate a radial or directional pattern using natural stone pavers. The labyrinth would be another design possibility for the pavement. Consideration for maintenance should be given especially when snow will be part of life. All-weather seats in the plaza could accommodate worshipers and visitors when the temperature is comfortable.

In urban centers plans could consider the reorganization of underutilized spaces contiguous to the church. Where there is enough setback space, the front steps could be reconstructed to create an expanded terrace that would allow people to gather outside the main doors. These spatial provisions encourage people to arrive early and then after the liturgy linger and visit. All this is vital to building community.

Artwork Outside the Church. The concern for vandalism should not deter the installation of outdoor works of art. The plaza or terrace could be used to display art celebrating the liturgical cycle, e.g., a crèche at Christmas or the cross during Lent. The pathway to the entrance of the Metropolitan Cathedral in Brasilia is lined with sculptures of saints to remind worshipers that others have taken the journey before them (fig. 33). Also, provision can be made for flying lanky architectural

74

hangings during festive occasions: along the streets and the sidewalks, elsewhere in the plaza and on the church building. The location of sleeves in the pavement and hardware on the building should be considered ahead of time. Permission from civic officials can be obtained to fly such banners from city street lamp posts.

Meditation or Memorial Garden. Honoring the memory of benefactors and other loved ones is an important gesture. A low-profile granite wall in a small garden area can set off a quiet area for contemplation. In urban settings, if space is available, falling water or a splashing fountain might serve as an acoustical buffer from the noise on the streets. An alternative location for a memorial wall would be in the commons itself, e.g., etched or carved names in the glazing. Some congregations embed memorial bricks or pavers inscribed with names into the pathways leading to the church. See the chapter on Memorials for other thoughts on the subject.

Bells and Bell Tower. Just as a *muazzin* calls Muslims to prayer during the day, bells traditionally have been used to signal times of prayer and call Christians to worship. A freestanding bell tower (campanile) could be designed to stand alongside the church. A carillon in an archway leading into the plaza is another option. Every effort should be made to maintain bells and their towers in older churches. In new churches true bells rather than a system using pre-recorded chimes is a worthwhile investment. They sound better. There are different types of bells: those that peal (two or more, up to eight), chimes (nine to 21) and carillons (21 and more). Bells removed from churches that have been closed can be purchased for much less than the cost of new ones. However, extracting them from one location and installing them in another can be costly.

Thresholds. An arch is a structural form that identifies a passage from one place to another. In religious buildings the arch transports the worshiper from the realities of the everyday world into a more liminal state. A lintel is an overhead horizontal beam that has the same Latin root as *limen*, a threshold in both a physical and spiritual sense. Whether we pass through a gateway to a Shinto shrine or the archway leading to a mosque, moving through a threshold signals the first crossing over from the outside world into the space where this community of sisters and brothers gathers. This passing through can add to the excitement that should accompany the arrival at a church.

Doors. The mythologist Joseph Campbell once remarked that anything is possible on the other side of a door to a sacred space. How do we

Fig. 34 *Great Bronze Doors.* Cathedral of Our Lady of the Angels, Los Angeles. Sculptor, Robert Graham. Photograph by Julius Schulman and David Glomb.

construct such a door to the house of the church where, it is believed, illness, loneliness, hunger and desperation are replaced by health, companionship, sustenance and hope? The doors bear a tremendous responsibility. They cannot look or feel like dull and monotonous doors to a shopping center. Although very different from each other, both Lorenzo Ghibherti's fifteenth-century north doors to the baptistery in Florence and Robert Graham's twenty-first century doors to the Catholic cathedral in Los Angeles help pilgrims, tourists and the faith community connect with the biblical and cultural roots of their faith and hope in God (fig. 34). These sacred portals enhance the religious experience and should not be overlooked in the design of newer places of worship. Doors in older churches often need to be refurbished.

One Common Doorway. In Scripture, John 10 provides an image of Jesus as the sheep-gate. Although adequate emergency exits are required, one and only one entrance should appear as the common "front" door to a church. All worshipers could be encouraged to enter through this door by walking through the open plaza or the cityscape terrace. Access to offices and meeting rooms in the church could be through distinct entrances or through the commons.

These are not ordinary doors. They should be strong, practical (easy to open), beautiful and in harmony with the architectural style of the building. The doors should be crafted using authentic materials in an artistic way. They could be taller than usual to help signify the importance of this entry. Concerns for durability, building security and personal safety should not be overlooked. One door in this common entrance should be automatic to accommodate the needs of elderly or physically challenged persons and people pushing strollers.

The Church Commons. Part of the mega-church phenomenon, which will be discussed in the final section of this book, is the element of hospitality and thus the important function of a large main entrance where all persons are greeted. A commons is the gathering place, an interior space we pass through (with time to linger) as we come to and depart from our worship and other events. In its design, this place is a continuation of the plaza or garden. It extends a ceremonial and processional pathway from the outside of the church to the main assembly area. Thus, this space should not look like an ordinary lobby in a school, theatre or museum. All surfaces as well as the lighting and works of art should be designed to draw us into the main worship center of the building.

But this is also a gathering place. In this sense there are areas in the commons designed to accommodate various projects that are part of the life of the community (e.g., food collections and clothing drives). Two things are important and sometimes they have to be held in tension: (1) Great care must be taken that this place not become cluttered or unkempt with random displays and notices. (2) Yet it should look like this is a place belonging to people involved in a great number of activities, projects and interests.

In older rural churches the only gathering place is the weather lock (the space between the outside doors and the inside doors) that provides protection from the wind and extreme temperatures. In other churches a narrow narthex provides some gathering space along the church's back wall. In these situations consideration could be given to the removal of some seats inside the worship area, near the main doors. This could provide the congregation with some room to prepare for processions or gather after the liturgy especially if there is no church hall. Sometimes, the church can be connected to another building so that the annex becomes the narthex or common gathering area (fig. 35).

Fig. 35 *Commons.*
Hoversten Chapel, Augsburg College, Minneapolis, MN. Architect, Edward A. Sövik, SMSQ Architects.

77

Art in the Commons. The presence of art in church buildings does not have to be limited to the area of worship. Settings for religious art along corridors or in designated areas of the commons should be planned in advance. A written program prepared by an art committee would establish the criteria for the art to be commissioned. Attention to lighting, temperature and security is important.

Clear Glass and Art Glass. Light is another ingredient of hospitality. A combination of art and clear glass windows could be planned for the commons. Abundant natural light could filter into the space through energy efficient clerestory windows and/or skylights. Ceiling to floor windows would make it possible to enjoy the outdoor landscape. As an alternative, art glass could be commissioned to begin a theme or narrative that would continue in the assembly part of the church.

Lighting in the Commons. The careful blend of natural and indirect electric lighting should facilitate the maximum use of this commons during the day or night. Different levels of incandescent lighting intensity should be controlled from a convenient and secured location. Fluorescent or high intensity discharge lamps would not be appropriate in this space. All lamps and fixtures should be easily maintained, unobtrusive and flexible.

Multi-lingual Indoor Signage and Guidebooks. Indoor signs should not provide direction to or identify liturgical spaces or furnishings. For example, there is never a reason to place a sign on the font that says "font." Such ritual objects and liturgical places (e.g., a reconciliation chapel) should be recognizable by their distinct designs. Anyone should recognize the difference between a pool in a mall and the baptismal font because of design, materials and location. In churches visited by tourists some signage may be important but should always be discreet. All directional signage and guidebooks could be written in the two or three languages most familiar to the community. Braille should be used as needed.

Support Spaces Near the Commons. In a new church building the commons often serves as a hub connecting many different spaces in the church complex. Another possibility is that the main entrance to the church could be connected by ambulatories leading to other support spaces in the complex.

In this chapter I have identified those spaces and objects that are important as a congregation gathers for worship. Acknowledging that some or all of these areas might not be possible in older churches, this is still a worthwhile checklist for planning a church building.

Chapter 16

The Church Baptizes

MANY RELIGIONS have provided areas for ablutions or water baths of initiation within or near their places of worship. Muslims wash themselves *(wudu)* to obtain a ritually pure state before entering the mosque to pray. Many Jews use the ritual bath *(mikvah)* for the purification of the body and, at times, to mark conversion to Judaism. In the Christian context the water bath is a crossing or threshold for both an individual and the Church itself. How is this a part of our common space?

In the early Christian Church new members were baptized in rivers and lakes. Then came bath-size pools in or near churches. Over time the increase in infant baptism coupled with a reduction in the number of adult initiations led to the use of smaller pedestal fonts. These shallow bowls where the water is hardly perceptible are still found in many church buildings.

Clearly the baptismal act became more efficient, less messy. But what was lost when the water—still more or less required—practically disappears? What is water? Why was it once not only required but full and powerful? The important polysensory connection made possible by immersion in a large body of water is entirely lost when only drops are dribbled on foreheads. The potential embrace of the underlying mystery *effected* by the ritual act of initiation is scorned. In the water bath the candidate and the community experience the passage from one way of life to another. This is not a mere cerebral experience.

In many Christian denominations there is a renewed emphasis on the presence of water in places of worship. The first liturgical focal point encountered in a church should be the baptismal font. With its abundant and moving water, it is a crossing where the Christian embraces and is embraced by the life, death and resurrection of Jesus Christ. The living water is a reminder of the death we died and the life we live, a constant presence to the church as we gather and disperse.

The size and location of baptismal fonts has varied throughout Christian history. In some places the large pools were located in separate baptisteries, e.g., at Ravenna and Pisa. When the small pedestal font came into use, it was usually located in or near the main entry to the church. Many fonts are still found in the baptisteries next to the narthexes or porches of older churches. In the buildings of other Christian churches, smaller basins for baptism are found in or near the chancel area. In churches where the font was tucked in some out of the way corner or missing completely, holy water stoups were added as surrogate fonts where people could "bless" themselves as they entered the building.

After the reforms of Vatican II, many fonts were placed near the altar table. Even though there is no clear historical precedence in the Catholic tradition for this practice, many parishes are still inclined to do so. This preference is based somewhat loosely on the principle of active and conscious participation: Should not everyone in the church see everything that is going on during baptismal liturgies? But seeing doesn't equate with participation. The baptistery and its font is an area meant for a ritual bath, while the altar table and the assembly seating area are designed for offering, eating and drinking during a ritual meal. These are very different human activities and each one requires its own setting. When the font competes for space and attention with the altar table (another major ritual furnishing), the clarity of each symbol is compromised.

In new churches every attempt should be made to create centers within the church, i.e., appropriate settings for important liturgical actions. Blending these areas dilutes the importance of each space and what goes on there. The development of distinct ritual places throughout the church will prompt the use of processions from one area to another. These separate settings are not and should not be merely convenient.

When the font is located in its most historical and symbolic location, in or near the main entrance to the worship center, it becomes a vital element in the processional act of moving through the main doors, through the baptistery and to the altar table (fig. 36). This passage is in fact our Christian life. When placed near the main entrance, the font provides worshipers with a chance to touch the water and remember their own baptism.

The rituals for other sacraments and devotions will often include processions from the main entrance of the church. Pausing at the font is an important gesture during celebrations of marriage, first communion, confirmation, and finally Christian death and burial.

Fig. 36 *Saint Jean Vianney Church,*
Baton Rouge, LA.
Architect, Trahan Architects.
Consultant, Marchita Mauck.
Photograph by Timothy Hursley.

Fig. 37 *Saint Francis de Sales, Morgantown, WV.*
Architect, Rafferty Rafferty Tollefson.
Consultant, James Moudry. Photograph by Steve Bergerson.

The Setting for the Font. When the baptistery is between the commons or entrance area and the space for Eucharist, then the baptistery
serves as a distinct *transitional* space or passageway. This bridge between
the two spaces is not a corridor but a spacious and wide promenade.
Something is lost when the font is crowded into the back of the center
aisle. The font should always be in a processional part of the church.
Like the altar table, the font needs a generous amount of uncluttered
space to accommodate baptismal candidates, sponsors, family members,
the presiding minister and members of the assembly. Other furnishings or seats should not encroach upon the font (fig. 37). Decorative
flooring materials could be installed around the font to distinguish the
baptistery from other areas in the church building.

Fig. 38 *Font.* Saint Charles Borromeo Church, Kettering, OH. Basin by Architectural Glass Art, Inc.

The Design of the Font. The font should be designed to accommodate infant and adult baptism by immersion (fig. 38). Some congregations object: "We don't do that here." They mean that the immersion of candidates, which is an option in the rites, is discouraged or not allowed. But the option is for the candidate or the parents or guardians of the children to be baptized. If the font is to be a powerful symbol, it must be large and full of living, moving water. Whether it is a single container or two containers (with water flowing one level into another) has to do with practical issues. The experience of passage is found in

the act of immersion—going into the water and then coming up out of it. The classic shapes (octagon, hexagon, cruciform, rectangle) have worked well for a long time.[1]

Sometimes an older font basin or other elements no longer used in the church (e.g., altar railing) can be incorporated into the new larger font. Care should be taken not to undertake this design approach unless the new and old materials complement each other in terms of proportions, materials and color (fig. 39).

Fig. 39 *Old font with new.*
Christ the King Cathedral, Superior, WI.
Architect, Architectural Resources, Inc.
Artisan, Saint Paul Fabricating and Decorating.
Designer, Richard Vosko.

[1] See T. Jerome Overbeck, S.J., "Ancient Fonts, Modern Lessons," in the *Meeting House Essays* (Chicago: Liturgy Training Publications, no. 9, 1998).

A connection is sometimes attempted between the font and the altar table by means of materials, but again one furnishing is for bathing while the other is for a ritual meal.

Items required for baptism (candles, linens, towels, books) could be stored in a nearby sacristy or cupboard and not within or upon the font itself. The control system that allows the water in the font to be re-circulated, heated, purified and emptied should be in a convenient but remote location. Although there is no requirement to empty the font into a dry well, a storm drain would be preferable to a sewer line.

A Setting for Wakes. The water of the baptismal font is about the mystery of death and life in Christ. Thus the font is an appropriate place for the vigil over the body of one who has died and for greeting that body during funeral liturgies. Space should be planned next to the font for the placement of the casket or the container of ashes during the wake or vigil rites. The common practice during funerals is for a casket to be placed on a folding metal dolly that is then rolled down the aisle by pallbearers. An alternative approach would be to carry the deceased body in its casket by hand or upon shoulders. When arriving at the font and then near the altar the coffin could be placed upon a finely crafted wooden stand or table. A container with ashes could also be placed on the same piece of furniture (fig. 40). The font can be designed so that the coffin may be placed on some part of the font itself.

Fig. 40 *Ossuary and Funeral Bier.*
Woodcarver, Jefferson Tortorelli.

Fig. 41 *Holy Oil Repository.*
Christ the King Cathedral, Superior, WI.
Artisan, Saint Paul Fabricating and Decorating.
Designer, Richard Vosko.

The Reservation of the Holy Oils. In recent years some congregations have placed the holy oils and the chrism where they can be seen, often near the font. The exact location for the reservation of the oils will differ from place to place. These oils are used at various times, not all with baptism, and in some places each vessel is stored in a different part of the church.

The ambry that holds the oil vessels could be designed as a fixed but freestanding tower or a cabinet recessed in a niche or mounted on a wall (fig. 41). This visible and lockable cupboard should be artistically made from durable materials. The design of the ambry must take into consideration the size of the vessels. In the case of a cathedral a decision about how and where large amounts of oil and chrism should be stored will be important. Nevertheless, for processional purposes, the scale and proportions of the vessels should not be overlooked.

The Easter Candle. This paschal candle with stand is located near the baptismal font throughout the year. This same candle is placed near the altar table and ambo during the Easter season. The paschal candle itself, crafted in proper proportion to its stand, should be scaled to fit in both of these settings. The symbolic weight of this candle should not be overlooked even if, literally, there is some inconvenience caused by its heaviness or size.

84

The Advent Wreath. The display of a wreath of greenery and candles is customary during Advent. The wreath could be large enough to be seen from most parts of the church. In an effort to keep the altar area from becoming cluttered with seasonal displays, the Advent wreath could be suspended over or near the font. An alternative location would be in the church commons, perhaps hung like a chandelier. Provisions might be made for raising and lowering the wreath.

Chapter 17

The Church
Celebrates the Eucharist

THE ASSEMBLY *and Its Furniture.* Standing during worship was commonplace in the early days of Christianity. Praying with outstretched or uplifted arms predated folded hands as the customary gesture. Kneeling, always considered a penitential posture, was also used to show reverence and respect. Prostration on the floor or ground was also a posture for specific times.

Typically there were no seats in the worship place. People stood about, watching and often walking along with the processions as they moved into and through the building. In some places benches were placed along the walls to accommodate weak or elderly persons, especially during long liturgies. It is hard to pinpoint the exact time when worshipers began to sit more during public prayer. Portable chairs were first used and are still found in many older church buildings in Europe.

The pew bench came into wide use in non-Roman churches after the Protestant Reformation in the sixteenth century. The benches came with the new emphasis on the preached word and the often lengthy sermons. In some places these benches were made with a tall backrest as a way to obstruct uncomfortable chilly drafts. In New England, for example, the pew box was originally created not so much to distinguish different classes (that came later) but as a way of keeping warm on wintry mornings. People would put pre-heated bricks or soapstones in quilted pouches and bring them into their pew boxes.

What kind of seat is appropriate in a church building? How are they arranged? Some congregations are resolved to use pews simply because they believe it is the traditional thing to do. Of course, this is not true. (Once again, the word "tradition" is often misused.) There are valid reasons for selecting one type of seating (chair, bench, pew) over another. Each type has advantages and disadvantages. The decision should be based first on function. How does a congregation imagine itself using its church? What kinds of community activities will occur there? Will the congregation ever want to rearrange the space to accommodate various liturgical and non-liturgical gatherings? In his description of a church as a "centrum," architect Edward Sövik wrote, "It is a place for more than one purpose, and must be so seen, and so used"[1] (fig. 42).

Most congregations want a dedicated place to worship in. However, this desire can be compatible with the ancient practice of utilizing a church or cathedral for other functions as well. While different activities like social gatherings, education and outreach programs (counseling, clothing stores, soup kitchens) may take place in other rooms or buildings, the actual place of worship can sometimes house diverse community activities in addition to the liturgies celebrated there. For example a church can be some or all of the following.

- A place for private devotions and prayer.

- A center for annual festivals and processions that mark the liturgical year.

- A place for the performing arts and lectures.

- A meetinghouse where the congregation gathers to discern its role in the world.[2]

- A place of refuge.[3]

There are some good examples of flexible seating plans in the United States. In Christ Church Episcopal Cathedral in Saint Louis, the nave was reordered to allow for maximum flexibility. Rather than yield to urban renewal and relocation, the cathedral congregation decided to breathe new life into their "tired dragon" as Edward Lynn would call it.[4] The entire building was upgraded but the interior modifications

---

[1] Edward A. Sövik, *Architecture for Worship* (Minneapolis: Augsburg Publishing House, 1973) 70.

[2] Consider how St. Peter's Basilica was used for the business meetings of Vatican Council II.

[3] It is well known that parts of the nave in the cathedral in Chartres were frequently used as overnight shelter for homeless people. The floor slopes toward the street so that the hot water used to wash down the nave before morning Mass would flow toward the plaza.

[4] Edward C. Lynn, *Tired Dragons: Adapting Church Architecture to Changing Needs* (Boston: Beacon Press, 1972).

Fig. 42 *Corpus Christi University Parish Church,
Toledo, OH.* Architect, The Collaborative.
Consultant, Richard Vosko.
Photograph by Anne Spenny.

Fig. 43 *Movable chancel modules.*
Christ Church Episcopal Cathedral, Saint Louis, MO.
Architect, Kurt Landberg, AIA. Photograph by Kurt Landberg.

Fig. 44 *Christ Church Episcopal
Cathedral, Saint Louis, MO.*
Photograph by Kurt Landberg.

are remarkable. The spectacular Caen stone *reredos* was cleaned and
maintained. However, the chancel area was extended into the nave
using handsomely crafted wooden modules that can be rearranged
into several different shapes (fig. 43). The pew benches were replaced
with chairs making it possible to create various seating plans on the
floor (fig. 44). Now, in the best tradition of the cathedral, this one houses

not only the worship of the community but also Church and neighborhood meetings and the performing arts (fig. 45).

Some congregations are concerned that chairs are not formal enough or that they create an unsightly or cluttered appearance. This perception is caused in part by the poor quality of some chairs used in churches. It also may have something to do with maintenance of the space itself. Wherever furniture is movable someone has to make sure that the space is kept orderly (fig. 46).

Sometimes a congregation decides to use benches (a bench for our purposes can be thought of as an open pew that is not attached to the floor but is heavy enough to be stable where it is placed). Such benches do not lock a community into a fixed seating pattern. Shorter, movable benches provide an alternative for congregations that might wish to rearrange the space once in a while. Saint Peter Lutheran Church in New York City is a good example of this. However, chairs and movable benches are not good options in churches with sloping floors. In this case fixed pews shaped to align with the floor must be used (fig. 47). Pews with high ends are sometimes selected for sentimental reasons.

Fig. 45 *Christ Church Episcopal Cathedral, Saint Louis, MO.* Photograph by Kurt Landberg.

Fig. 46 *Movable chairs.* Saint Thomas More, Paducah, KY. Fabricators, New Holland Furniture.

Fig. 47 *Pews.* Unknown.

Fig. 48 *Saint Catherine Church, DuBois, PA.* Architect, Edward A. Sövik, SMSQ. Consultant, Richard Vosko.

This style can create a feeling of being boxed in and hinder ease of movement in and out of the rows.

Some places introduce a combination of fixed and movable seats. The movable chairs or benches would be placed on the flat floor while benches or pews would be installed on the tiered or sloped sections. In older churches with heavy pews, some movable chairs or benches make sense as replacements for several front and back rows (fig. 48). These spaces are then able to accommodate the needs of various liturgical and non-liturgical events. For example, when a wake occurs near the font, the chairs could be arranged in a choral setting facing the casket nestled next to the font. During marriage liturgies, movable chairs in the front rows would allow different seating arrangements for the wedding attendants and families.

So there are many factors and much history and a great deal of feeling involved in the choice of furniture for the assembly. When the liturgy itself has been thought through and discussed as the primary factor shaping the worship space, questions about the assembly's furniture become quite important. This furniture immediately conveys to everyone—visitor and member alike—what takes place in this space. A room dominated by heavy pews suggests that the room, for many people, is a place to settle in, watch and listen to a few people in the "stage" area. Aidan Kavanagh once wrote, "Filling a church with immovable pews is similar to placing bleachers directly on a basketball court: it not only interferes with movement but changes the event into something entirely different.[5] No furniture for the assembly at all (as in most Orthodox churches in Europe and Asia and some Roman churches in Europe) may suggest that here there are no onlookers, only participants. Chairs and lighter benches are somewhere in between, partially depending on how they are arranged.

Whether or not the seats for the assembly are upholstered should depend on the advice of the acoustical consultant.

Among Catholics, as the laity participated less and less during the liturgy they became preoccupied with their private prayers or with the pageantry carried out by the clergy and choir. During the Mass they focused on the elevated host and chalice. Kneeling became the normative posture for venerating the Blessed Sacrament. Today, although kneeling is still a posture used by Catholics, not every church has kneelers. The provision of kneelers for congregations that continue to kneel for any length of time can be a convenience and comfort for many.

Sight Lines and Distances. The merits of a centralized plan become more obvious as the seating capacity of the church or cathedral increases. The sight lines are enhanced when worshipers are seated in concentric circles around the ritual focal points. Typically, in a congregation of a thousand, no one should be more than seventy feet from the table. This suggestion is based on the design of open-stage theatres.[6] This is generally considered the maximum distance before it becomes increasingly harder to see and hear what is going on. While speech

[5] Aidan Kavanagh, *Elements of Rite: A Handbook of Liturgical Style* (New York: Pueblo Publishing Co., 1982; Collegeville: Liturgical Press, 1990) 21–22.

[6] See *The Theatre Checklist: A Guide to the Planning and Construction of Proscenium and Open Stage Theatres*, The American Theatre Planning Board, Inc. (Middletown, CT: Wesleyan University Press, 1969) 6. A reference to the *British Theatre Technician's Booklet* sets the visual limit for seeing plays at seventy feet from the setting line.

reinforcement systems can solve some acoustical concerns, only the projection of the ritual action on large screens or monitors will resolve the poor sightlines.

On the other hand, it may be helpful to note that it is not absolutely essential that everyone see everything during worship. This is not a theater. If we believe that the liturgy is the action and responsibility of every person in the assembly, the questions shift. But even in this proper concept of liturgy, there is a tremendous problem when a large assembly is strung out through a long, narrow space where all that is seen by most people is the backs of those in front of them.

During liturgy all of the senses should be triggered by the full use of our rich symbols, by speech articulation and by poetic choreography. Nor does the focus need to be in just one location. Rather, the pilgrimage aspect of Christian life should be expressed in liturgical processions that move from one liturgical center in the church to another. Assemblies should acquire good habits for various postures, for moving at various times, even for dance.[7] Imagine if the liturgy were thought of as a dance in praise of God.

So a good sightline is a relative issue. The provision of a clear visual field is dependent on the stature of a worshiper and where he or she chooses to sit. Those who wish to see the ambo and table and the actions that surround them without obstructions should arrive early. In a church designed in a sociopetal plan, where the assembly surrounds the liturgical action it is doing, everyone can be seated in the midst of the liturgy. In this plan there should be a number of "front row" places, ideal for families with very young children.

Typically, fifteen square feet per person net, including circulation space, is recommended in a worship setting. A thirty-six-inch pitch between rows will make it easier for worshipers to move in and out of their seats. A space with a capacity of approximately a thousand should have about twenty to twenty-four mainstreamed places set aside for physically challenged or elderly people and their companions.

The width of the aisles should be generous to permit the processional activity of the worshiping assembly without hindrance. The apron space around the altar and ambo should be generous but not

---

[7] See *Varietates Legitimae*, The Congregation for Divine Worship and the Discipline of the Sacraments, Vatican City, March 29, 1994. No. 42 says that swaying and dance during liturgy must always be in the spirit of prayer and not performance. See also videos by Thomas A. Kane, c.s.p., *The Dancing Church of the South Pacific* and *The Dancing Church: Video Impressions of the Church in Africa* (Mahwah, NJ: Paulist Press, 1998 and 1991).

92

Fig. 49 *Cathedra.* The Philadelphia Cathedral, Philadelphia, PA. Architect, George Yu. Consultant, Richard Giles.

put the assembly more that fifteen to twenty feet away from the altar table. The main ceremonial aisle could be ten to twelve feet wide. All other aisles should be wide enough (a minimum of seven to ten feet wide) to accommodate persons in wheelchairs and the frequent processional activity of the assembly during liturgical celebrations. An ambulatory around the perimeter of the entire seating area would also provide a gracious way for worshipers to move about the church. Care should be taken to utilize all aisles in the church for liturgical processions and not just the main one. Also, attention should be given to the actual layout of the seats. Codes will allow only so many linear feet in a row before a break is required. Aisles that do not run through the entire length of the assembly area are awkward dead ends and can create congestion during processions.

Of course, these recommendations are more useful when building a new church. However, the underlying principles can encourage those responsible for liturgy in older buildings to re-imagine their churches and be courageous in exploring all the possibilities.

Seating for Different Ministries. The word "cathedral" is derived from the Latin word for "chair," *cathedra.* This chair of the bishop is present in every cathedral and has a strong symbolic meaning. First, it signals the presence of a bishop or archbishop who is the chief liturgist and teacher in the local church. The design of the *cathedra* should signal the importance of this office but does not have to be ostentatious or regal in any manner (fig. 49). The chair is not personal to the sitting bishop or archbishop but is a sign of the "unity of believers"[8] with the

---

[8] *Ceremonial of Bishops,* no. 42.

rest of the Catholic world. Thus the common practice of incorporating the coat of arms into the furnishing should be reconsidered. It would be better to place the bishop's coat of arms in another location, e.g., at the main entrance to the building. The bishop's staff or crook is a better symbol than any motto or coat of arms.

The *cathedra* should be ample, gracious and comfortable for most bishops who will normally be wearing their vestments. The design should provide for discreet pockets or sleeves to hold participation aids that are easily accessible to the bishop. The *cathedra* is normally a fixed furnishing, but there may be occasions when it could be shifted or turned depending on the liturgical event. The style and material of the *cathedra* may or may not match that of other chairs in the cathedral. Although distinct because of its symbolic significance, some design connection to all other seats in the building might make an important statement about relationships between bishops and other members of the Church.

Ideally the *cathedra* is located so that the bishop can preside at liturgy. This means it is a place where the bishop can be seen and where he can see the assembly clearly. In the earliest cathedrals the location of this chair was in the apse of the building, a most remote location derived from the place of the emperor's throne. In many of our older cathedrals the *cathedra* awkwardly faces the opposite wall. Most likely this arrangement occurred when the altar table itself was moved to the far wall once occupied by the bishop and so a new place had to be found for the bishop and his chair. Then when the tabernacle was set into the *reredos* or *retablo*, it was considered inappropriate, even for bishops, to sit with their backs to the reserved Sacrament.

Significant distances and changes in elevations magnify divisions between the hierarchy and the laity, while the understanding of the liturgy as the work of the entire Body of Christ suggests that all seating arrangements should symbolize the sacrament of unity. A less remote setting for the *cathedra* is a significant sign of service and leadership. Some of the better examples where the *cathedra* is distinct but not separate from the assembly may be found in the Catholic cathedrals in Los Angeles, Seattle, Milwaukee, San Antonio and Rochester, New York.

A single presider's chair may be designed and crafted out of wood or other appropriate material. The shape and materiality of the chair does not necessarily have to match that of other chairs in the space. However, some stylistic connection signals the relationship between the presider and the assembly. There could be the discreet incorporation of pockets or sleeves in the chair to hold participation aids needed by the presider. This is an alternative to the bookstand or table nestled next to the presider's chair that has become an unfortunate accessory in many churches.

This chair stands as a symbol of the function of the priest presiding within the assembly. The proximity of this chair to the assembly constitutes a significant gesture of unity. The chair could be located on the main floor of the worship area in proximity to the altar table and ambo and in the first row of the assembly (fig. 50). The elevation of the chair may not be required in new church buildings where sightlines throughout the assembly are taken into consideration in the planning stages. In older churches care should be taken to provide elderly or physically challenged priests with easy access to the chair. In a cathedral setting the chair for the presiding priest should not compete for attention with the *cathedra*.

The chair for the deacon is to be designed in a way that distinguishes it from the presider's chair. The choice of materials and finishes could complement all seats in the church. The deacon's chair is usually placed to the right of the presider's chair, but only when a deacon is present for the liturgy. Otherwise, it should be removed. The deacon or other liturgical leader may use this same chair when presiding at various services (e.g., Liturgy of the Hours or the Liturgy of the Word with Holy Communion).

Servers should sit near the credence table in order to have easy access to books and vessels. They do not have to sit immediately to the left and right of the presider or the deacon. Their seats should match those in the assembly. It is recommended that all other liturgical ministers take places in the assembly and come forward to serve as lector or Communion minister or other roles.

Where are other bishops and priests to be located? In Catholic tradition, the presbyterate and other bishops would flank the local bishop seated in the *cathedra* as a sign of collegiality and cooperation. If room is available, the diaconate would be seated in the same area. Although this part of the church is known as the *presbyterium*, it is frequently called the sanctuary. I discussed earlier different ways in which the hierarchical nature of the Church can be affirmed without the creation of separate areas for the clergy and laity. Also in new cathedrals and churches designed in a more sociopetal plan, the room may appear to be less compartmentalized than in older ones. Again, care should be taken not to create a sense of division between clergy and laity especially at the eucharistic table. During the Eucharistic Prayer, for example, concelebrants should not stand in places that cut off the sightlines of the assembly. In practice, in cathedrals with little or no space around the altar table, this means that the presbyterate and diaconate sit with the assembly. What a wonderful picture of the Church gathered together for the worship of God!

The place of the choir and instrumentalists should be distinct but not separate from the rest of the assembly. This in itself helps to form in everyone the notion that these people are first and last present as members of the assembly. This influences their posture and manner throughout the liturgy. In the centralized plan the music ministry would be located in one section of the circle. The type and exact location of the seats for the music ministry is dependent on a number of factors that will be discussed in the next chapter.

Because it is primarily a place for the worship of God the church must be an inspiring place. But, that inspiration may also come from the biography of the faith community as well as the architectural or artistic ambience. The choice of seats will depend on how a congregation decides to use its new or renovated church building. That decision will depend on the mission of the community and its understanding of the liturgy.

Fig. 50 *Chair.* Old Saint Joseph Church, Saint Norbert College, DePere, WI. Architect, Hammel Green Abrahamson. Consultant, Richard Vosko.

Chapter 18

Music Ministry, Instruments and Acoustics

THE ASSEMBLY sings the liturgy. The music ministry does many things in the service of the liturgy. (1) It supports the rest of the assembly. (2) It gives familiar hymns new energy when it sings descants or harmonies with the assembly. (3) It sings antiphonally with the assembly (e.g., the psalms and hymns). (4) It performs musical selections that the assembly could never learn to sing or hear or feel.

Like other liturgical ministers, choirs and instrumentalists are members of the assembly who perform a service for that whole assembly. But they are, first of all, members. In this sense, they are not separated from the rest of the worshipers.

When designing a setting for the music ministry, the first step is to involve the architect, the liturgical designer, the director of music, an acoustical consultant and the organ builder. Before any plans for the building are created, the musical instruments' committee should meet with this professional team to address a number of key issues.[1] When building a new church the first "musical" task is to determine where the music ministry is to be located. Each community will have its own preference. Ideally singers and instruments are not separated. Therefore, the preferred location of the choirs also becomes the favored location for the musical instruments. The entire church building is then acoustically designed and tuned to honor this decision.

Various Locations for the Music Ministry. A choir loft is not the ideal location for the music ministry for at least two reasons: (1) It is removed

---

[1] See "Acoustics for Liturgy," in the *Meeting House Essays* (Chicago: Liturgy Training Publications, no. 2, 1991) and Dennis Fleisher, "Concerns For Pastoral Musicians in Built of Living Stones," in *Pastoral Music,* June–July 2001.

from the assembly and (2) it is usually inaccessible to physically challenged and elderly persons. It becomes a difficult decision to relocate the choir when the organ in the loft is in good condition and when it would be fiscally unfeasible to move it. In places where the major instrument is not in good condition, the better option is to replace it with a new one not located in the loft.

In smaller churches the problematic time lapse experienced in larger or longer buildings may not be a concern. (Some acoustical consultants say that it takes less than one-tenth of a second for sound to travel from one end of a hundred-foot long nave to another.) Thus, it may be quite possible to keep the instrument in the loft and work to develop an appropriate setting for the singers and other instrumentalists somewhere else in the assembly area. A well-trained song leader can keep the organist, choir and assembly singing and playing together. Sometimes in very large and long churches, the organist in the loft will rely on a video monitor to keep time with the choir director. Another option is to use a much smaller organ console where the choir is located while leaving the organ (the pipes) in the loft.

Almost any location for the instruments and singers is possible in terms of acoustical issues. Consider some modern concert halls where the audience actually sits around the symphony and the choirs. Again, gathering together a reputable professional design team is essential in the early stages of discussion.

In many new churches there is no real front and back. Everyone is part of the assembly gathered around the ritual focal points. Saint John's Church in New Freedom, Pennsylvania, locates the music ministry and the rebuilt pipe organ behind the assembly, which is arranged in a semi-circle around the altar table (fig. 51). The choir setting is

Fig. 51 *Choir behind assembly.*
Saint John the Baptist, New Freedom, PA.
Architect, Crabtree Rohrbach and Associates.
Consultant, Richard Vosko.

Fig. 20 *Saint Peter's Church, Boerne, TX.*
Architects, Davis & Rexrode Architects, Inc.
Photograph by Larry Pearlstone.

Fig. 26 *Saint Francis de Sales, Morgantown, WV.* Architect, Rafferty Rafferty Tollefson. Consultant, James Moudry. Photography by Steve Bergerson.

Fig. 36 *Saint Jean Vianney Church, Baton Rouge, LA.*
Architect, Trahan Architects. Consultant, Marchita Mauck. Photograph by Timothy Hursley.

Fig. 37 *Saint Francis de Sales, Morgantown, WV.*
Architect, Rafferty Rafferty Tollefson. Consultant, James Moudry. Photograph by Steve Bergerson.

Fig. 42 *Corpus Christi University Parish Church, Toledo, OH.* Architect, The Collaborative. Consultant, Richard Vosko. Photograph by Anne Spenny.

Fig. 55 *Jesus Christ Word and Sacrament Retablo.*
San Fernando Cathedral, San Antonio, TX.
Artisan, Leonardo Soto Recendiz. Photography by Christ Cooper Photography.

Fig. 57 *Cross in Center.* Corpus Christi University Parish Church, Toledo, OH.
Architects, The Collaborative. Consultant, Richard Vosko. Photograph by Anne Spenny.

Fig. 86a *Oratory in Holy Rosary Church.*
St. Amant, LA. Trahan Architects. Photo by Tim Hursley.

Fig. 63 *El Cristo Negro.*
San Fernando Cathedral, San Antonio, TX.
Photograph by Chris Cooper Photography.

Fig. 95 *San Fernando Cathedral, San Antonio, TX.*
Architects, Rafferty Rafferty Tollefson and Fisher Heck. Photograph by Chris Cooper Photography.

Fig. 96 *Saint Francis de Sales Church, Morgantown, WV.*
Architect, Rafferty Rafferty Tollefson. Consultant, James Moudry. Photograph by Steve Bergerson.

Fig. 100 *Courtyard.* San Fernando Cathedral.
Architects, Rafferty Rafferty Tollefson and Fisher Heck.
Consultant, Richard Vosko.
Photograph by Chris Cooper Photography.

Fig. 101 *Plaza.* Cathedral of Our Lady of the Angels, Los Angeles.
Photograph by Julius Shulman and David Glomb.

Fig. 102 *Commons.* Saint John the Evangelist Cathedral, Milwaukee, WI.
Photograph by KOROM.COM.

Fig. 103 *Old with new font.*
Saint John the Evangelist Cathedral, Milwaukee, WI.
Designer, James Shields. Consultant, Richard Vosko.
Photograph by KOROM.COM.

Fig. 104 *New font.* Sacred Heart Cathedral, Rochester, NY.
Architect, Williamson Pounders, Inc. and LaBella Assoc. Consultant, Richard Vosko.
Photograph by © 2005 Tim Wilkes/www.timwilkes.com.

Fig. 108 *Cathedra.*
Saint John the Evangelist Cathedral,
Milwaukee. Photograph by KOROM.COM.

Fig. 109 *Chapel of Eucharistic Reservation.* San Fernando Cathedral, San Antonio, TX.
Architects, Rafferty Rafferty Tollefson and Fisher Heck.
Consultant, Richard Vosko. Artisan, Leonardo Soto Recendiz.
Photograph by Chris Cooper Photography.

Fig. 52 *Choir in midst of assembly.*
Saint Benedict the African Church,
Chicago, IL. Architect, Belli and Belli.

slightly elevated above the assembly and was chosen before the designs
for the church were made. From this place the choir boosts congregational singing. The song leader near the ambo and the choir director
synchronize the assembly and choir. Ample space is provided for
instrumentalists at different times of the year.

In the Saint Peter's Lutheran Church in New York City, the music
ministry and pipe organ are placed to one side of the assembly. The
tiered seats and floor of the music area are made of hard wood creating a wonderfully resonant worship environment. Because of the intimate design of the church the instrumentalists and singers are very
much part of the assembly.

In the renovated Saint Francis Xavier College Church in Saint
Louis, the choir is now located in front of a magnificent stone *reredos*
facing the nave and transepts of the building. The placement of the
main instrument and choir behind the altar table (in front of the assembly) is not common in Catholic churches, but many other religious
traditions have long located the organ and choir in their chancel or
sanctuary area. Acoustically this location is just as rewarding as the
other end of the nave especially if the shape of the church is rectilinear.
The disadvantage of this location is one of perception. Many worshipers would say that the choir in that location is a distraction, but if
all choir members as well as the congregation understand themselves
to be members of this one assembly, how could they be distractions?

Saint Benedict the African Church in Chicago utilizes a flexible
plan where the worshipers are seated around the ritual furnishings.
The music ministry area is located within the midst of the assembly
(fig. 52). This location, or one that is at the end of a semi-circular
arrangement, is becoming more acceptable. It is also a good location in

churches with choral or antiphonal seating plans. The advantage of this setting is that the instrumentalists and singers are perceived, first, as members of the congregation and not primarily as entertainers. From this location the whole community can see and hear the music ministers very well. In fact, because of the seating arrangement, the assembly becomes part of the choir. This interaction can foster lively participation throughout the liturgy.

In Saint James Cathedral, Seattle, the altar table is exactly in the center of the cruciform space allowing the assembly to gather completely around it. The normal location for the music ministry is at the east end of the nave, where one of the two pipe organs in the cathedral is located. Ample room is provided on an elevated level for choirs and instrumentalists. The ministry also occasionally uses the gallery at the west end of the nave where the other pipe organ is located. At times the choir may even sing an anthem from one of the two transepts.

Perhaps the most popular location for the music ministry is to the left or right of the altar table area in a horseshoe or semi-circular seating arrangement. In this plan there is good visibility for all and the ministry, as in other plans, is very much part of the assembly (fig. 53).

Finding the best location for the instrumentalists and choirs in an older worship space can be complicated. There may be a fine pipe organ already in the loft or gallery. In these situations a difficult decision has to be made. Should or can the instrument be moved? Can the singers carry out their role in the assembly space when the instrument is far away from them?

Fig. 53 *Choir and Pipe Organ.*
Saint Hugo of the Hills, Bloomfield Hills, MI.
Architect, Harley Ellington Pierce Yee and
Associates. Consultant, Robert E. Rambusch.

We have learned how important it is to design worship spaces that are completely accessible or barrier-free. Although getting into the building may be easier now, moving about inside may not be. Access to the altar table, the ambo and the music ministry area is equally important. This is one reason the loft is not a good place for the music ministry. In an older worship space every effort should be made to re-locate the choir and even the instrument if possible. If the organ and the choir must remain in the loft, the installation of an elevator should be seriously considered. In new spaces the word "loft" should not even be mentioned.

There will be different solutions for different worship places. Moving the choir out of the loft to the front of the church near an older side altar may bring mixed results. First, that part of the church was, most likely, designed for devotional purposes. Typically, choirs and instrumentalists squeezed into this area will spill over into the aisles and may block an emergency exit. Further, placing a choir and instrumentalists in the corner of a church may not work acoustically. Attention has to be given to the immediate environment. The materials and shapes in the walls, ceiling and floor will affect the way sound travels. In an older church designed in a rectilinear plan one end of the room (loft) or the other (apse) are probably the only two best locations for the music ministry. The lateral reflectance value of the walls in a long narrow building enables sounds to carry clearly through the room.

The most important thing to do when considering different locations for the music ministry is to engage the design team—architect, acoustical consultant, liturgical designer and organ builder—in a conversation with music ministers *before* final plans are made.

Places for Specific Ministries of Music. In older church buildings a single space was required for the organ, the organist, the choir and occasionally other instrumentalists. Usually, this was in the loft or gallery of the worship space although many larger churches and cathedrals had magnificent organs in the chancel or choir area between the apse and nave of the building. Today we need to accommodate a larger variety of music ministers, especially song leaders and cantors or psalmists. Many different instruments are also used in worship today. In addition to the organ and its console, there may be a piano, hand bells, strings, brass, woodwinds and percussion. The architectural setting for music must take into consideration the needs of these various ministries and different instruments. The setting should also be flexible enough to accommodate diverse musical styles and additional instruments at different times. This whole area should be pleasing to the eye even when not occupied by the full choir. Who are the ministers of music and what are their needs?

The psalmist or cantor is that person blessed with a most wonderful voice and entrusted with studying the psalms and canticles and learning how to sing them for the assembly, usually with the assembly alternating with a refrain. The psalmist is also entrusted with the verse in the alleluia acclamation. The preferred location for the psalmist is the ambo, which is used for the proclamation of the Word of God. If it is decided not to sing these pieces from the ambo, the alternative lectern should be crafted to distinguish it from ordinary music stands.

Unlike the psalmist or cantor, the song leader may or may not have the most beautiful voice in the community. However, he or she does possess a certain kind of charisma that can animate the whole assembly while singing the liturgy. This person also coordinates the antiphonal singing of the congregation and the choir (e.g., the penitential rite, the general intercessions, the Lamb of God). The preferred place for this minister is at a lectern near the choir but in a place that can be seen by everyone in the congregation. This ministry is usually not carried out from the ambo. As an assembly becomes familiar with and good at its role in singing the liturgy, the song leader is needed less often.

The music director at a liturgy should be easily seen by all instrumentalists and choir members. When the director is also the song leader, the assembly must also see that person. In some communities the organist is also the choir director and the song leader! This is too much to ask of any one person. The more appropriate long-term solution is to train members of the community to carry out the different ministries of choir director, psalmist (cantor) and song leader.

The choir members are best arranged on tiered risers so that their voices can carry forward and so they can see the director. The amplification of the entire choir is a difficult thing to accomplish successfully. Few communities can afford the sophisticated equipment, microphones and mixers required to amplify or record choirs. If the room is acoustically reverberant, the choir should be able to carry out its ministry without amplification. Consider also how often an amplified song leader or choir "drowns out" the assembly. Maybe one weekend each year the sound system should be completely turned off so all liturgical ministers would have to learn how to use their natural voices to project into the assembly.

The benches or chairs for the choirs and instrumentalists should not be cushioned. Ideally, the singers are located on risers behind the instrumentalists. All instruments are clustered in an area in front of the choir where everyone can see the director(s). The walls, ceiling and floors in the music ministry area ideally should be hard surfaces. In a new church the architectural integration of a soundboard or canopy over the choir area may be helpful in directing the sound out to the assembly.

The rehearsal room, music library, and office for the director of music are essential places in a church. I will review these places in the chapter on Auxiliary Rooms later in this section.

The Pipe Organ. Studies have shown that, if the community is serious about purchasing a fine instrument for the worship space, the best long-term investment is still the authentic pipe organ. Other instruments have been developed to sound like the real thing but, in fact, they do not. Why not call it that instead of claiming that "it sounds just like a true pipe organ and only a trained ear can tell the difference"? Even the hybrid organ (part pipe, part digital) is really another kind of instrument.

In this age of never-ending technological advancement, anything is possible. I am writing this on a computer and not a typewriter. Both are writing tools and can help me produce the manuscript. The difference is that the word processing program makes editing much easier. It also corrects my spelling. The advent of the musical instrument digital interface (MIDI), the use of synthesizers and even pre-recorded music all make it possible to utilize many new and exciting musical options for the public worship of God. I am not suggesting that a congregation should not buy anything but an authentic pipe organ. I am recommending that the decision to invest in another kind of organ should not be driven by cost factors but a desire to use different kinds of instruments for worship.[2]

Often a community cannot find or afford to employ someone who can actually play an organ. Perhaps the best investment in that case is to buy a good piano. There is a Catch-22 situation here. We often do not invest in good organs because it is hard to find good organists to play them. We cannot find good organists because reputable organ teachers will only train students on good pipe organs, which are hard to find in churches.

In the absence of instrumentalists it may be a great temptation to utilize canned music available on compact discs or stored in MP3 players to accompany congregational singing. This malpractice falls into the list of sins that includes the use of artificial flowers (they don't

---

[2] The Organ Clearing House (http://www.organclearinghouse.com) is a good source for finding old, rebuilt pipe organs just waiting for a new home.

smell like flowers), electric candles (they have no real flames) and wafers (they seem only remotely related to what people call bread). While recorded music may sound better than even a well-rehearsed choir, what kind of message is being sent when authentic things are no longer used for worship? Assemblies singing unaccompanied and slightly off-key is still liturgy. There is a significant amount of liturgical repertory available today that can be sung without accompaniment.

Acoustics. A liturgical space must accommodate speech, song and the sounds of various instruments. Creating an acoustical setting that works for all these is difficult. On one hand, the ideal worship space should be very resonant allowing for singing and playing instruments. On the other hand, clear speech intelligibility is absolutely essential if the spoken word is to be heard. Unlike the theatre or concert hall the acoustics in a church setting must make it possible for all worshipers to hear each other.

In a new church there is no reason why a wonderful acoustical environment cannot be attained, but a competent design team is important early in the planning stages.[3] The first step is to determine the desired reverberation time in the room. Help comes from the acoustical consultant, the organ company and the director of music. Most experts will say that two to three seconds of reverberation time (RT) should be the target in a space accommodating eight hundred worshipers when full. This results in an architectural allowance of approximately three hundred to four hundred cubic feet per person. A longer time may be more effective in a larger place of worship. The surfaces in the room should be hard and irregular in order to achieve a desired RT.[4]

The second step is often referred to as sound enhancement. This procedure is utilized frequently in older buildings. The idea is to tune the building by modifying (adding or subtracting) the amount of absorptive materials on the floors, walls and ceiling. It may even require altering some of the shapes of the interior, which could be costly. When absorptive materials must be added to tone down an extremely lively space, these are often placed on the ceiling or walls or even used as seat cushions. Aidan Kavanagh once advised, "The ambience of a carpeted church is too soft for the liturgy, which needs hardness, sonor-

---

[3] Dennis Fleisher and Joseph Fête, *Acoustics for Churches and Chapels.* See this excellent summary of concerns, guiding principles and recommendations for acoustics in the construction and renovation of worship spaces (The Catholic Diocese of Columbus, 1997).

[4] Ibid., 3.

ity and a certain bracing discomfort like the Gospel itself."[5] Carpeting does more than absorb sound; it changes our perception of the space and should be avoided.

The third step is to have the acoustician on the design team develop specifications for a sound reinforcement system that will provide clear speech intelligibility for the assembly.

Fixing a poor acoustical situation in an older worship space is challenging. The first step is to try to enhance or re-tune the space itself before buying a completely new sound system. Then a reputable consultant or vendor should specify a new system or speakers to work in that building. A common mistake is to attempt to fix poor acoustics with new microphones. Microphones are only as good as the loud-speakers that are used with them. Loudspeakers are designed to amplify or reinforce sounds. Occasionally, they also distort them. When the sound leaves the loudspeaker it has to travel somewhere. The amount of (or lack of) absorptive material in the walls, the floor, the ceiling and the clothing of the worshipers will affect the amplified sound. The best thing to do is retain a good acoustical consultant who is not interested in selling you a new sound system but who is capable of helping you adjust the acoustical characteristics of your church through sound enhancement.

Acoustical Equipment. Once the acoustical character of the room is established organically or by a process of enhancement, a sound re-inforcement system should be specified for the church. The system should be designed for worship and non-worship events and should feature the most up-to-date recording and playback components. There are different opinions about controlling the system manually. Usually, the vendor or the acoustical consultant will set the system and store the key so no one tampers with the settings. Some companies can control a system from a computer not on the premises. If a congregation has a very creative music ministry or liturgy planning team that require variations in the sound system settings, or if the church is used for non-liturgical events, there may be a good reason to have complete manual control over the acoustical system. The location of these controls as well as the main panel should be determined in consultation with the owner.

Acoustical experts generally agree that no single loudspeaker system can be used to amplify all the sounds used during worship. Although there are loudspeakers that can handle a wide range of fre-quencies, they are enormous in size and would be distractions in the

---

[5] Kavanagh, op. cit., 21.

church. An alternative is to use different loudspeakers to amplify or reinforce different sounds. For example, the sound of electronic instruments would not be driven through the same loudspeakers used to amplify the spoken word. In this case all electrified instruments would have their own amplifiers and loudspeakers.

Because each worship space is unique there is no one best location for the loudspeakers. Ideally, everyone in the assembly should be able to hear clearly without noticing where the amplified sound is coming from. It is disconcerting and very unnatural to see someone in front of you move their lips while you hear their voice coming from behind you. A centralized loudspeaker cluster may work well in some spaces. Loudspeakers mounted on walls or columns may be better in others. Some acoustical professionals say that placing loudspeakers under the seats is the best solution (but not possible with flexible seating arrangements). Competent professional help is vital from the beginning.

Acoustical provisions and/or devices, e.g., the Assistive Listening Device (ALD), should be made available so that persons with hearing impairments can participate in all worship and non-worship activities without inconvenience or embarrassment.

There should be a sufficient number of microphones in the church to accommodate the worship of the community as well as non-worship events. Because movement about the church is inevitable for some ministries, alternatives to hard-wired microphones are practical. The clip-on microphone and the handheld wireless microphone (which may be inserted into a stand) are the most popular. More congregations are beginning to use wireless headsets like those employed in the theatre. These almost invisible units are worn over the ear. Everyone who has a speaking part during the liturgy would wear one of these microphones. There is a tremendous amount of freedom when one does not have to worry about standing only at the right angle to a microphone or adjusting it to the right height. One does have to remember to turn off the microphone when finished speaking or singing. These head-set microphones are not popular with some cantors who prefer to move to and from the microphone while singing. Wireless headset models are still more expensive than the conventional ones.

Any hard-wired microphones and stands should be as unobtrusive as possible, completely flexible and not attached to any finely crafted liturgical furnishings like the altar table and ambo (though most acoustical designers prefer attaching microphones to these furnishings). Ample discreet outlets for hard-wired microphones should be placed flush to the floor at the necessary locations (the apron space around the altar table, the presider's chair, at the choir, ambo, altar table, font, main door, church commons, as well as in different parts of the assembly space).

The elimination of interior noises (e.g., mechanical systems and light fixtures) and exterior noises (e.g., traffic) is highly desirable in the church building. When asked to pray or sit still for a moment, the assembly should experience a very quiet environment. The acoustical consultant can be helpful with specifications.

Care should also be taken to provide ample electrical outlets for musical instruments, music stand lamps, outlets for mixers. Remote controls for both the lighting and the sound-reinforcement systems are wonderful inventions and should be considered.

Visual Distractions. When there is the opportunity to install an authentic pipe organ (either new or rebuilt) the design of the organ case for the instrument is important. Principles governing the role of art in houses of prayer may be helpful. Art work should be placed so that it does not serve as a potential source of distraction during the liturgical action. The same could be said about the design of organ cases, which can be wonderful works of art. It is possible that a highly ornate case located in the visual field of the assembly could be a distraction.

Likewise, the organ console and various other instruments could be considered sources of distraction. The console (typically ten inches higher than a person's eye level when seated) could block sightlines. Low profile consoles are available. Likewise, the lectern for the song leader should not compete for attention with the ambo.

Some worshipers occasionally will remark that the many different ministers, busy about their roles during the liturgy, unwittingly can become sources of distraction. Decorum is the key. Proper attire, posture and discreet mobility are part of learning one's ministry. So is the consciousness, that first and last, all music ministers are assembly members and must learn and model that role. The music ministry and its instruments are not liturgical focal points. Thus, the location of the choir and all instruments must be in deference to the altar table and ambo and not sources of distraction in the visual field of the assembly.

Chapter 19

The Role of Art in Worship

CATHOLIC CHURCH buildings are traditionally understood to be places of art. The windows, sculptures, paintings, ornamentation, the furnishings and the buildings themselves all comprise the worship ambience. Many would say that since Vatican II our churches manifest a lack of artistry. The Constitution on the Sacred Liturgy states that the number and location of images in a place of worship should not be distracting and that, in matters of art, the goal is noble beauty and not extravagance.[1]

This neo-iconoclastic period came as a surprise to many because these same works of art once served as primary objects of devotion even as the liturgy was "said" by the priest. Over time many things not required for worship became normative in the church building and, often in the absence of engaging liturgy, these images were extremely significant to parishioners. People continue to visit famous churches and cathedrals not so much for the worship but for the art. While art should always be in the service of the worship that is done in the space, it often seems as if these accidentals are more important than that which is essential for the public worship of the assembly.[2] Out of all this, the role of art and artists is taking on a whole new dimension in the Catholic liturgy. This chapter is dedicated to this subject.

The veneration of saints and martyrs began in the early days of Christianity. The practice of creating images in their likeness followed. The reverencing of icons and sculptures eventually took on cultic proportions especially in the eastern part of the Roman Empire. The first

[1] Constitution on the Sacred Liturgy, 124, 125.
[2] It is fair to say that austerity in church environments is not something new when one considers the strength, beauty and simplicity of some medieval monasteries and churches built in modernity.

(730–787) and second (813–843) iconoclastic periods halted the practice of venerating icons because, it was thought, it had pagan similarities.

The veneration of saints even during Mass became popular when lay participation in the liturgy diminished. Throughout the history of the Church images of holy women and men have survived many controversies and will probably always have a place in church buildings. This is entirely as one would hope and expect.

The appreciation of art in the history of the liturgy, however, should not be limited to paintings and sculptures. The work of the artist is also evident in the careful attention to details and ornamentation found in the ceilings, floors, walls and columns of many religious buildings. Likewise, the innumerable building styles of *martyria,* churches, cathedrals and monasteries comprise a most remarkable treasure in the history of architecture. The artistic hand is also found in the fabrication of fonts, pulpits, altar tables, rood screens, *retablos (reredos)* and stained glass windows.

A variety of art forms play different roles in Roman Catholic places of worship at different times.

- Art that is required for public liturgy, e.g., altar, font, crucifix.

- Art that may not be required for liturgy but is important to the devotional practices of diverse peoples, e.g., the Stations of the Cross, images of Mary, the tabernacle.

- Art that is seasonal, i.e., art that is not always present in the church, e.g., Advent wreath, nativity crèche, flower arrangements.

- The media arts, i.e., the utilization of projected imagery during liturgy.

- Ornamentation, which will be addressed in Part Three of this book.

Every effort should be made to accommodate these different art forms in a manner that is appropriate to the customs of the faith community and the artistic and architectural vernacular of the region. In every case the needs of the faithful in terms of public liturgy and private devotions should be honored. Further, my earlier reference to the language of space suggests that a place of worship depends on artistic forms in order to convey theological messages. The arts must always be seen not as ends in themselves but servants to the worship life of the community. In this sense, the purpose of different objects of art in churches needs clarification.

Most congregations cannot afford to commission all desired works of art for their church at the same time. Even so, appropriate settings should be planned in and around the building for installations that may come in later phases. A master plan should be developed for all works of art that are worthy of a place in and around the church. Leaving these areas empty is a better solution than filling the designated settings with commercially produced ersatz images. A church is always a work in progress and the voids just might entice new benefactors to make contributions to the art program. When memorial opportunities are presented to the community, care should be taken so that everyone understands that the financial underwriting of a particular work of art or a ritual furnishing does not mean that that piece belongs to a group or individual. There is a chapter on memorials later in this section of the book.

ART FOR PUBLIC WORSHIP

This section includes the altar table, the ambo, auxiliary lecterns, the cross and crucifix, the processional cross, candlestick appointments, vesture, vessels and books.

The Altar Table. In the early church a simple wooden table was used for enacting the eucharistic liturgy. The banquet aspect of the sacrament was apparent. Eventually the emphasis was placed on the sacrifice of Jesus on the cross. The Mass was then understood as a dramatic reenactment of that sacrifice and a means of producing the sacrament for purposes of adoration more than Communion. At this time the altar simulated a sarcophagus or tomb and was often ornately crafted out of stone. Eventually, it was placed against the apse wall. To indicate its importance, ornamental canopies (e.g., baldachins and testers) were erected above the altar table. In some places the prayer of the priest was considered so secret that drapes would be drawn about the altar during the words of institution. Frequently, a *confessio* or burial place for martyrs and other famous persons would be constructed beneath the altar table. The size of the actual altar top *(mensa)* increased as prayer cards, candles, statues became part of the composition. The number of altar tables in a single church was multiplied to accommodate many liturgies going on at the same time. This was a response to the popular requests of the laity who were granted indulgences for the stipends they offered.

To express unity in the eucharistic experience today, there is to be only one altar table in every church. As a symbol of Christ it stands in the midst of the gathered assembly (fig. 54). In the case of older buildings where other altars and perhaps their backdrops (a *reredos* or *retablo*) have been appraised as works of art or where these pieces are important to the congregation for historical reasons, every effort should be made to maintain them as long as they do not compete for attention with the ritual furnishings used in the liturgy. In this case they are best thought of as part of the architectural features of the building and should not be decorated or used in any way. In Saint Andrew's Cathedral in Grand Rapids, the program called for the old *reredos* to be refurbished and for new sculptures of saints to be installed. In San Fernando Cathedral in San Antonio, the art program called for three new *retablos*, which were then crafted by artisans from Mexico City (fig. 55).

Fig. 54 *New stone altar.* Sacred Heart Cathedral, Rocheser, NY. Architects, Williamson Pounders, Inc. and LaBella Associates. Consultant, Richard Vosko.

Fig. 55 *Jesus Christ Word and Sacrament Retablo.* San Fernando Cathedral, San Antonio, TX. Artisan, Leonardo Soto Recendiz. Photograph by Chris Cooper Photography.

Fig. 56 *Wooden altar.* Saints Peter and Paul Cathedral, Indianapolis, IN. Architect, Edward A. Sövik, SMSQ Architects.

Fig. 57 *Cross in Center.* Corpus Christi University Parish Church, Toledo, OH. Architects, The Collaborative. Consultant, Richard Vosko. Photograph by Anne Spenny.

A fixed altar table is typically made of stone. A movable altar table is made of wood or a combination of materials (fig. 56). Today, even in flexible church settings where concerts or other events may occur, the altar remains in its place as a reminder that the place is primarily used for the liturgy. At times it may be desirable to move the altar table for ritual purposes. For example, on Good Friday the Corpus Christi University Parish, Toledo, moves its centrally located altar. They then insert a life-size cross into a sleeve in the floor where the altar stood. The processions that accompany the veneration of that cross follow the path of the labyrinth engraved in the floor (fig. 57).

Whether fixed or movable the altar table should have a strong presence in the church. It is designed so that one person can easily preside at it even during liturgies when many priests concelebrate. Although worshipers throughout the church should be able to appreciate the proportions and beauty of the altar table, it does not have to be so large that it loses its gracious and human scale. The finest artisans should be commissioned to design and/or make this furnishing.

True relics, where they exist, are to be buried in the floor beneath or next to the altar table. They are no longer embedded in or on the tabletop. A cross may be engraved or carved in the floor to mark the location of the reliquary. As an alternative, the relics could be placed in a chest or cache mounted on the floor directly beneath the altar table (fig. 58). If the relics are objects of occasional veneration by the people, provision should be made to remove them from the reliquary at appropriate times of the year. In Rochester, altar stones with their relics were collected from many diocesan churches and buried beneath the new altar in the renovated Sacred Heart Cathedral.

The Setting for the Altar Table. Similar to the pavement surrounding the baptismal font, the floor beneath and around the altar table could be designed using a symbolic pattern, e.g., a cross or radiant sun. The placement of tall processional candles around the altar area would further highlight and distinguish this space during the liturgy of the Eucharist.[3]

When there are no steps around the altar table, the church becomes a completely barrier-free environment. While this is easier to achieve in a new church, there is no reason why access to this area could not be inclusive and gracious in every older place of worship. In fact,

Fig. 58 *Relics under table.*
Saint Benedict College Chapel, Saint Joseph, MN.
Architect, Hammell Green Abrahamson.
Consultant, Frank Kacmarcik.

[3] The *General Instruction of the Roman Missal,* 2000, no. 295, refers to the sanctuary as the place for the altar, the ambo and where all ministries exercise their offices and that this area should be marked off from the body of the church somewhat by elevation or by "a particular structure and ornamentation."

many states require it according to code. To avoid steps and ramps, consideration should be given to placing the altar table exactly in the middle of the assembly on a flat floor.

There should be sufficient space around the altar table to facilitate the gospel procession, the dressing of the altar table, the presentation of gifts and the Communion procession. These movements should not be encumbered by a lack of space or the interference of other ritual objects like the ambo or candlesticks. This is most possible when the altar is in the true center of the church. If the altar table must be placed on a platform the circulatory space immediately around it should be approximately five feet wide. This means that the actual size of the platform is greatly reduced providing enough space for the presiding priest and a deacon or acolyte. Concelebrating priests would participate from their places. Bridal parties as well as candidates for the sacraments of initiation could be accommodated in various locations in the space near the altar table. For example, brides and grooms would occupy places of honor near other seats in the assembly rather than on a "sanctuary" platform. Candidates for other sacraments, e.g., confirmation, would approach the chair of the presiding bishop or priest. Caskets would also be set in the place of honor on the floor near the altar table.

When smaller older churches do not lend themselves to such a configuration, a simple de-cluttering of the altar table area may be necessary to create extra space. Fundamentally, nothing else should detract from the significance of the altar table. Decorating the area with elaborate flower displays that obscure the ritual furnishings should be avoided. Candles and processional crosses should not encroach upon the altar table and so interfere with the ritual movements around it.

The Ambo. Lecterns were probably not common in early house-churches. Elevated places for proclaiming the Word and preaching were introduced in buildings where the crowds were large. The word "ambo" is derived from the Greek infinitive *ambein* meaning a place to mount. In some cases the ambo was a fixture in the choir. These furnishings were elevated so that voices would carry throughout the building. Eventually, when the liturgy was done without concern for the laity present, the Scriptures were read silently and preaching was considered an extra-liturgical event. Pulpits were placed closer to the people so they could hear. Each age provided different artistic versions of the pulpit, often with elaborate ornamentation, inscriptions and diminutive sculptures. Many pulpits incorporated fan-shaped sound-boards overhead to amplify the spoken word.

Only one reading desk or ambo for the proclamation of the Word of God is allowed in every church. While a permanent ambo (fig. 59) may be the ideal way to signal its importance, a movable one makes more sense in churches where even occasional flexibility is desired (fig. 60). It serves as a functional furnishing crafted as a place where the Scriptures are proclaimed. Form can follow function. For example, some new ambos are being designed with mechanical or electrical controls to adjust the height of the reading desk for persons with different statures and physical abilities (fig. 61). In these cases the style and shape of the ambo is determined to some extent by the way in which the piece operates.

Fig. 59 *Fixed ambo.* Sacred Heart Cathedral, Rochester, NY. Artisan, Brian DiBona, Oakwood Custom Woodworking.

Fig. 60 *Movable ambo.*
Old Saint Joseph Church, DePere, WI.
Fabrication, Rick Findora.
Designer, Richard Vosko.

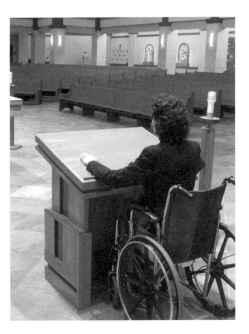

Fig. 61 *Accessible ambo.*
Saint Margaret of York Church, Loveland, OH.
Architect, Cole + Russell Architects. Consultant, Joanne Kepes.

Although the Liturgy of the Word is as important as the Eucharist, the ambo does not have to look like the altar table to signify this equity. Similarly, while there is a liturgical connection between the font, the ambo and the altar table, there is no reason why all of these pieces should look the same. The altar is a symbol of Christ (it is anointed at the rite of dedication), but the ambo does not really symbolize anything. On the other hand, the ambo often appears undersized when compared to the scale of the altar and font.

The size of the desktop of the ambo should be spacious enough to cradle the largest Scripture books used during the liturgy and to give the furnishing presence in the church. The desktop can be as large as two feet deep and three to four feet wide. Although a discreet shelf in the ambo could be a useful place for notes, it should not be used for storing the Scripture books or other paraphernalia.

Any shelf on the front of the ambo (for displaying the Book of Gospels or the Lectionary) compromises the primary function of the ambo, which is to serve as a reading desk. It is not a display unit. Nor does this practice honor the Word of God. See the section on Scripture books below.

The Setting for the Ambo. The ambo should not have to compete for space with the altar table nor should the ambo be placed right next to the altar table where it could inhibit movement around both furnishings. Distance is needed to lengthen the processions with incense and lights that take place prior to the proclamation of the gospel. If the ambo must be placed on a platform the circulatory space immediately around it should be approximately five feet wide. The two furnishings could be separated in large churches or even small chapels when a different seating plan is chosen for the assembly. For example, in a choral plan the ambo could be located at one end of the space while the altar is toward the other end. Placing the ambo on the same grade with the altar table will eliminate the need for ramps.

Ideally no microphones or light fixtures are attached to the ambo, which should be a finely crafted furnishing. Ample lighting from above and a good speech reinforcement system should be provided.

Auxiliary Lecterns. The singing of psalms and canticles by a cantor or psalmist may occur at the ambo or some other suitable place. It is recommended that two auxiliary lecterns be designed for the church. A lectern for the song leaders (and cantors if they are not using the ambo) should be visible to the entire assembly. The other is a podium for the choir director. These are movable furnishings, which could be adjustable to accommodate persons with different statures and physical abilities. They may also be elevated if necessary although access to these furnishings should be barrier-free. Again no microphones or light fixtures need to be attached to these furnishings unless required by the music ministry. Adequate overhead lighting and a good speech reinforcement system should be provided. During the Easter Vigil ample candlepower is preferred to "itty-bitty" snap-on lamps or flashlights.

Cross and Crucifix. Early in Christianity the cross was used as a sign of victory and was often ornately decorated with precious stones and/or images of Christ depicted as a king. Images of Jesus dying on a cross gained popularity in the late Middle Ages as Christians began to focus more on his passion and death. Large crucifixes became focal points in the *reredos* or *retablo* behind the altar. This is probably where the idea for a cross of the altar came about.

The crucified Jesus is an important image for the Church today and is required during the celebration of the Catholic liturgy. Because it is referred to as "the cross of the altar" there are some questions. Where exactly should it be placed? How big should it be? Should it be carried in only for worship or should it be permanently installed? Are any other crosses ever allowed?

The requirement for a cross of the altar can be satisfied with either a large fixed crucifix or the portable processional cross with a corpus.

Where should the crucifix be located? While visiting a small church in Otavalo, Ecuador, I watched a young mother teach her son how to venerate a very large ornately decorated cross standing in the corner (fig 62). I witnessed the same devotion in San Fernando Cathedral in San Antonio, where people kiss and caress El Christo Negro mounted on a wall near the font (fig. 63). I thought then as I do now that a cross or crucifix in a church, like other objects of devotion, should not be mounted high on a wall or suspended from the ceiling in such a way that people cannot physically embrace it.

Fig. 62 *Otavalo cross.*

117

Fig. 63 *El Cristo Negro*.
San Fernando Cathedral, San Antonio, TX.
Photograph by Chris Cooper Photography.

Fig. 64 *Crucifix*.
Cathedral of Our Lady of the Angels, Los Angeles.
Artist, Simon Toparovsky.
Photograph by Julius Schulman and David Glomb.

For example, the architectural volume of the Cathedral of Our Lady of the Angels in Los Angeles is 3,300,000 cubic feet. One idea was to suspend a heroic-size crucifix high above the altar table in scale with the vast interior. Now, instead, a most evocative and powerful life-size crucifix stands on the floor behind the altar where people line up to venerate the cross and kiss the feet and other parts of the corpus (fig. 64). Some will say that this practice is unique to Latin countries. However, in another example, the parishioners of Saint Bede Church in Williamsburg, Virginia, began the practice of using the same crucifix for all ritual activities throughout the liturgical year. They even remove the body from it during the Easter season when it is cleaned and hung in the sacristy.

118

Fig. 65 *Processional crucifix.* Christ the King Cathedral, Superior, WI.
Sculptor, Alexander Tylevich.
Cross by Saint Paul Fabricating and Decorating.

Processional Cross. When a processional cross also serves as the cross of the altar it must have an image of the crucified Jesus on it (fig. 65). In churches where a crucifix is already embedded in the *reredos* or *retablo* or where a crucifix stands near the altar, the processional cross could be one that has no corpus on it.

Different processional crosses could be crafted for the church, e.g., a cross with precious stones or jewels *(crux gemmata),* a cross with an image of the risen Christ, a cross with Jesus crucified. These crosses may be used at various times during different liturgical seasons. Every effort should be made to avoid the multiplication of crosses and crucifixes in the church. As a symbol, one cross or crucifix with a strong presence is sufficient.

In order to have a presence as it is carried in processions the crucifix could be as big as three feet high and mounted on a pole that is about seven feet tall. Because a processional cross is intended to be portable it should be as lightweight as possible. Older servers or acolytes should be able to bear this cross without difficulty. The cross would be inserted into a low-profile stand somewhere near the ambo or altar table. A bulky base would take away from the stature of the cross. Sometimes the bases look more important than the cross itself. The recent practice of setting the portable cross into the framework of a much larger empty cross permanently located in the altar area dilutes the symbolism of the cross. A cross is not a display case even for another cross.

119

Candlesticks and Candles. The Easter candle, also known as the paschal candle, is the most important symbol of the light of Christ in the church and was discussed in the section on baptismal fonts. Its flame is taken from the new Easter fire.

The earliest indication of the use of lights (lamps and candles) during Christian worship is found in Acts 20:8. The liturgical purpose is not clear. When bishops took on civic prominence, lights were used for honorific reasons especially in processions. The usage of candles on and near the altar table during liturgy probably began in the late Middle Ages as the liturgy accumulated more ceremonial appendages. The number of candles varied according to custom. Today two candles may be used for liturgy, and up to seven when a bishop is present. This number is a reference to the seven lamps in Revelation.

The use of candles makes sense during liturgy when everyone can see them as they accompany certain ritual actions. They can be used to lead the entry procession, to escort the Book of Gospels to the ambo and then to its place of reservation, to accompany the presentation of gifts at the altar table and to guide the final procession. However, these lights need to be tall and plentiful in order to mean something and have a presence in the church (fig. 66). This is especially important when the whole assembly joins in a procession. Up to seven light-weight candleholders approximately seven feet tall could be designed for use during various liturgies. At this height they will easily be noticed from anywhere in the assembly. They should be placed into low-profile stands or sleeves in the floor in various locations. However, in order not to impede processional activity they should not encroach upon the altar table and ambo.

Fig. 66 *Processional candlesticks.*
Cathedral of Our Lady of the Angels,
Los Angeles.
Artist, Marirose Jelicich.
Photograph by Julius Schulman
and David Glomb.

The dedication of a church includes the lighting of four or twelve candles that are mounted on the walls marking the areas where the building is anointed (fig. 67). The number twelve could refer to the tribes of Israel or the apostles. The candleholders as well as the candles should be scaled to fit into their architectural context. Often a cross is incorporated into the design of the candleholder. The candles are lighted again not only on the anniversary of the local church building but also the dedication of the Lateran Basilica in Rome, the episcopal seat of the pope as bishop of Rome. There is no reason why these candles could not be lighted on other festive liturgies, e.g., Midnight Mass or the Easter Vigil. The practice of anointing the walls has taken on a new significance. I have noticed in many dedication liturgies that the oil is not just dabbed on a tiny dedication cross but is now actually smeared directly on the wall or column in the shape of a cross.

All candles used in the church, especially the paschal candle, should be of proper proportion and scale in order to be sensed and appreciated by all. A short, thin Easter candle is lost in the vast architectural volume of a big church. And they should be authentic candles. The use of oil as a substitute or imitation is inappropriate for liturgical use. Electronic or artificial (permanent) candles also have no place during the liturgy.

Vesture for the Liturgy. In the early Church liturgical vesture was not much different from the ordinary clothes worn at the time. Changes occurred as the liturgy developed and appendages were added. For example, the maniple, an ornamental handkerchief or napkin originally carried by people with rank, was worn on the left arm of clergy and had no practical application during Mass.[4] Also, stylistic changes in the making of vestments are evident in different periods of history.

Every worshiping community should try to afford one good chasuble for each liturgical season. The collection ideally is tailored to fit the person wearing the clothes. This is a difficult thing to achieve because of the different stature and girth of presiding clergy. The hue of the vestments could incorporate color schemes and various subtle patterns to harmonize with the finishes in the environment (fig. 68). The décor that changes from season to season should complement the color palette in the vesture collection even if an occasional visual counterpoint is desired.

---

[4] In common practice this handkerchief or napkin was draped over the forearm or tucked into the fold of a garment because there were probably no pockets in the togas.

Fig. 67 *Dedication candle.*
San Fernando Cathedral, San Antonio.

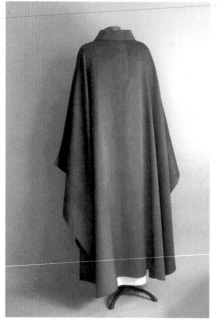

Fig. 68 *Chasuble.*
Designer, weaver, Katreen Bettencourt.

Chasubles for concelebrants and vesture for all other ministries should be well coordinated. The alb is the white garment common to all baptized members of the Church and may be worn by different liturgical ministries according to local custom. Albs should be made to fit various body sizes. There is no reason why women should have to wear garments designed with only men in mind. In every case competent and reliable regional or local weavers and tailors should be considered for all vesture. Lastly, most vestment designers suggest that chasubles are best stored flat. Provisions should be made for this.

As previously mentioned, the altar table, a symbol of Jesus Christ, is the focal point of the eucharistic liturgy. In the early Church it is unlikely that the altar was clothed in an ornamental manner. Later, when liturgical ceremonies became more affected, elaborately woven cloths placed over the table obscured it. Today a simple cloth may be placed on the flat surface of the altar table. The practice of doing so during the preparation of the altar and gifts is occurring more frequently. Some places also remove the cloth at the end of the Communion rite. The cloth used during liturgy should not remain on the table after the liturgy. Instead a seasonally colorful dust cloth should suffice to protect the altar.

Another important vestment is the one placed over the casket during rites of Christian death and burial. Referred to as a "pall," it is a reminder of the baptismal garment and the Christian dignity of the deceased. Although palls may be purchased from church goods stores, the local congregation might wish to commission an artist to weave one that reflects the spirit of the local community.

There were banners in my childhood church. They belonged to organizations like the Altar Rosary Society and the Holy Names Society. They were carried in all liturgical processions inside the church and around the block on the feast of Corpus Christi. Although not required for worship, architectural hangings have found their way into many contemporary places of worship to provide an extra air of festivity. Although there is something to be said for homemade banners—which, one could argue, reflect a kind of popular art form— all textile art should be commissioned to professionals. In some congregations the artist will provide templates and actually guide the local decorative arts committee in fabricating of the pieces.

Textile or fabric art can provide a flowing or billowing atmosphere to the pathways leading to the church as well as different interior spaces. An alternative to banners hanging from columns, pilasters or ceilings is the installation of canopies free flowing to and from different elevations in the church (fig. 69). These streams of color could be opaque or sheer and made from different materials like nylon or even paper.[5] Appropriate storage spaces for all architectural hangings should not be overlooked.

Vessels. Many vessels are required for the celebration of liturgy. At least one complete set of tableware should be custom designed for the church and its use encouraged at every Sunday liturgy. One reason for this is similar to the one given for vesture. Every building is different and the major altar table vessels for wine and bread should be of a scale

---

[5] Nancy Chinn, *Spaces for Spirit* (Chicago: Liturgy Training Publications, 1998) and David Philippart, *Clothed in Glory: Vesting the Church* (Chicago: Liturgy Training Publications, 1997).

Fig. 69 *Nylon canopy.*
Grace Cathedral, San Francisco, CA.
Textile artist, Nancy Chinn.

large enough to be perceived by everyone in the assembly. Further, the actual design of the vessels could emulate a particular stylistic pattern that may exist in the interior of the building.[6] But there is a larger reason: even in the vessels the liturgy should be clearly the work of the assembly, not the action of a priest alone.

The service vessels handled by ministers of Communion may be smaller. The design of the flagon(s) for wine as well as the pitcher and basin for washing hands and feet could all match. Pewter, silver or some other appropriate material indigenous to the region could be considered. In those places where glassware is used, the vessels should be unbreakable.

Containers to accommodate the sprinkling of holy water as well as for the use of incense should also be custom designed. The vessels for chrism and holy oils were discussed in the section on baptismal fonts. In every case competent and reliable regional or local artists and artisans should be commissioned. Something important is lost when these items are "store-bought." Just as the church building is a reflection of the local assembly, so too is everything else that is used for liturgy. Generic appointments and artifacts purchased out of catalogues or from church goods stores will express nothing of the local culture.

Often a congregation will possess something (e.g., a chalice) that has been used in the liturgy for generations and is part of the heritage

---

[6] *Basket, Basin, Plate, and Cup: Vessels in the Liturgy,* ed. David Philippart (Chicago: Liturgy Training Publications, 2001).

124

of the community. Sometimes there may be a question about the appropriate use of such treasures or whether to bring them along when a new church is constructed. It is important to gauge the sentimental and real value of such artifacts. The input of appraisers as well as older members of the congregation can help in making a decision to keep some appointments and properly discard others.

Books for the Liturgy. Before Gutenberg invented movable type in the fifteenth century, scribes wrote the Scriptures and ritual books. Many of these manuscripts also contained magnificent illustrations. More attention could be given today to the books that contain the Word of God for they should also be considered works of art. Although some publishers have made an effort to produce remarkable covers and illuminated pages for the Scripture books, most of the books parishes use appear quite ordinary and plain. In the print world where thousands of fonts and mass production are commonplace, the art of calligraphy is lost as a ministry in the Church. Even today, in the Jewish tradition, a *sofer* handwrites the Torah scrolls.

Why could not each congregation commission a calligrapher to write the Scriptures according to the current three-year cycle? This collection of Scriptures could also be illustrated, depicting passages from the Bible.[7] The faith community would then have its own original bound books of Scripture that would be cherished and passed down from generation to generation. If this is not possible, every effort should be made to obtain the finest of commercially produced books.

Another part of the Jewish heritage that Christians could emulate is the manner in which Jews cover their Torahs with decorative mantles and store them in the Ark. Catholics are respectful of the real presence of Christ in the reserved sacrament but fail to show the same reverence for the presence of Christ in the Scriptures. Consider how carelessly Scripture books are handled before, during and after the liturgy. The Book of Gospels, for example, is carried gracefully in the entrance procession and then placed on the altar table. But, after the proclamation of the gospel, this book most often ends up on the shelf of the ambo or a side table. A more appropriate alternative would be for the deacon or priest to carry it in procession, accompanied by candle bearers, to a place of reservation (fig. 70). Different locations are possible, (e.g., in the commons, near the ambo or in the chapel where the Eucharist is reserved). The advantage of reserving these Scriptures in or near the commons or baptistery is two-fold. It would be where the processions

---

[7] See, for example, the extraordinary *Saint John's Bible,* the seven-volume handwritten and illuminated Bible (Collegeville: Liturgical Press, Volume One, 2005).

Fig. 70 *Book Repository*. Christ the King Cathedral, Superior, WI.
Artisans, Saint Paul Fabricating and Decorating. Designer, Richard Vosko.

begin and it would be accessible to people. It could even be venerated with a kiss in such a place. Perhaps the congregation could be encouraged to venerate the Word of God as treasured by the Church in its book, as they do the reserved Sacrament. Christ is really present in both.[8] The cathedrals in Superior and San Antonio both have ambries for the reservation of all Scripture books.

DEVOTIONAL ART

I remember watching a person walk directly in front of the altar table and assembly during liturgy to light a candle by the image of his

---

[8] *Holy Communion and Worship of the Eucharist Outside Mass*, no. 6.

Fig. 71 *Retablo.* Santa Maria de la Paz, Santa Fe, NM.
Consultant, John Buscemi.
Artisans, Marie Romero Cash and Félix López.

favorite saint. To what extent should a place of worship, primarily designed to house the common liturgy of the assembly, also accommodate popular devotions? How can the church house works of art that
are not required for the celebration of the sacraments? Acts of personal
piety, although important, are always subordinate to the Liturgy of the
Eucharist. At the same time, the inculturation of that liturgy cannot
ignore the devotional practices that many Catholics adhere to.[9]

The principle to follow is that all works of art should be crafted to
reflect the customs and traditions of the local faith community. This
means that churches will not look the same. The same works of art will
not be present in every church. For instance, strange as it may sound,
some congregations do not have a custom of strong devotion to a particular saint. That church may have few images in it. On the other
hand, a church that has a long tradition of venerating a particular saint
may have many images of that same individual. The significance of
having multiple images of the same saint should be reevaluated in
these places.

Church art is not decoration to identify the building as Catholic or
as "New England" or as used by Latinos or Poles. Images of saints and
Scripture stories are to be considered part of the narrative that helps
people remember their place in the larger religious family. Most of us

[9] See the *Directory on Popular Piety and the Liturgy* (Vatican City: Congregation
for Divine Worship and the Discipline of the Sacraments, December 17, 2001).

understand how relationships can develop between human beings and saints. They are spiritual partners or companions on the journey (fig. 71). At the beginning of every building or renovation project, it is essential to document the popular devotions, customs and traditions of the members of the congregation.[10]

Older Catholic church buildings typically have a collection of statues or paintings depicting the once-favorite saints or scenes from the Bible. They are located in various parts of the church or in the niches of a *reredos* or *retablo*. The evolution of this practice dates back to the early Christians. As the liturgy itself became more clericalized, the cult to the saints and martyrs grew and resulted in the proliferation of images in almost every church building. The exuberant ornamentation of churches created stimulating backdrops for these images. Wealthy patrons commissioned artists and artisans to produce works of devotional and decorative art.

Unfortunately the quality of most of the images found in twentieth-century North American churches, even though considered precious by the people, is artistically uneven and generally lackluster. Much of the statuary has been purchased out of catalogues and appears to have little to do with the cultural characteristics of the local faith community. On the other hand, some of the imagery is first-rate because of the good taste of the pastor or someone in the congregation. Today there is no reason why a congregation should not be able to find and commission an artist to make an image for a place of worship. The renewed interest in liturgy prompted by Vatican II also triggered a new appreciation for works of art in the worship environment. This has led, in turn, to a new relationship between artists and faith communities.[11] Some resources that can put the congregation in touch with artists and artisans are listed in the bibliography.

The setting for each work of art is important and should be planned ahead of time in the construction of a new church. Otherwise, the sculptures or paintings will end up being randomly placed wherever there is room left over, usually on some wall. Ideally all artists should be commissioned during the schematic design phase to assure that spaces are considered early in the project. It is recommended that

[10] See also, John Buscemi, "Places for Devotion," in the *Meeting House Essays* (Chicago: Liturgy Training Publications, no. 4, 1993) and Michael Jones-Frank, "Iconography and Liturgy," in the *Meeting House Essays* (Chicago: Liturgy Training Publications, no. 6, 1994).

[11] See Pope John Paul II, *Letter to Artists* (Chicago: Liturgy Training Publications, 1999).

devotional settings be designed to accept each image. The size of these areas can vary from smaller niches to larger chapel-like settings. It is important to determine how people will have access into the space and whether candles will be available for devotional purposes. Larger chapel settings should include benches and kneelers.

Different media could be considered for all works of art. Wood, metal, bronze and marble are popular materials for sculptures. However, paintings, tiles and tapestries could also be considered for other art pieces. Some studios employ artisans who know how to work in different techniques (e.g., frescoe, intaglio, mosaic, relief, *repoussé*). The proper approach should be decided to harmonize with the worship environment.

Mary. What is common to every church is an image of Mary, Mother of God, a title dating back to the early Church. Since then Mary has been honored in many ways. Under the title Immaculate Conception, Mary is the patron of the United States as well as Spain, Tanzania and the Democratic Republic of the Congo. Also, she is the patron of the Americas under the title of Our Lady of Guadalupe, which commemorates her appearances to Juan Diego, an Aztec Indian, at Tepayac Hill near Mexico City in 1531 (fig. 72).

Fig. 72 *Our Lady of Guadalupe.* Cathedral of Our Lady of the Angels, Los Angeles. Artist, Lalo Garcia.

Fig. 73 *Mary the Teacher.*
Corpus Christi University Parish Church, Toledo, OH.
Sculptor, Steve Shields.

Fig. 74 *Mary with Child.*
Sacred Heart Cathedral, Rochester, NY.
Sculptor, Matteo Moroder.

The ways in which Mary has been artistically portrayed are count-less and depend a great deal upon the cultural traditions of the region. In recent years more congregations are commissioning artists to depict Mary in ways that are more realistic and less romantic. For example, at the Corpus Christi University Parish in Toledo, there is a life-size copper sculpture of Mary the Teacher showing Jesus how to walk (fig. 73). The effort to see Mary and Jesus in ways that are familiar to the local com-munity is not new. Very personal and compassionate interpretations were the hallmark of the Renaissance art community. For example, the tender and intimate images of Mary breastfeeding her child are most popular in Spain, Portugal and Italy but seldom seen in North America, most likely because nursing is still not an acceptable public practice.

The trend to humanize images of the saints is refreshing because one of the attributes of art, any art, is found in its power to shape attitudes and value systems. Works of religious art that relate to the everyday experiences of people can reinforce or challenge their con-victions. Instead of placing Mary on some ideological pedestal, new works of art showing her human side could provide an important lesson for young and old Christians alike (fig. 74). The statue of Mary

Fig. 75 *Communion of Saints tapestries.* Cathedral of Our Lady of the Angels, Los Angeles. Artist, John Nava. Photograph by John Nava.

teaching Jesus how to walk mentioned above is a favorite of young-sters in that community because they can actually walk up to it and compare their height to that of the youthful Jesus. Similarly, parents and guardians will connect with Mary as a teacher and come to know that it is possible for them to model their ordinary lives after her.

The same can be said of any work of art that depicts any saint, whether the patron of the parish or one of the saints or blessed ones on the universal list.

The Communion of Saints. The largest collection of tapestries any-where in the world depicting the communion of saints hangs in the Cathedral of Our Lady of the Angels in Los Angeles (fig. 75). The origi-nal plan was to surround the assembly with images of holy women, men and children who join the living faithful in the praise of God. The model for this collection is found in San Appolinare Nuovo, a sixth-century basilica in Ravenna where the holy martyrs all face the altar in procession.

But the presentation of the iconic figures in Los Angeles prompts a slightly different act of devotion. They are suspended along the lengthy and soaring walls of the cathedral, which are made of finely honed architectural concrete. The artist John Nava used local models to paint the images before they were digitally mastered for the weaver's

131

Fig. 76 *Communion of Saints tapestries.* Photograph by John Nava.

loom in Belgium. Also, in addition to the saints and blessed ones[12] who were selected to reflect the multi-cultural make up of the local church, a number of images are anonymous as are most of the saints.

Collectively the tapestries invite a different devotion that is more communal than individualistic (there are no votive candles to be lighted near the tapestries). Those in the assembly are both invited to focus on the individual saints and, at the same time, be swept up in a long parade of ancestors who have completed the journey. Worshipers frequently comment on the overwhelming feeling of walking in the Communion procession—along with the saints and blessed ones (fig. 76). This is

[12] See *Newsletter,* USCCB Committee on the Liturgy, for information on the public cult in honor of a blessed one (vol. XL, August 2004, 35).

132

what art can achieve in a liturgical environment. In addition to serving as objects of personal piety, the art provides an opportunity for the whole assembly to be drawn deeper into the mystery of the Body of Christ. This is the common purpose of liturgical and devotional art. This is the purpose of the whole environment for worship.

The colorful "Dancing Saints" by the iconographer Mark Dukes are painted along the high walls in Saint Gregory of Nyssa Episcopal Church in San Francisco (fig. 77). According to Richard Fabian, Gregory of Nyssa's commentary on Psalm 150 gives "his vision of the world's peoples in harmony—not just audible harmony, but active dancing harmony."[13] In this church the all-inclusive liturgical style incorporates dance. As the worshipers move through the church, which has different centers for the word and sacrament, the saints dance along with them creating a remarkable sense of harmony among all persons living and deceased. The *Catechism of the Catholic Church* asks, "What is the Church if not the assembly of all the saints? The communion of saints is the Church."[14] This traditional understanding of sainthood has been depicted inside and outside church buildings for

Fig. 77 *Dancing Saints.*
Saint Gregory of Nyssa Church, San Francisco, CA.
Artist, Mark Dukes.

[13] Richard Fabian, *The Dancing Saints: Who Are These Like Stars Appearing?* (Saint Gregory of Nyssa Episcopal Church, San Francisco). An essay on the project.
[14] *Catechism of the Catholic Church* (Allen, TX: Tabor Publishing, 1994) no. 946.

Fig. 78 *Kateri Tekakwitha.*
Christ the King Cathedral, Superior, WI.
Sculptor, Sister Margaret Beaudette, S.C.,
DePaul Sculpture Studio.

ages. Encircling the living Church with images of the saints can present a renewed opportunity to ponder the relationships between not only the living and the deceased but also heaven and earth.

Although there are many popular and familiar saints and blessed ones in the Catholic Church, congregations in North America now have an indigenous list. These would include Isaac Jogues, René Goupil, John LaLande, Katherine Drexel, Elizabeth Ann Seton, Frances Xavier Cabrini, John Neumann, Venerable Solanus Casey and Blessed Kateri Tekakwitha (fig. 78). Of course, as congregations become more culturally diverse, choices from the ever-growing list of saints and blessed ones can be made. The parish membership could be invited to participate in the selection process. Some Latino congregations have lined the walls of their churches with niches that contain santos, carvings of their favorite saints and blessed ones. I have wondered how soon it will be before images of the holy ones will appear in churches as holograms. Imagine entering a chapel setting and being greeted by an interactive image of your favorite saint who just might wish to tell you her story and encourage you to live out yours. This technology is begging to be developed for worship environments.

Stations of the Cross. Also not required for public worship but important to Catholic custom are the Stations of the Cross. Similar to

134

Fig. 79 *Station of the Cross.* Saint Joseph Church, East Millstone, NJ. Artist, Charles Wells.

Fig. 80 *Station of the Cross.* Cathedral of Our Lady of the Angels, Los Angeles. Sculptor, Christopher Slatoff.

the labyrinth, the Way of the Cross is a mini-pilgrimage for those who cannot journey to the Holy Land. This devotion has been a popular practice since the Franciscans, who were responsible for the holy places in Jerusalem, introduced it in the fourteenth century. In addition to the familiar stations comprised of nine gospel scenes and five stories from tradition (e.g., Jesus falling three times), other formats are available. These would include a recent version that focuses on the women who were present to Jesus at the time of his passion and the scriptural stations introduced by Pope John Paul II in 1992.

The stations may be fabricated in almost any material and style that complements the worship environment (fig. 79). In addition to mounting them on the walls of a church ambulatory they are some- times embedded in the floor or etched in the windows. In some places they are portable and brought into the space only when larger crowds gather during the season of Lent. The stations are also found along

135

Fig. 81 *Iconostasis.* Unknown.

pathways outside a church building (fig. 80). Still other congregations favor the enactment of the Way of the Cross by the youth in the community. If it is perceived that the devotion is popular, care should be taken so that individuals have access to the stations anytime.

Icons. The recent practice of placing icons in Latin Rite Catholic churches is a curious one.[15] The reasons for this trend could be related to the ecumenical spirit of Vatican II. The council encouraged more understanding of the Orthodox churches, which in turn prompted more dialogue. This led to a new appreciation of the rituals and the art that plays an important role not only in the piety of individuals but also in the liturgy of these churches (fig. 81). The increased interest in Eastern mystics has prompted a desire to connect with some of the imagery associated with that spirituality.

However, the popularity of icons has led to some concerns on both sides of the dialogue. First, in the authentic tradition, the iconographer should be a person who trained under a "master" iconographer. That artist is also someone who leads a prayer-filled spiritual life that guides the personal and artistic journey. Prayer must be an important part of the iconographer's practice especially before and after writing an icon. In fact, the very act of writing an icon is considered a

[15] See Mahmoud Zibawi, *The Icon: Its Meaning and History* (Collegeville: Liturgical Press, 1993).

prayerful act. The icon represents the manifestation of God or a saint as experienced through the spiritual life of the iconographer. Time is also important in writing an icon. It could be a fruitful exercise for the congregation to become aware of the difference between an original icon and a copy.

Another concern has to do with the veneration of the icon, which is quite different from the customs surrounding a painting found in Western Christian churches. A true icon is not considered a portrayal but the embodiment or "real presence" of God, Mary or some other saint. This is why the manner in which the icon is used in the church and how it is venerated should be considered before a congregation commissions one. My mother's family was Ukrainian Catholic, and although I was not raised in that tradition, we would go to the family church, Saint Nicholas, for weddings and funerals. As a youngster I noticed how the people took time to venerate the icons with a kiss as they entered and left the church. Candles burned constantly near them. Today, when icons are found in Roman Catholic churches, they are treated often like other statues and paintings, almost like decorations. They are hung in lobbies or on the walls of the church and seldom do you see a worshiper venerate them. It would be important for a congregation to learn more about the meaning of icons before placing them in their churches.

Votive Candles. Lighting votive or vigil candles is a very important religious practice for many people. It provides them with a way of connecting or interacting with a favorite saint or blessed one. It is also a way to remember someone or an event. An absence of candles for individuals to light may mean that the members of the congregation no longer practice the custom, or the local fire marshals have prohibited them. The former reason could be considered another example of how religious customs change over time. The latter reason should be challenged.

Ventilation, maintenance and safety factors are important wherever candles are used. New stands for votive candles should be designed specifically for the devotional areas in the church. While oil lamps may be used in the lamp near the tabernacle, wax is required for all other candles used in the liturgy. The use of electronic candles, even as a way to satisfy safety and health concerns, is inappropriate in a church building. They totally extinguish the symbolic significance of the flame, not to mention the very act of lighting the candle.

Flags. There are no requirements for either the nation's flag or the Vatican City state flag (often mistaken as the papal flag) during the celebration of the liturgy. "Although the art and decoration of the liturgical place will be that of the local church, identifying symbols of particular cultures, groups, or nations are not appropriate as permanent parts of the liturgical environment."[16]

SEASONAL ART

There are works of art that are not required for worship but may be important to a particular congregation at different times of the liturgical year. In most cases the custom of decorating the church in a particular way will reflect the culture and traditions of the local community. However, architectural hangings, flower arrangements, the Advent wreath, the crèche and Christmas trees are embellishments that should not encroach upon major liturgical focal points. I once saw a large baptismal font that was filled with poinsettias at Christmas and sand during Lent. And, I once could not see an altar table because it was hidden behind banks of lilies at Easter. Such innovations are symptomatic of a lack of understanding and appreciation of the symbols in the Church.

The locations planned for the display of seasonal decorations are important. For example, although the candles on the Advent wreath may be lighted in the midst of the community, this aliturgical custom could easily take place in the commons or near the main entrance to the church before the liturgy begins. Hardware provisions should be planned for the proper hanging of all art forms in the building.

Plants and Flowers. Flower arranging is an art. Much could be learned from the ancient Japanese practice of *Kado,* also known as *ikebana,* which takes into consideration the choice of plants and flowers in relationship to their containers and settings. Plants and flowers should be used as accents in worship environments rather than focal points. One or two properly proportioned and scaled displays strategically placed could be an attractive alternative to rows and banks of seasonal plants and flowers that often conceal major liturgical furnishings like the altar table and ambo. Also, it is helpful to think of flowers in relation to the whole room and not certain sections that may have been considered more important in the past.

Art Exhibits. Occasionally a church building can be a place for the exhibition of religious works of art, works that are not related to the

---

[16] *Environment and Art in Catholic Worship,* ibid., no. 101.

ritual practice of the congregation. For example, scenes from the Bible comprise a significant part of the Church's artistic heritage. Down through the ages many artists have interpreted familiar biblical texts and personages in a wide variety of styles. Current generations should not be deprived of the gifted artists who continue to express themselves in a spiritual context.

The exhibition of such work could take place in the lobby, along the corridors of the building or even in the ambulatories of the worship place. Security, lighting and humidity controls are some of the environmental factors important in attracting local or regional artists who may wish to display. Receptions and lectures by the artists could be an effective way for the congregation to gather and explore contemporary artistic interpretation. Again, care should be taken so that the art does not become a distraction during liturgical events.

THE MEDIA ARTS

The Catholic Church continues to rely on a primal symbol system to shape the life of the Church and its members. Elements like water, fire, oil, bread, water and wine are used as part of the ritual language of the Church. These flourish in the environment in actions of immersion, burning, anointing, eating and drinking. Any minimalist approach to these powerful non-verbal symbols during liturgy is regrettable. These symbols are to flourish in the liturgical environment.

But this often is not the case. Overwhelming reliance on the spoken word (poor translations included) has contributed to the dissatisfaction many have with the liturgical life of the Church today. Often the rich ritual language of the Church has been reduced to the cerebral experience one finds in lecture halls. In part this is the fault not of the reformed rites but of the manner in which they are enacted. This dullness contrasts with much in popular culture. There are now almost two generations of Catholics born after Vatican II who grew up with wide-screen televisions, computers, Play Stations and Game Boys in their homes and schools. These things are interactive. Movie theatres show films using video and acoustical technology that stimulates the sensual appetites of young and old alike. There is little wonder why the liturgy seems dull in an age when the media arts have been integrated into just about every nook and cranny of life. Liturgy need not compete in technology, but too often it is ignoring its own powers of engagement.

There is the concern that the use of the media arts in church will turn the liturgy into a time of entertainment rather than worship and that it will promote more passivity than ever before.[17] These worries cannot be overlooked. Any efforts to improve the celebration of the liturgy should begin by paying attention to the manner in which primary symbols are celebrated. But do we ignore the developments taking place in the field of media arts? Like all art in a church building, the media arts would have to be understood as servants in the worship of God rather than objects of worship.

Another concern is the way in which everything in the electronic world changes so rapidly. It is possible that whatever equipment is installed in a church building will soon be out of date. The problem becomes exacerbated when the ministries become more preoccupied with having the latest and best technology rather than focusing on what the purpose of worship is to begin with.

How can the media arts be used in liturgical environments? Eileen Crowley believes that the media arts will eventually be considered liturgical art because they can be "integral and appropriate to the liturgical actions of a community's worship."[18] There are indications that more churches are using the media arts during worship. The technology is becoming affordable so that even smaller congregations can purchase and use basic equipment. However, much more needs to be learned before this art form takes its rightful place in the context of the liturgy.

What exactly are we talking about here? In Saint Patrick's Cathedral in New York City, color monitors have been attached to the columns along the nave. It is disconcerting to watch people looking at the images on the monitors rather than engaging with the rituals being enacted in the very same room. The use of media technology in this way is most unfortunate. Rather than working to celebrate the rituals in a manner that embraces all worshipers in the cathedral (including the tourists who drop in for a visit), the planners are apparently content with projecting whatever goes on in the sanctuary just so people can see. In other places the use of media technology means the mere projection of images or words on a screen.

A more effective use of the media arts would be to incorporate the screens and projection equipment in such a way that they embellish the worship experience. The screens would have to be incorporated into the very fabric of the building on the walls or from the ceiling so that

---

[17] Quentin Schultze, *High-Tech Worship? Using Presentation Technologies Wisely* (Grand Rapids, MI: Baker Book House, 2004).

[18] Eileen Crowley, http://www.calvin.edu/worship/theology/liturgical_media_art.htm.

all members of the assembly would be able to see what is projected on them.

It would be inappropriate to use media technology to enlarge live liturgical actions or a particular liturgical ministry as if it were a television broadcast. This approach will result in more passivity during the ritual action. Instead, the imagery (words or pictures, still or moving) could serve as almost subliminal backdrop to the actual liturgical action. Is it not reasonable to think that the proclamation of Scripture could be enhanced by the use of projected imagery in an age where such media is so ubiquitous in the everyday world? The challenge is to design media arts systems (e.g., all hardware) so they are integrated into the architecture of the building just like other building components.

The use of media technology during worship will require a commitment to employ new ministers of the arts. It will require budgets for training programs and the purchase of equipment. As with all art in the church a program should be written to state the rationale for investing in the media arts. It should also describe the specific ways in which these arts will be used during liturgy. Because the field is so new it would help to retain a media arts consultant to guide conversations and assist in creating this program. Once this document is completed professionals should be retained to prepare specifications for the building plans. Until all of these related issues are addressed the use of the media arts in church buildings should be considered a work in progress.

Chapter 20

Light and Color and Glass

COLOR AND LIGHT are siblings in any church environment. Each has an influence on the way the other performs. Did you ever try on a jacket or dress in a store only to find out when you got home that the color was just not right? The reason for the variation was the different light sources in the two locations. This is a simple example of what light can do to color and vice versa. Let me start with a few principles concerning light in a worship space.[1]

Light is important in every place of worship for reasons of function, security and aesthetics. But it is also a significant symbol. The Church is a beacon to the world (fig. 82). This is not just an architectural analogy. It is a theological metaphor. The building needs to be a beacon

Fig. 82
*Cathedral of Our Lady of the Angels,
Los Angeles.* Architect, Rafael Moneo
and Leo A. Daly. Photo by Julius
Schulman and David Glomb.

---

[1] See Viggo Bech Rambusch, "Lighting the Liturgy," in the *Meeting House Essays* (Chicago: Liturgy Training Publications, no. 7, 1994).

because the Church, the Body of Christ, is a light to the world. How the building is illuminated inside and out will make a difference in the way it is perceived and understood by the worshipers and the neighborhood community. The exterior lighting of the property and the building was discussed in the section on the gathering of the Church. The lighting plan for the interior will be dependent on the functions that take place there. In churches where flexibility is required for different liturgical and non-liturgical events a more creative lighting system will be needed.

Lighting. A qualified lighting consultant and designer should be retained to develop a comprehensive lighting plan to facilitate daytime and nighttime activities in the church. Many architects will insist that they have the ability in their firms to create the lighting plan. Some do, but review what they have done in other places. If their only experience is with schools, gymnasiums and office buildings, then it would be wise to get a consultant. Along with acoustics, a good lighting plan for a church is essential.

In a liturgical context, the lighting system should be designed to achieve the following:

1. Architectural and artistic highlighting. This lighting would illuminate the ceiling and walls as well as any desired artwork or ornamentation. It can be achieved with the introduction of up lights, pin spot lamps and gradient wall washers. Approximately ten- to fifteen-foot candles would be sufficient.

2. Task lighting. This lighting provides illumination over the assembly, including the clergy, and the music ministry areas. It could be accomplished with a combination of up-light sources that reflect off the ceiling and down-light sources. Approximately thirty-foot candles would be sufficient. It is important to note that some experts say that up lighting does not help much in providing appropriate foot candles at book level. This will depend on the height of the ceiling. The objective is to illuminate the clergy and laity so that they appear to be part of the same assembly in the same place.

3. Focus or accent lighting. This lighting provides illumination over primary ritual furnishings when they are used—font, ambo, altar and cathedra. Approximately ninety-foot candles would be sufficient. When these furnishings are in the midst of the assembly, they will not appear as objects of devotion but essential elements in the worship practice. For example, it may

be desirable to highlight the ambo during the proclamation of Scripture during the Easter Vigil while the light level in the rest of the assembly is dim.

Recently three types of lamps have been used in church projects. Incandescent, fluorescent and high-intensity discharge lamps are each very different from one another. A qualified lighting consultant is the best one to explain the advantages and disadvantages in a worship setting.

Many times a lamp is chosen because of energy efficiency and maintenance concerns. The compact fluorescent lamp has been used for these reasons. Although some of these lamps do possess extremely warm spectrums, the overall quality of the illumination is still uneven. No doubt the fluorescent lamp is the best choice for restrooms, offices, classrooms and meeting rooms.

There are three types of high-intensity discharge (HID) lamps: metal halide, mercury vapor and high and low pressure sodium vapor. These are best used for retail stores, commercial office spaces, manufacturing plants, warehouses, sports venues, parking lots and roadways.

Neither the fluorescent nor the HID lamps can be completely controlled for lighting intensity. This is an inconvenience during those liturgical occasions when the congregation will desire to control the amount of light in the church.

While weighing the effect of any type of lamp on the energy cost, remember that much depends on the amount of time the lamps will actually be in use. Estimated times should be determined before decisions are made to use lamps that, otherwise, are not conducive for worship. The desire for a certain aesthetic effect and the need to control the intensity of light using dimmer switches is a compelling reason to use lamps from the incandescent family, e.g., the tungsten halogen lamp.

Unobtrusive fixtures are all important. All fixtures should be arranged so that there will be no glare in the eyes of worshipers, no dark spots over seating sections and no shadows on the faces of the assembly or liturgical ministers. Every effort should be made to lamp the church as discreetly as possible. The selection of fixtures should take into consideration not only the architectural nature of the space but also the desire for a harmonious visual field. Careful analysis of the architectural volume and design of the ceiling should take place before specifying suspended fixtures. While some fixtures might be considered works of art in themselves, more often than not they detract from the design of the ceiling.

144

Fig. 83 *Saint John Church, Hopkins, MN.*
Architects, Rafferty Rafferty Tollefson. Consultant, Frank Kacmarcik.

Lighting is a work of art and like all art in churches it should be in the service of the worship of God. As with the acoustics of a building, no two situations will be the same.

Different computer-based, pre-set zones and levels of lighting intensity should be controlled from one or more suitable locations to facilitate a variety of desired lighting effects for worship and non-worship events throughout the church. Wireless control panels offer added convenience. However, liturgy is not a show. Although there may a great temptation to "play with the light board," the rule of thumb is to set up the program and then leave it alone.

Windows and Glass Art. Some cathedrals and churches are known for their stained glass windows. Once considered the illiterate person's Bible or catechism, these windows portrayed scriptural and saints' stories for the education and delight of worshipers.

Early churches erected in the Romanesque style used clerestory windows allowing light to bathe the space below. The lower levels of these buildings were usually solid and devoid of any fenestration. The reason was a structural one. The thick walls of these buildings held up the roof. Anything that penetrated these vertical elements would weaken the structure. The discovery of the flying buttress, an exterior arch or brace placed up against the wall of the building, made it possible to construct churches with lighter walls and so allow more windows. Modern building techniques make it possible to introduce windows just about anywhere the designer wishes.

Consideration could be given for employing a combination of clear glass and art glass in a church. The shape of these windows should honor the architectural style of the building. Clear glass could be utilized at the clerestory level (fig. 83). On the main level of the

Fig. 84 *Rose window.* Neue Wallfahrtskirche Maria, Königin des Friedens, Neviges, Germany. Architect, Gottfried Böhm.

church, clear windows will often cause glare and backlighting. Creativity in the building's design will often overcome this and allow the use of clear glass on the main level to provide indirect sources of natural light. A light canopy or cupola *(Oculus Dei)* over the central part of the assembly would allow natural light to enter the church while providing a place to conceal accent lights needed to highlight the altar table area below. The use of low-E windows with different shading coefficients (SC) should be selected depending on the climate. Photovoltaic arrays can convert any light, not just sunlight, into electricity. These can be integrated into the design of the building, on roofs, in walls, windows, window frames, skylights, etc. Both types of windows should be considered as significant energy saving devices that could be incorporated into the church building.

"Architectural glass art" accurately describes the type of glazing used in places of worship. The term "stained" glass, although common, has a limited meaning. The glossary of art glass includes: antique, Dalle de Verre (faceted), Cathedral, Favrile (iridescent), flashed, drapery, frosted (sandblasted), dichroic, opal, opak, reamy and others (fig. 84). Some artisans will use different types of glass in the same church windows. The list of glass artists in North America is very long and the committee will need to do a serious search. Like other artists commissioned for work in the church, the glass artist should display an understanding of the role of art in a worship environment and how it is always in the service of the worship of God. It is often advantageous to work with an individual artist rather than with a larger company where the congregation may never meet the person actually designing the windows. Close collaboration between glass artist and architect is essential to assure the proper installation. Glass art may be installed in

146

the main part of the church as well as in other parts of the building, e.g., the chapels (fig. 85).

Many contemporary office buildings are hermetically sealed containers where the windows do not open. How the windows function in a church could be an issue for congregations desiring an aesthetic way to be energy efficient. For example, in those regions where air conditioning is not essential, it would be important for some or all of the windows at the floor level of the church to be manually operable.

Colors and Textures. Both natural and electric lighting are important to color rendering and materiality in any environment. The entire church building should be treated according to an appropriate interior plan, taking into consideration various colors and textures in harmony with the nature of the building. Factors like the region and the budget will also help determine which finishes are most appropriate and affordable. There should be no reason to paint an entire interior various shades of white unless there is a compelling design rationale for doing so. Other colors could be considered to create warmer or cooler atmospheres. Wood and plaster are alternatives to the gypsum board systems in ceilings and walls. Decorative work on these surfaces may be appropriate in some building styles. Suspended ceilings would not

Fig. 85 *Chapel window.*
United States Catholic Conference, Washington, DC.
Artist, David Wilson.

147

be appropriate in churches. Stone and brick are other wall materials that could be used. Stucco is often associated with mission-style churches. Various possibilities for the floor would include: marble, terrazzo, travertine, porcelain tile and stained, colored or painted concrete. The choice of surface texture (heavy or smooth) of all materials used is also important. Decorative patterns in the floor could be used under and around the important ritual furnishings and in the aisles. Hardwood is another flooring possibility. Environmentally friendly bamboo, for example, is 25 percent harder than red oak. Vinyl composition tile and carpet should be avoided in worship settings.

The coordination of color, light and materials should be entrusted to the most competent professionals. Acoustical and lighting consultants should be involved in all decisions pertaining to surface materials, color and light. While the input of the congregation is important, no one committee should be solely responsible for creating the color and material palette for the church.

Chapter 21

Chapels

CHAPELS WITHIN churches are small areas with a specific focus for the devotion and prayer of individuals or small groups. Chapels give an opportunity and an invitation for parishioners and visitors to make private devotional practices and common prayer. In a new building especially, but also in a renovation, the planners should consider at least three different enclosed chapel settings: for public liturgies, for the reservation of the Eucharist, for the sacrament of reconciliation.

A Daily Chapel. A daily chapel can accommodate the celebration of the liturgy of the Eucharist on weekdays, the Liturgy of the Hours, small gatherings for weddings, wakes and funerals, reconciliation liturgies and a variety of parish prayer groups, e.g., those who wish to pray the rosary together. This chapel would also be a more suitable place for celebrating the Liturgy of the Word with children than a classroom or church hall.

Ideally this chapel has its own outside entrance. It can be accessible while keeping the rest of the church closed and secure. This would also eliminate the need to heat or cool the entire facility. However, the chapel should also be constructed as part of the church building so that it can be utilized when desired, e.g., for children's Liturgy of the Word on Sundays. Where possible, and especially in new churches, this chapel could be near or even contiguous to the chapel for the reserved Eucharist and the reconciliation chapels. The close proximity of all three places could create the ambience of a small church. This means that support spaces like kitchens, toilets and maintenance rooms would be best located in another area of the building.

In older churches there may not be adequate space for such a chapel. Often a sacristy or meeting room can be suitably renovated to serve this purpose. Sometimes in larger rectories or office buildings a room is set aside for daily liturgies. The information in this section could be adapted in any situation.

Like the church, the door to the chapel is a reference to Christ and should be distinct from ordinary doors. There should be easy access and egress for physically challenged and elderly persons. The size of the chapel will depend on local requirements. Usually eighteen to twenty-five square feet is allowed per person net, including internal circulation and space for liturgical focal points. Because the chapel may be used for different liturgies by various age groups, chairs rather than fixed pew benches would be more functional. Each chair should allow storage of a worship aid, if bookshelves are not built in near the entry. It should also be possible to stack and gang the chairs. A nearby storage room will be essential in this regard. Individual bolsters could be considered as an alternative to attached kneelers. They also become comfortable cushions for younger children gathered in the chapel.

Sometimes, these chapels are also places of private prayer. The tendency is to arrange the seats in a rectilinear or sociofugal pattern. In new churches the seating plan should be the same in both the daily chapel and main worship place. If this chapel is in an older church building with a rectilinear seating plan that cannot be altered for one reason or another, the chapel should still be arranged to foster participation in the liturgical action.

This room should have a quiet atmosphere conducive for prayer. This environment is best created by the texture, color, volume, scale and utilization of the space rather than by the presence of religious artifacts. In addition to assembly seats, the essential furnishings in this chapel include one altar table, an ambo, a table for eucharistic gifts, a chair for the presider and a credence table. Like the rest of the church the chapel should be finished according to an approved interior plan with detailed attention to the floor, ceiling and walls.

There could be a blend of natural and artificial lighting in the chapel. The natural light source might be through a cupola in the ceiling or clerestory windows (fig. 86, 86a). Different levels of incandescent lighting intensity should be controlled from convenient switches. The use of fluorescent or high-intensity discharge lamps would not be appropriate in this chapel any more than they are in the main assembly place. The incorporation of glass art would add to the character of the room. Often when a congregation has to leave its older church, it will relocate all or portions of the stained glass windows from that building to the new daily chapel—if they are appropriate.

Frequently a congregation will name the chapel after one of the holy women or men of the church or a person connected in some way

Fig. 86 *Interfaith Chapel.*
Miami Valley Hospital Interfaith Chapel,
Miami Valley, OH.
Architect, Orin Group.
Designer, William Schickel.

Fig. 86a *Oratory in Holy Rosary Church.*
St. Amant, LA. Trahan Architects.
Photo by Tim Hursley.

to the history of the parish. Many chapels are dedicated in honor of "Our Lady," or the Immaculate Conception, the patron of the United States, or Our Lady of Guadalupe, the patron of the Americas. This is the place where an appropriate image of Mary could be honored. The processional cross for major liturgies in the large church could also serve as the cross of the altar in this chapel. If the congregation has a designated place for a life-size crucifix in the main church, there would be no reason to duplicate that image in this chapel. Care should be taken not to clutter the daily chapel with too many statues or other religious items.

Adequate acoustics are important: those who gather here must be able to hear themselves pray and sing. Carpeting should be avoided. In

Fig. 87 *Oratory tabernacle.* Old Saint Joseph Church, DePere, WI. Architect, Hammel Green Abrahamson. Consultant, Richard Vosko.

large chapels a portative organ could be considered even if not used at daily Mass. The acoustical consultant should be involved in decisions about surfaces and all that relates to sound. Depending on the size of the chapel, it may not be necessary to use microphones for those who read Scripture or lead the prayer. That would be ideal.

The chapel should be zoned independently for complete climate control. The heating and cooling system should not make distracting noises.

Sometimes, this chapel is located contiguous to the assembly area so that it can be used for overflow seating. This should not be a regular occurrence because of poor advance planning. When this does happen everyone in the chapel section should be able to participate fully in the liturgy as members of the assembly. Also, this chapel should never be used as a "cry room."

Although a tabernacle is frequently found in these daily chapels, they are not the place to be set aside for the reservation of the Eucharist. The distinction between the celebration of the sacrament and the reservation of the sacrament is to be kept clear.

The Chapel for the Reserved Sacrament. The history of the reservation of the Eucharist in the church is familiar and well documented.[1] Further,

[1] See Archdale A. King, *Eucharistic Reservation in the Western Church* (New York: Sheed & Ward, 1964).

152

the fundamental difference between the celebration of the Eucharist and the adoration of the reserved Sacrament is also clear in doctrinal and pastoral practice.[2] The reasons for reserving the sacrament after Mass also help us understand the importance of the reserved Eucharist in the life of the Church. The first reason is to take it to the sick or dying members of the community. The second reason is for private adoration[3] (fig. 87).

In spite of this clear and authoritative information, the location of the tabernacle and the design of its setting continues to be a contentious issue in the recent experience of the North American church. Although such argumentation over the Sacrament is not new,[4] it may be helpful to note that Christ is also really present in the life of the community. We should never act as if the experience of Christ's presence is limited to the substantial presence in the Sacrament.[5] One must wonder, therefore, why the visible presence of the tabernacle is such a preoccupation for some, especially during the celebration of the Eucharist (when, in fact, the adoration of that Sacrament is not at all appropriate). Perhaps more catechesis stressing the other ways in which Christ is really present would be beneficial for some congregations. It will help to begin giving due reverence to the Scriptures and to the assembly itself.

What role does the tabernacle play during the eucharistic liturgy? Number 321 of the *General Instruction of the Roman Missal* states that the breaking of the bread will express more clearly the "importance of the sign of unity" when the one bread is shared by the assembly. Distributing the reserved Sacrament weakens the sign value of giving thanks, breaking bread together and sharing in a common meal. When this is done habitually, the value of these central actions, actions at the very center of Catholic life, is worn away. For pastoral reasons it may be necessary on rare occasions to distribute the reserved Sacrament when not enough bread has been prepared for the entire assembly. But this practice must not be the norm. Even though it is the place for reserving the fragments that are left over after the Communion rite, the

---

[2] Nathan Mitchell, *Cult and Controversy: The Worship of the Eucharist Outside Mass* (New York: Pueblo Publishing, 1982; Collegeville: Liturgical Press, 1990) and *Real Presence: The Work of the Eucharist* (Chicago: Liturgy Training Publications, 1998).

[3] "Holy Communion and Worship of the Eucharist Outside Mass," in *The Rites* (New York: Pueblo Publishing, 1976; Collegeville: Liturgical Press, 1990) no. 5.

[4] Miri Rubin, *Corpus Christi: The Eucharist in the Late Medieval Culture* (New York: Cambridge University Press, 1991).

[5] "Holy Communion and Worship of the Eucharist Outside Mass," ibid., no. 6.

tabernacle is not a ritual focal point during the eucharistic liturgy. The reserved Sacrament is not essential for the celebration of the Eucharist. If logic were to prevail, one might deduce that the tabernacle need not be located in the same place where the Eucharist is celebrated.

These statements are intended to point out that the adoration of the Sacrament is quite different from the celebration of the Sacrament. There is a time and place for veneration and a beautiful chapel setting can encourage the custom.[6] Quite simply the adoration of the reserved Sacrament is not a high priority for most Catholics. Nor has it been in the history of the Church. This does not mean that Catholics do not believe in the real presence. There is really no reason to argue about this issue any longer.

The current legislation of the Church offers two options for locating the tabernacle. They are: behind the altar table but apart from it (fig. 88) or in a place that is distinct but still visible from the main part of the church.[7] While the exact location in a given church may be governed by a local bishop, one hopes that, presuming space is available, whatever place in the church is chosen will provide a chapel-like setting conducive for prayer and adoration.[8] Certainly the Sacrament has been reserved in the main space of large and small churches for a long time. When the churches are locked, access to this space is denied. Today, issues of energy conservation, security and handicap accessibility are also important. A separate chapel could be kept open for a reasonable time during the day to allow people to enter and pray. These climate-controlled places could also be barrier free and secure.

Wherever the tabernacle is located today the setting should be designed to foster prayer. This requirement has design implications. The architectural specifications for such a chapel are different from those used to build a large church for public worship. Perhaps cathedrals, where the Sacrament is located in a chapel separate from the body of the church, are the best models.[9]

In new churches a dedicated chapel for the reserved Sacrament is unquestionably a viable option and there should be no reason to compromise the primary purpose of this chapel by also using it for public liturgies. The principle is obvious. In order to preserve an atmosphere for private prayer and adoration the space needs to be designed in an

---

[6] See the Apostolic Letter, *Mane Nobiscum Domine*, October 7, 2004, where John Paul II encourages more frequent adoration of the Sacrament.

[7] GIRM 315.

[8] "Holy Communion and Worship of the Eucharist Outside Mass," ibid., no. 9.

[9] *Ceremonial of Bishops,* no. 49.

Fig. 88 *Chapel of Eucharistic Reservation.*
Christ the King Cathedral, Superior, WI.
Artisan, Saint Paul Fabricating and Decorating.
Metalwork, Rick Findora.

Fig. 89 *Chapel of Eucharistic Reservation.*
Mepkin Abbey, Moncks Corner, SC.
Architects, Hammel Green and Abrahamson.
Consultant, Bro. Frank Kacmarcik.

intimate scale (fig. 89). When a space is designed for the enactment of the eucharistic rites, the seating plan is quite different and should focus on the altar table and ambo. Like all other chapels in the church the location of this reservation chapel should be obvious to all.

In the new Saint Bede Church in Williamsburg, the tabernacle is a chapel that is distinct but not separated from the main part of the church. This carefully appointed room has clear glass walls and doors. There is no doubt about its presence. However, because of its location behind a section of the centralized seating plan it is not a focal point during worship.

Such a dedicated chapel in older churches may not be easily achieved. Perhaps this is why a second option is now offered in the Roman Missal. The thought is that it would be better to leave the tabernacle in the apse of the church rather than risk placing it in another area that is less conducive to private prayer and adoration and susceptible to disrespect. While this seems to be a reasonable alternative, care should be taken that the tabernacle be arranged so that it is not a focal point during the actual celebration of the Mass. Where possible the tabernacle should be as far removed from the altar table as possible. The use of lighting or the incorporation of chapel gates and screens could help to signify the importance of the chapel before and after the public liturgy.

No matter where the chapel is located it should be in a part of the new church that is accessible to all, including persons who are older or with disabilities, allowing all to enter into the space even without having to go through the nave. The doors or gateway into the chapel should be artistically and architecturally distinct, suggesting the passage into a "holy of holies" place.

The size of the chapel would depend on the requirements of the congregation. Again, more options prevail in the design of a new church. The chapel may be furnished with cushioned pew benches or individual chairs and kneelers or bolsters. It should be a quiet place conducive to prayer and meditation (another reason why a distinct chapel setting is more appropriate). Consider that the whole chapel is the "house" (the word *tabernacle* means "tent") for the Body of Christ as well as the eucharistic bread reserved for the sick or dying members of the community. It is *the* place for the private adoration of the reserved Sacrament.

Another compelling reason for reserving the Sacrament in its own chapel, distinct from the main part of the church, is to avoid the potential disregard for its presence when the cathedral or church is used for concerts, lectures, ecumenical and inter-faith events. While this gesture does not imply that the tabernacle be disrespectfully placed in an out-of-the-way closet, it does suggest that respect for the Sacrament requires that it be reserved in it own distinct and secure chapel.

To the extent possible the architectural style of the reservation chapel should be distinct from but sensitive to the style of the building. This serves to indicate its location and importance. A single oil lamp or candle should be suspended over or near the tabernacle or just outside this chapel. This oil lamp or candle is constantly burning and should be visible from the nave of the church. There are no liturgical requirements for votive candles or artwork; if used, they should be

156

integrated into the very design of the room, e.g., appropriate ornamentation and art glass windows.

The focal point in this chapel is the tabernacle for the reservation of the Sacrament. Nothing else in this space should detract from the beauty of this container. History shows that a wide variety of tabernacle designs have been produced. Some early containers resembled a dove. Later some were tall, freestanding towers while others were cupboards mounted to the wall. The normative shape and location since the Council of Trent (although they surely existed prior to it) was a cupboard embedded in the center of the *reredos* or *retablo*. The same variety is possible in this age not only in locations but also in designs. The tabernacle should be fixed and lockable. The presumption that glass may not be a suitable material for the tabernacle is one that is based on safety and security more than any other reason.

The intensity of direct and indirect incandescent lighting sources should be planned to highlight the tabernacle and provide adequate task lighting for the people praying in this chapel and to make the chapel colorfully visible from the exterior. The lights should be controlled from convenient switches. Again, the use of fluorescent or high-intensity discharge lamps would not be appropriate in this space. A combination of art glass and clear glass windows may be installed. A prismatic skylight or series of clerestory windows above the tabernacle could also be considered to allow ample natural light into the room.

The chapel should be independently zoned for complete climate control and finished according to an approved interior plan with detailed attention to the floor, ceiling and walls.

The Chapel of Reconciliation. The reform of the sacrament of penance included little direction for the actual design of the place where the sacrament could be celebrated. One school of thought suggests that any area of the church building could be used, e.g., at the presider's chair. Occasionally the daily chapel or the main church may be appropriately arranged to facilitate the rite. However, it seems that most people who frequent the sacrament prefer a private room. Such a room fits our norms as a chapel.

The number of chapels set aside for celebrating reconciliation will depend on the needs of the local community. With a shortage of presiders, most new churches get by with just one chapel. The best location is contiguous to the daily chapel and the chapel for the reserved Sacrament. One could make a case, as I have done, that somewhere near the baptismal font would be suitable. The reconciliation chapel should be set aside only for the celebration of the sacrament. Thus, the room is not used for storage or any other visitation or counseling sessions. The room itself should be designed to convey a warm, inviting and hospitable impression.

The usual size for the chapel is approximately 150 to 200 square feet. The room should allow a person using a wheelchair to make a complete turn around on both sides of the screen. A five- to six-feet turning radius is sufficient for this purpose. The door should have hardware (lever handles or push bars rather than knobs) designed to accommodate elderly or physically challenged persons.

Each chapel should afford the opportunity for anonymity without embarrassment (fig. 90). A person who chooses to be anonymous should have a place for kneeling or sitting. A small reading desk or a nearby table will facilitate the reading of Scripture by the person during the rite. A person who chooses not to be anonymous should also be provided a place for kneeling or sitting. There could also be a table for the book of Scriptures and a kneeler for those who prefer that posture.

The desire for anonymity is to be respected when individuals avail themselves of this sacrament. This option is satisfied when there is a screen or room divider. The materials for the screen can vary. There should be three chairs in each chapel: one on the anonymous side of

Fig. 90 *Reconciliation chapel screen.*
Saint Thomas More, Paducah, KY.
Designer, James F. Williamson.
Consultant, Richard Vosko.

the screen and two on the other side of the screen, one for the priest and the other for the penitent. Straight back, armed chairs are recommended. Chairs found in living rooms, family rooms or offices would not be appropriate in these chapels.

Usually the availability of each chapel is indicated by an open door. Mechanical or electrical "traffic" signals (little red and green lights) and signs ("face-to-face" or "anonymous") above or near the door are not required. Convenient switches would control the intensity of indirect, incandescent lighting levels. The lighting ambience should be warm. There should be no glare or harsh lighting that could cast shadows on the faces of the participants. The use of fluorescent or high-intensity discharge lamps would not be appropriate in this chapel.

Each chapel may be decorated with artwork that suggests the theme of reconciliation: a sculpture, painting, weaving or tapestry could be provided. A crucifix is often hung on the wall or placed on the table. A lighted candle is appropriate.

There may be architectural art glass windows in this room. Consideration may be given for the re-use of existing windows. In order to provide a modicum of security as well as anonymity in each chapel, some consideration should be given to the amount of glass incorporated in each door. The recent abuse scandal in the Church has prompted some congregations to install windows in the door of the reconciliation chapel. If the architectural layout of the building allows it, there could be a second door leading to the sacristy or hallway that could be used by the minister of the sacrament.

Each chapel should be designed with an acoustical rating that respects the privacy of the penitent. For this reason, the floor may be carpeted but the carpet pile should not make mobility difficult for anyone. The walls may also be finished with suitable material. Each chapel should be zoned independently for complete climate control and finished according to an approved interiors plan with detailed attention to the floor, ceiling and walls.

Chapter 22

Memorial Places

MEMORY PLAYS a substantial role in the creation of the environment for worship. It does so by helping a person make connections between what is present and known in the church building and what has been personally or collectively experienced in the past. Images, smells, sounds, pathways and seats are some of the ways we hold the past dear. Some might call this experience one of nostalgia but no human being can escape it. In a mysterious way, memory can trigger possibilities for the future.

The word "memorial" is used to describe the Eucharist. Think of how the Jewish community keeps the Passover not just as an historical event but as an event that continues now. The word for memory is *l'zikkaron* and is hard to translate literally. It means that what was past is also part of the present. The act of remembering or "memorializing" somehow brings that historical moment into the present in such a way that people today participate in the event. Imagination and hope work together in the expectation that the future will usher in a time of peace and justice rather than more oppression and captivity. The last lines in the Haggadah are: "Next year, Jerusalem." This is a yearning for a tomorrow where the world will be devoid of oppression.

To participate in the Eucharist is to embrace and embody the paschal event as one's own life experience. The work that God has already begun continues in the Church. The members of Christ's body are entrusted with this paschal event.[1] Further, it thrusts the believer into the realm of possibilities "as we wait in joyful hope for the coming of the Lord." In this sense the eucharistic memorial links the past with the present and the future.

---

[1] See all *Eucharistic Prayers for Masses for Various Needs and Occasions* (Collegeville: Liturgical Press, 1996) 19, 29, 39, 49.

Fig. 91 *Contemporary Saints*. Solanus Casey Center, Detroit, MI.
Architect, Hammel Green Abrahamson. Sculpture by Karen Atta.
Exhibition by DMCD. Consultant, Richard Vosko.

Places of worship are not monuments. They are not tributes to individuals or to groups of people or to historic events, but places of memory. I have noted the importance of this factor in earlier parts of this book. The purpose of a church or cathedral is precisely to link the past with the present and the future. Built on strong foundations, the contemporary Church longs for that time when all people will experience the full realization of God's gracious presence. Thus, places of worship also challenge and invite people to live in new ways.

A good example may be found in the way some are re-imagining shrines. Traditionally these are places of pilgrimage that, in some way, honor a person or events considered holy. The objective in any spiritual journey is growth of mind, body and spirit. However, as one might expect, most shrines tend to emphasize only the life of the person honored, focusing on his or her biography, failures and achievements. Many are like museums.

When the Capuchins built the Solanus Casey Center in Detroit, they wanted it to be a different model for places that memorialize people who have done good work. They certainly wanted the Center to focus on the humble but remarkable life of Solanus Casey. The journey, which begins on the outside of the building, guides the visitor to the tomb of Solanus. However, it does not end there. Like our church buildings the purpose of this Center is to foster a transforming experience for the pilgrim and to prompt a spiritual reply. Thus the architectural path takes the pilgrim beyond the tomb to the baptismal font and into the church where the Eucharist is celebrated. The understanding is that, after being exposed to the life of Solanus Casey, the pilgrim should be inspired to renew her or his baptismal promises to work for justice and peace (fig. 91). The sustenance for that work is not found only in devotion to Solanus but more in the celebration of the Eucharist or, better yet, by embracing the paschal event. The Solanus Casey Center models a different approach to the idea of shrines because architecturally it is designed to do more than a monument or a museum built to memorialize a person or event.

How can this notion of a memorial place contribute to the understanding of a place of worship? The churches and cathedrals that house the public prayer of the Church also serve as memorial places. They are not only vessels of cherished stories of faith, they are places that should inspire a renewed commitment to doing good work in the present with the hope for a better future. Thus the art and architectural plan for these buildings could challenge the visitor or worshiper to re-imagine his or her life as a Christian by depicting images of Mother Teresa and Oscar Romero alongside traditional saints. If the art or exhibitions focus on the deeds of the past without any indication that the work of the Gospel continues today, it is memorializing only part of the story. These same places can also serve to memorialize members of the local congregation who participated in the life and work of that community.

Mausoleum or Columbarium. Many older churches have cemeteries next to them or nearby. It can be a powerful experience to walk through a graveyard on the way to a church. One is reminded of the many people who have already taken this journey of faith. Other churches were constructed over burial places. These underground sanctuaries helped to connect the entire communion of saints in the worship of God. They also made a metaphorical and architectural statement about the living Church built upon this foundation. Canon 1242 indicates the dead may not be buried in church buildings today. This law was most likely put into effect to discourage abuses. Care should be taken when incorporating a burial ground in or near a church or cathedral so that exclusivity is avoided. For example, it would be a wonderful gesture in all cemeteries or mausoleums owned by the Church if spaces were set aside for the burial of indigent people. The potter's field is still a good and gracious idea (Matt 27:3-6).

Fig. 92 *Columbarium.*
Metropolitan Community Church, Washington, DC.
Architect, Suzane Reatig.

Fig. 93 *Columbarium and Labyrinth.* Saint Joseph Church, Richardson, TX.
Architects for design, Landry and Landry. Architects and Planners and Architects of Record,
Good, Fulton, and Farrell, Inc. Photograph by Donald L. Fischer.

The Metropolitan Community Church in Washington, DC, has a ministry to people with HIV/AIDS. The community prides itself on how it is present·to those who are afflicted with the disease especially as they approach death. After death, these AIDS victims are honored as their memory is held dear. One can see the urns filled with the ashes of cremated persons nestled in niches along a wall as you enter this church (fig. 92). This is another way of reminding us how fragile life is. Saint Joseph Catholic Church in Richardson, Texas, has a circular stone columbarium and labyrinth courtyard to honor the cremated remains of the deceased. There are 1,285 niches in the columbarium. A circular walkway follows the walls on both sides, allowing people to touch the niches (fig. 93). The labyrinth is available for anyone who wishes to walk it.[2]

[2] See *Faith & Form: Journal of the Interfaith Forum on Religion, Art and Architecture,* vol. XXXVII, no. 1, 2004, 8, 13.

Treasury or Museum. One of the interesting rooms to explore when visiting cathedrals in the European Union is the treasury. There one finds innumerable clues to the people who founded and worshiped in the church as well as some insights pertaining to their customs. Perhaps because the Church is still young, there are not such museums or treasuries in most churches or cathedrals in North America. Still the practice is a good one to consider. It would not take much to endorse the research and collection of artifacts and documents, vessels, vesture and works of art that could be housed in a room that would be visited by pilgrims and parishioners alike. This room is especially important in displaying the history or exhibiting remnants of an older church building that was either closed or destroyed by fire or severe weather. Even the smallest of country churches has a history that could be lost if not documented and exhibited in a place accessible to all. When considering such treasuries or museum-like spaces, provide lighting, climate control and security measures to assure the proper care of all materials.

Memorializing the Dead. Consideration could be given to creating memorials for deceased members of the community without distinguishing the cause of death. For example, all names could be inscribed by a calligrapher in a beautifully designed public book alphabetically and chronologically. Perhaps this book could be part of the daily chapel or in an area near the font—spaces that are also used for the vigil (wake) over a deceased body. This idea makes good sense in a new church building where the setting can be designed into the plans. In older churches somewhere inside the church and near the font could be considered. On All Saints and All Souls and throughout November this book could be honored with candles or incense burning near it during Sunday liturgies.

Consideration could be also given to inscribing names of the deceased into the glass or stone fabric of the building rather than purchasing a commercially produced memorial system (fig. 94). Many congregations are incorporating an idea that has become popular in some civic communities. Inscribed bricks in the pathways to churches and cathedrals can be another way to create a memorial walk. Some climates, however, are not conducive to this idea. Further, thought should be given to how names will be added and not mixed in with donors' names. Perhaps the memorial book is the best way to accomplish this.

Honoring Donors. Inevitably the success of every church building project relies on financial donations from members of the community. Participating financially in the construction or renovation of a church is still often connected with spiritual welfare. Many financial campaigns rely on emotional responses to themes that indicate you will be "doing something for God" or that "your reward in heaven will be great." Also there is no end to the ways in which someone is recognized for having made a contribution to the project.

No one wants their donation to go toward the electrical, mechanical or structural components of the project. The attractive "big ticket" items are the baptismal font, the altar table, the tabernacle, the crucifix, a window, a sculpture. These items should be perceived as belonging to the entire faith community. If there are members who, because of their resources, can make it possible to obtain these furnishings and works of art, they should do so without expecting to be honored or have their name attached to the item or space. The best solution is not to attach inflated currency values to the art, ritual furnishings or rooms in the project however common this practice has become. The publication of a shopping list only fosters an individualistic consumer mentality when, in actuality, the project is a time for sharing resources.

Although most gift givers are not that interested in highlighting their contributions some congregants still insist upon recognition. Etching names in glass or stonework stirs up a wonderful connection to 1 Peter 2 that reads, "You are the living stones." What better way to remind everyone that the Church is really the people and not just bricks and mortar? A recent method for listing donors' names is the fanciful attachment of trees with leaves inscribed with names to the walls of the building. Why introduce such a novelty when the very fabric of the building provides a more organic place for memorials?

Perhaps the best way to recognize donors is in another handsomely crafted book where the names are inscribed by a calligrapher. Everyone who gave something for the project would be listed alphabetically no matter how large or small the gift. Extreme care should be taken not to distinguish names based on the amount of the gift.

In the past names of donors were often attached to artifacts and furnishings. This practice, which is no longer acceptable, could present a sensitive situation when the church is being renovated or a new church built. What should be done when certain items or spaces already memorialized are not going to be incorporated in the plan? There is no question that valuable works of art or historic pieces should be maintained. If these are not liturgically suitable, they could be placed in the treasury or museum mentioned above. Sensitivity is required in addressing this issue to assure that common good is served. The book honoring all donors could also list the names of donors of those pieces or spaces no longer being used in the church.

The book honoring donors should be clearly distinct in appearance and location from the memorial book for the dead. If many books are produced over time consideration should be given to the manner in which all volumes are displayed together. I will discuss the way in which memorial opportunities are presented to the congregation in the section on "stewardship" later in this book.

Chapter 23

Auxiliary Rooms

SUPPORT SPACES are essential in every place of worship. The programmatic requirements will vary according to the needs of the congregation. Although the provision of many of these places will not be possible in an older or smaller church, the principles could be adapted. Here is a listing of some of the rooms or areas that could serve a church building today.

Parish Parlor. Certain parish activities may require this room. For example, should the church be utilized for wake services, it may be necessary to provide a private and comfortable place for family members where they can meet before or after viewing hours. This same room could be used to secure the casket (as may be required by law). The parlor would be located in or near the church commons.

This room is where the catechumens, the elect and the candidates for baptism would go upon dismissal from the assembly during the liturgy. Some parishes call this room a *catechumenon*.[1] This same parlor could serve as the bride's room where the wedding party can make final preparations.

This hospitality parlor could also be used for different purposes including: a reading room, liturgical ministry preparation, Bible study, adult enrichment programs, youth group meetings, sacramental preparation programs, etc.

This parlor would differ from other meeting rooms because of its "living room" ambience. It should be outfitted with comfortable furnishings, a coat closet and a washroom with toilet. A built-in tack board and porcelain board, ample shelving, a closet and cabinet space will facilitate the use of the room by different groups.

---

[1] There was a large complex north of the Basilica Urbana in ancient Salona (Solin), Croatia that consisted of a *catechumenon* (hall for religious education) and the baptistery.

A combination of incandescent and indirect fluorescent lighting could be used. The intensity of the lighting should be controlled from an accessible but secure location. It should be barrier free and zoned for independent climate control.

Coatroom. Provision could be made so that visitors and worshipers could store their coats when visiting the church. This space is a welcomed convenience especially in wintry regions and in those church complexes used for different events, e.g., if the lobby of the church also leads to other meeting or social rooms. An alternative is to line the walls of some nearby corridors with hooks.

Toilets, Telephones and Drinking Fountains. Restrooms should be located next to the commons or in some other convenient location. Usually, the drinking fountains are nearby. Although cellular telephones are common, one public pay phone for outgoing calls is essential. Maintenance, security and insurance issues should not be overlooked in the design of the restrooms. There should be easy access, use and egress by handicapped and elderly persons. The minimum number of water closets, urinals and sinks should be governed by the code. Strong consideration should be given to the provision of extra space and extra toilets in the women's room. Ideally, the childcare room (see below) should have its own restroom with a toilet for "little people."

There could be a small area in both restrooms with a full-length mirror to afford hospitality particularly for wedding guests. There should be a changing table in both restrooms to accommodate the needs of parents and guardians with infants.

When adults and babies are baptized by full immersion there will be the need for a drying and dressing room. In a new church the restrooms could be equipped with a built–in bench and wall pegs for clothing and towels. These amenities should be available to all, especially persons who are older or with disabilities. In older churches other accommodations may have to be provided (e.g., a contiguous rectory or parish center).

Gift Shop or Information Center. These places are important especially in cathedrals and other major church buildings frequented by tourists. Mementos, books, candles, souvenirs and materials about the church would be made available to visitors and members.

Child-care Rooms. The child-care spaces could be located somewhere in the nearby parish center. While these rooms should be easy to access, the safety and security of the children should be a high priority. Silent beepers could be provided for parents and guardians to alert them during liturgy when an emergency situation occurs.

The ideal child-care program uses two rooms. One space, designed for sleeping, should be furnished with cribs and rocking chairs. The second room, designed for children to play in, should have child-size tables and chairs, storage cabinets or cubbies for toys, chalk boards, video or DVD players and shelving for books. The area should have a telephone with intercom and a first-aid kit.

Appropriately scaled toilet and washroom facilities with changing tables should be adjacent to the nursery. The use of natural light, a sunny exposure, washable walls, a carpeted floor, incandescent and fluorescent lighting, a good acoustical rating, operable windows and independent zoning for climate control are recommended for this room.

The Dressing Sacristy or Vestry. It is recommended that this sacristy be located adjacent to the commons where it can serve the chapel areas as well as the main church. Access to it is through the commons. All ministers who wear special vesture for the liturgy would use this room to dress and compose themselves for worship as well as finalize details of their ministry. There is no reason to separate ordained persons from those who are not ordained. Some clergy may argue that the priests' sacristy is also a "green" room where they can reflect before beginning the liturgy. This type of preparation is helpful to all ministries. Praying together just before the entrance procession is becoming more frequent in parish churches.

This sacristy should include a closet, drawer space (chasubles are best stored flat), a counter, bookshelves, a message board, a coat closet (for various ministers), a telephone with intercom and a full-length mirror. Only those vestments, vessels and books necessary for the current liturgical season should be kept in this room. Appointments such as the processional cross, candles and charcoal/incense vessels should also be kept here because liturgical processions usually begin from the main entrance of the worship space. In new churches this sacristy could be located so it can also serve the daily chapel.

The room should be independently zoned for complete climate control. Carpeting and a combination of incandescent and fluorescent lighting are recommended. The sacristy room must be a lockable space.

Work and Storage Sacristy. Where possible this room should be located close to the actual altar table area of the worship setting to facilitate the preparation of ritual furnishings and appointments. In a centralized plan it could be accessible from somewhere along the ambulatory that encircles the assembly. Flower arrangements for various events can also be made here. Horizontal drawer storage space is required for altar table linens. Other appropriate storage space is required for art forms (banners, etc.), candles, candleholders, and those vestments, vessels and books that are not in use during the current liturgical season. A safe would also be required to house precious vessels. These rooms are also used to clean the vessels that are in use for current liturgical celebrations (e.g. Communion cups and plates used during weekend liturgies). A generous work sink is essential in this room.

This room needs at least ten feet of counter space in addition to a large worktable and chairs. There should be louvered closets, a message board for schedules and other important messages, cabinets with drawers for vesture, a safe for precious vessels, an ironing board and a space for cleaning materials. Cupboard space, a broom closet, a hamper and a hanging area for clean laundry should also be available.

There should be a small refrigerator for Communion wine and temporary storage of fresh baked Communion bread. A *sacrarium* (sink that drains into a dry well or storm drain) for the cleansing of Communion vessels should also be provided. Various liturgical ministers (servers and eucharistic ministers) will frequent this room as they make immediate preparations for liturgical celebrations. The vesture for these ministries could be kept in this sacristy if this serves better than the vesting sacristy.

If it is technically convenient, this room could contain the controls for the media, lighting and acoustical systems. This room should be independently zoned for complete climate control. Fluorescent lighting and a tile floor are recommended. This space must be lockable.

Music Rehearsal Room. A music ministry office and rehearsal room should be planned for a new church. Ideally, in older churches these rooms should not be too remote from the place of worship. Although some choirs prefer to practice in the church, warm-up sessions just before liturgy could be distracting. The rehearsal room should include ample space for the choir, a rehearsal piano, the storage of instruments, music stands, choir vesture and the music library. In an ideal situation there are risers for the choir. This room should be designed with good acoustics in mind so that activities in adjacent places would not be distracted during rehearsals. Both the office and rehearsal space should also be independently zoned for complete climate control and good ventilation. Fluorescent lighting and a tile floor are recommended. This space must be lockable.

Storage. Ample room to store all seasonal artwork and liturgical artifacts and appointments should be provided. There is never enough storage space in church buildings.

PART THREE

Further Planning

I began this book with an outline of the building or renovation process. Then in Part One I presented a foundation for building and renovating places of worship. My strongest possible recommendation is that issues concerning the life of the church be addressed before decisions are made about the design of the building and the layout of the interior. Such discussions provide a framework for understanding the place and function of church buildings in the modern world.

Part Two offers a program of ideas that could be used in building or renovating a worship environment. This final part focuses on the issues I believe need further attention by anyone involved in creating places of worship. My hope is that this section will stir the imagination and lead to discussions about church art and architecture today.

Topics in Part Three include:

- Art Education for Pastoral Leaders

- Finding and Working with Artists

- Preserving and Enhancing Older Churches and Cathedrals

- Inculturation in Our Places of Worship

- The Architectural Style of Church Buildings

- Megachurch Models

- Cathedral Models

- Stewardship Concerns

- Environmental Stewardship: An Ethical Concern

Chapter 24

Art Education
for Pastoral Leaders

ONE AREA that needs urgent and consistent attention is the training of pastoral leaders in the arts.[1] At one time the artistic and architectural style of the church depended largely on the direction of the pastor. Many of them had acquired good taste in the arts. They collected works of art and ideas; often they traveled widely. They wanted to retain the very best artists and architects. There were others who had little knowledge and appreciation for the arts, but had the same responsibility for creating places for worship.

Designing and constructing a cathedral or church today is more complex and demanding. No one person, not even the professionals, can possibly know all there is to know about creating an environment for worship. This is why teamwork is so important. This is also why it is important for present and future pastoral leaders to enroll in courses that will help them foster a deeper appreciation for the role of the arts in worship. These learning opportunities will help to develop a new sense of priorities for the participants when it comes time to build or renovate a worship environment.

Finding such courses to enroll in is not easy. Most theology schools or continuing education programs have not yet figured out how to offer such tailor-made courses in the curriculum. First, it is important to employ teachers who know how to expose students to the living arts. Although illustrated classroom lectures can serve as helpful foundations, the real learning will take place in the studios of artists, in

---

[1] Here I am using the word "arts" in a very broad sense to include the fine arts, popular art, music, dance, literature, crafts, furniture design and so on. All of these arts will in some way have a role to play in any house of prayer.

173

concert halls, museums and galleries. Second, the arts curriculum should not be confused with a single mandatory three-credit-hour "arts appreciation" course. The course load could include sessions with dancers (how to hold your body when presiding or in other ministries), musicians (how to improvise), hotel managers (how to be gracious hosts), actors (how to project when speaking, praying and proclaiming), media technicians (how to incorporate projected images into worship), artisans (how to recognize a work of art) and architects (how to learn about the impact of the worship environment on ritual making).

A good example of how theology students and pastoral leaders can be exposed to the art world may be found at Union Theological Seminary in New York City. Here is a scenario. It is time for class on "Worship and the Arts." Instead of gathering in the classroom on campus the students meet their teacher, Professor Janet Walton, and head for the subway. They are off to see *Blue Man Group*, an off-Broadway show that has enjoyed years of success. Is this a field trip? A day off? Not at all. This is hard work for the students and for Walton who has been teaching about worship and the arts at the Seminary for twenty-five years. It would be a lot easier to lecture, show slides and play music right in the cozy atmosphere of the classroom. Instead, she believes that students preparing to lead worship have to make connections with the *living* arts if they are to learn how to practice the art of worship.

Walton schedules her classes to take in diverse artistic performances and meet with a variety of artists in New York. More often than not she invites the artists to lecture in her classes or to demonstrate their arts up close. The exchange between the artists and her students is invaluable, something that no lecture or textbook can match. Together they learn about improvisation, imagination and the creative process. Walton says she wants "students to learn from the inside of themselves first and then discover words to describe it, a method that applies to worship as well as the arts." She continues, "First we have an encounter, and then we remember it and imagine our lives through it . . . We feel it in our skin and under our skin, we pay attention with all our bodies; we feel disruption, we feel hope, and then we try to see how relationships are affected, both human and with God."

Learning how to absorb and embody the work of art is important to the artistic experience and can be helpful in learning to embody the paschal event. This is why Walton wants her students to "feel" the artistic experience in their bones. This is what "full, conscious and active participation" in the Mass really means. It is not just about singing and praying out loud together. It is more about how we actually *embrace* the paschal event.

The arts curriculum in any ministry training program may not produce world-class musicians, artists or presiders. But it can at least expose all students to the artistic process with the hope that sensitivity to the arts will enrich their ministries and the worship experience of the congregation. It can also help them gain the confidence needed to work with artists and architects.

Chapter 25

Finding
and Working with Artists

NO ONE would think of building or renovating a church or cathedral without an architect. Likewise, no project should be undertaken without commissioning various artisans and artists to make art, furnishings and other artifacts for the worship environment. How does one find the right artists and then work with them in a creative process?

Finding an Artist. The first step is to prepare an art program for the church. This is the responsibility of the liturgical design consultant and the architect in concert with the local art committee. The program will describe what art, furnishings and appointments should be placed in the church. It is important to do this very early in the process in order to establish a budget for artwork. Early estimates for the arts and furnishings budget can be based on the experience of the liturgical design consultant and the architect. Whether or not the artist can do the work for a pre-determined budget should be discussed during the interviews. The professional design team can assist the committee in searching for the best artists for the commissions.

There are three ways to go about this search:[1] (1) Choose a particular artist with no interview process. (2) Interview three or four candidates. (3) Create a competition for a small number of invited artists. The first option is easy. The artist is selected without interviewing others simply because of her or his reputation.

If the committee is not ready to commission a particular artist because of reputation, a list of potential candidates should be created. Research is required: searching websites, visiting galleries and studios,

---

[1] These approaches are similar to the ones used for finding an architect. However, congregations seldom select an architect by means of a competition.

viewing previous commissions. The liturgical art consultant and the architect as well as committee members can be good resources. The best reference may be another congregation that highly recommends an artist with whom they had a good experience. The caution here is that what an artist does for one congregation may not work for another. Searching nationally can be rewarding especially if it is difficult to find someone in the local region. Once the list is formed the committee should ask the artists to submit their portfolios.

Some artists who are eager to gain employment will immediately begin to show ideas for the commission. This is premature because there has been no real opportunity for dialogue with the committee. The objective at this time is to review all portfolios and narrow the search to two or three artists who will be invited to submit a more specific proposal. Now the committee can focus on this shorter list by visiting the studios and inviting each artist to come for an interview. The request for a proposal should include the written expectations of the committee pertaining to the work of art in question. The interviews will provide a good time for an exchange of ideas between the artist and the committee. The artist can present previous work, describe a philosophy of art and discuss how the collaboration will unfold.

In the third approach the committee establishes a competition. When the search process is completed, each of the two or three finalists is paid the same amount of money to prepare a sketch or maquette (small model) showing how they would respond to the commission. Prior to this response it is expected that the artists would take the time to learn more about the congregation and the narrative that is to be expressed in the art form. Within a designated time frame they would present and explain their work in front of the committee. The best submittal would get the commission and the work begins. In this approach it is important that the expectations of the committee be clearly spelled out so that each artist can comply with the rules of the competition. For example, if the committee requires each artist to submit a maquette, a cost estimate and a timetable then each artist should comply. This will eliminate the possibility of one artist outshining another because he or she prepared more exhibits and information.

What kinds of credentials and experiences should an artist have in order to qualify for a commission? Is an extensive portfolio of award-winning works enough? Will the artist be willing to work in a collaborative manner? Will the artist respect the input of the committee? Does the artist who may not share the same faith of the community show respect and sensitivity for that tradition? Will the artist attempt to create something unique that resonates with the stories of the congregation?

Finally, will the artist be willing to be transformed by the process of making something new for the congregation? These are the more compelling questions that should be considered in the interview process and not questions of cost. Many committees are attracted to the artist who charges the lower fee. It becomes frustrating when the artist who is favored by the committee is also the one who charges the most. This is another good reason for establishing a budget ahead of time and informing all contending artists of that number. Then the artist can decide whether or not to pursue the commission. Many artists are willing to negotiate. Setting the art budget in advance also reverses the unfortunate practice of purchasing art with funds that are left over once the building is constructed or renovated.

Working with Artists. There are three ways to work with artists who have been chosen. (These are similar to working with an architect.) In the first, the committee picks an artist and then expects that person to create something that reflects exactly the ideas of the committee. Although some artists are willing to comply with this approach it does not do justice to the artistic process, the congregation or the artist. In the end, the artist is paid to fashion something that may be precisely what the owner wanted but will not be an expression of the artist. Of course, it is the committee's prerogative to ask the artist to produce something just like another piece that is in another church. This request is hard to fathom when the objective is to create something that uniquely expresses the local faith community.

The second approach is the other end of the spectrum, letting the artist determine everything. This is not ideal either. It is seldom advantageous to give the artist a completely "free hand" in creating something for a worship environment. The exchange and growth of ideas through the dialogue process is lost and the final work will be less than it could have been.

The third approach, a middle ground, is more workable. The committee chooses an artist who displays the ability to listen carefully to the committee, observes the worship patterns of the assembly, and then creates a work of art that will contribute to the narrative of the faith community. In this approach the committee shares with the artist as much information about the congregation and the project as possible. Then it trusts the artist. The stages of the process will then include opportunities for the committee to review sketches or maquettes prepared by the artist. Both artist and committee need to be challenged by the dialogue and development of the work. A point then comes when the committee agrees to accept the final product without compromise.

In this approach the artist may challenge the assumptions of the owner, sometimes bringing a needed insight from the outside. A risk is taken as both parties work in this collaborative manner.

Visual Artists in Residence. It would be difficult to find a congregation that does not sing or play musical instruments during liturgy. In most cases there is a full- or part-time director responsible for the music ministry. It would be difficult to find a congregation that does not incorporate the arts in some way in its worship practice. However, few places have visual artists in residence. There may be volunteers serving on church decorating committees, but seldom is there someone on the pastoral staff who is trained in the arts.

A salaried person would provide continuity in the congregation. Like the directors of music and liturgy, a professional visual artist would take responsibility for the incorporation of the arts into the life of the community. This individual should have an interdisciplinary background in the fields of liturgy and the visual arts. Ideally the person is a practicing artist who has an extensive portfolio. In some instances grants are available to help fund resident artists.

The resident artist could have a number of responsibilities:

- Developing a long-term plan for the arts in the congregation

- Coordinating the decoration of the worship environment for the different liturgical seasons

- Overseeing the budgetary requirements for all art-related matters (e.g., the purchase of liturgical appointments)

- Inviting local and regional artists to exhibit works of religious art in the church or other part of the complex

- Producing appropriate events for the parish and larger community

- Training others in the congregation in making works of art for the church

- Being a resource to the RCIA, school and religious education personnel on integrating arts into all aspects of formation

- Participating in all staff planning meetings, especially those dealing with the worship life of the congregation

Learning to find and work with artists is a realistic possibility for every congregation. The long-term reward will be a greater appreciation for the role that the arts play in growth of the members of the community and in their worship.

Chapter 26

Preserving and Enhancing Older Churches and Cathedrals

HERE ARE FIVE concerns having to do with older churches and cathedrals: (1) The preservation of buildings currently used by vibrant congregations. (2) Finding funds to maintain important properties when there are not enough resources. (3) The impact of a landmark designation upon religious property. (4) The adaptation of landmarked churches for use according to the reforms of Vatican II. (5) The responsibilities of the owners and users.

Preserving Church Buildings.[1] According to the National Trust for Historic Preservation there are different reasons for wanting to preserve a particular building. (1) Some buildings are good to look at. (2) Some buildings are still useful. (3) Some buildings link us with the past and help us understand who we are.[2] No doubt the concern for saving older places of worship is based on all three reasons.

Certainly there are many places of worship that deserve to be preserved simply because they are architectural masterpieces. Historic preservation organizations are usually the arbiters who designate such places. The problem is not with the beauty of the building but the function of it in the community. Is it a museum-like place without a congregation? Or, if structurally sound, is it still useful as a place of worship? The problem has to do with the presence of a community and its ability to maintain the property. This is why some dioceses will

---

[1] Professionals define the word "preservation" in a particular way to distinguish it from "restoration" and "conservation," which also have specific meanings. My intention here is not to detail the differences but to address the issue of maintaining worthy church structures.

[2] See http://www.nationaltrust.org.

not close a church but merge the congregation with another. Whether a church building is closed or a congregation is merged the maintenance and sustenance of old places of worship is a contentious issue.[3] The third reason for preserving a church building—that it links us with the past and helps us to understand who we are—is, by far, the most compelling one.

When a church is closed and either sold or demolished, it brings tremendous sadness to the congregation. For generations the church may have been the place for the celebration of birth, death and everything between. Also this is the place where people worship but it is also the place where they gather to socialize, plan events and educate children. It is like destroying a home. Churches are touchstones. They are organic symbols of the vibrant faith of a congregation. Pastoral leaders must attend to this time of grieving.

If there is any possibility for objectivity in discerning the future of a church building, a difficult question must be asked. Aside from the emotional or even nostalgic reasons for keeping a church open, does it have any real value *per se*—as a place of worship, architecturally and artistically speaking? Even when this architectural question is answered, the ultimate issue has to do with the "mission" of the Church in that neighborhood and what will happen should that congregation be dispersed. The impact of the "presence" of the Church in a particular community has to be evaluated especially in poor neighborhoods. Will the lives of the people there suffer if a congregation has to move to another place? What if a congregation that is proactive in justice issues (hunger, domestic abuse, crime, sub-standard housing) is merged with a congregation that does not share the same values?

If it is determined by a diocesan pastoral plan that the presence of the congregation in a particular neighborhood is important to the life of that community then the work of finding funds to maintain the properties becomes crucial.

Finding Sources to Maintain Properties. When a congregation has dwindled to a small number of households with little or no disposable income to finance the church, it becomes very difficult to maintain the properties. In some cases the diocese subsidizes the congregation but eventually the coffers run dry. The convents and schools get closed. Eventually the rectory and the church buildings meet the same fate.

---

[3] The closing of churches coupled with merging of faith communities has created tensions in many United States dioceses especially when congregations and their pastoral leaders disagree with officials and claim they are solvent and vibrant communities.

The alternative use of these properties requires responsible tenants and they are hard to lure into the downtown area. Unlike some countries in the European Union where the government contributes to the upkeep of religious buildings, most congregations in North America have to rely on private funding even when the property in question has been designated by civic agencies as landmarks. It seems illogical that government agencies have the authority to protect old buildings by declaring them landmarks while that same government is not allowed to subsidize the property.

Some not-for-profit organizations (e.g., Partners for Sacred Places) help congregations establish a plan of action for keeping and funding significant church buildings. Co-directors Diane Cohen and A. Robert Jaeger write, "Preservationists should work closely with congregations, denominational organizations, and civic and philanthropic leaders to make the case for our collective stake in the survival of sacred spaces."[4] But the resources are not always there and the process for obtaining funding can be laborious. In some instances developers will purchase a church to convert it into residences, offices or art centers. Often other denominations will buy or lease the building. Some churches have been transformed into restaurants or taverns.

Another source of funding is possible, interestingly enough, because the faith-based initiatives of the United States government have made it possible for a religious organization to receive grants, even for places of worship, as long as some part of the physical complex serves the larger community. Recently, according to the *San Francisco Chronicle*, the Senate authorized ten million dollars in federal funds to help restore California's twenty-one Roman Catholic missions.[5] The California Missions Foundation has to match the funds. Other major religious buildings have received similar grants. The historic Touro Synagogue in Newport, Rhode Island, the oldest synagogue in the country along with the Old North Church in Boston, The Eldridge Street Synagogue in New York and Mission Concepcion in San Antonio were granted large sums of money for preservation purposes.[6]

In 2004, the Cathedral of the Immaculate Conception in Albany received an $800,000 Clean Water/Clean Air Bond Act grant to restore

[4] Diane Cohen and A. Robert Jaeger, "Affirming Our Collective Stake in Safeguarding Sacred Places," in *Historic Preservation News*, February–March 1995, 6.

[5] http://sfgate.com/cgi-bin/article.cgi?f=/c/a/2004/10/12/ MNGV597GL11 .DTL.

[6] See "Notes & Comments," in *Faith & Form: Journal of the Interfaith Forum on Religion, Art & Architecture*, no. 2, 2004, 25.

exterior stone surfaces of the building, as well as to renew integral aspects of the third oldest cathedral still in use in the nation. "The Cathedral which has been listed on the State and National Registers of Historic Places, has embarked on a three year, $4.25 million restoration project that will dismantle and replace the stone facade of the north tower and repair and replace the west side clerestories, walls and parapets. The Roman Catholic Diocese of Albany has committed and raised more than $3 million for this project, and the 1996 Clean Water/ Clean Air Bond Act grant will play a major role in getting the Diocese closer to achieving the project's financial goal."[7]

These initiatives could offer some interesting possibilities for new collaborations on the local level. Susan Ellis, president of Energize, Inc., a company specializing in volunteerism suggests that social agencies connect with congregations in the neighborhood to see if there are any programs that they could sponsor together and possibly qualify for federal funds, which could benefit both operations.[8]

Church Buildings Designated as Landmarks. The closure or sale of a church can also be hampered if the building has been designated as a landmark. The rules and procedures for landmarking a building differ greatly from one municipality to another. Further, the membership of local landmarking or preservation commissions changes and the interests or opinions of individual members affect whether a particular church building is landmarked. Here is one example of a landmark situation that has been contested by leaders of different faith traditions.

The Landmarks Preservation Commission of New York City (LPCNYC) says, "a landmark is a building, property, or object that has been designated by the Landmarks Preservation Commission because it has a special character or special historical or aesthetic interest or value as part of the development, heritage, or cultural characteristics of the city, state, or nation. Landmarks are not always buildings. A landmark may be a bridge, a park, a water tower, a pier, a cemetery, a building lobby, a sidewalk clock, a fence, or even a tree. A property or object is eligible for landmark status when at least part of it is thirty years old or older."[9]

I was involved at Saints Paul and Andrew Church, a designated landmark on the Upper West Side of Manhattan. This United Methodist congregation was financially strapped by the demands of the building

[7] See http://www.state.ny.us/governor/press/year99/dec30_3_99.htm.
[8] Susan Ellis, http://www.energizeinc.com/hot/01jul.html.
[9] See http://www.ci.nyc.ny.us/html/lpc/html/about/.

and wanted to make major modifications in order to attract other agencies to lease some of the space. I was retained to establish a case for modifying the building to suit the mission of the congregation. The LPCNYC did not change the designation of the church. This forced the congregation to spend money on legal proceedings and on the care of the property. An Interfaith Commission to Study the Landmarking of Religious Property (ICSLRP) was created to respond to this case. The final report of this group was prepared by the Committee of Religious Leaders of the City of New York. It concluded that the control of LPCNYC is "diverting resources dedicated to religious ministry to the non-religious cause of architectural preservation." Further, it says that the existing landmark laws put local commissions in "an unacceptable role in decisions respecting the conduct of religious ministry, which is abhorrent to our national heritage of liberty of conscience and freedom of religion." That report is dated January 26, 1982, and may be found on the Web.[10]

In 1984, the director of the Queens Federation of Churches, the Reverend N. J. L'Heureux, Jr., wrote, "A landmarks designation of a piece of property makes the aesthetic welfare of that building the top priority of the owner. The synagogue or church with a landmarked building is compelled by law to subordinate the funding of its religious ministry in order to accommodate this governmentally imposed priority. Thus, the building which was dedicated to the Glory of God for religious ministry becomes a monument to architecture. The other assets of the congregation—all contributed for ministry—must be placed fully at the disposal of this extraneous preservationist priority."[11]

Congregations should take notice of all landmarking laws before making decisions pertaining to the church building. Another issue to be aware of is when small groups organize to oppose liturgical modifications to a church.[12] These groups insist that nothing should be done to alter the interior of the church because of its architectural, artistic or historical significance. In one New York State case a group dissatisfied with the reforms of the Church tried unsuccessfully to obtain "landmark" status for the church in order to prevent any changes to the exterior as well as the interior of the building. The majority of the local

[10] See http://www.queenschurches.org/Partners/IFC/Final_Report_ Contents .htm.

[11] See http://www.queenschurches.org/Partners/IFC/GIRA2.htm.

[12] The City of Bourne, Texas v. Flores, Archbishop of San Antonio, et al. was decided on June 25, 1997. The U.S. Supreme Court struck down the Religious Freedom Restoration Act and ruled in favor of the preservationists. The Archdiocese claimed the RFRA would hinder plans to renovate the church building.

Fig. 95 *San Fernando Cathedral,*
San Antonio, TX. Architects, Rafferty Rafferty
Tollefson and Fisher Heck. Photograph by
Chris Cooper Photography.

congregation was in favor of the enhancements and noted that the real
reasons why some members objected to the liturgical adaptations had
to do with their displeasure with church reforms rather than any
honest artistic or architectural concern for the building.

Enhancing a Church for Worship. Even if a church or cathedral has
been designated a landmark (local or national), it is possible to enhance the building for worship to accommodate the current ritual life
of the congregation. The primary purpose of the church is the worship
of God. In the case of the Catholic Church, Vatican II initiated the
liturgical reforms. The manner in which the congregation worships
then has been affected by new legislation governing liturgical matters.
In order to accommodate these changes the building must be altered.

It is not easy for a landmarks commission to prevent the Church
from making liturgically related changes to the interior of a place of
worship. For example, San Fernando Cathedral in San Antonio is
listed on the National Register of Historic Places, is a registered Texas
Historic Landmark, is a contributing structure in the Main and Military Plazas National Register Historic District and is included in the
Main and Military Plazas Historic District of the City of San Antonio.

Yet, the entire cathedral complex was successfully stabilized, restored and modified to accommodate the reformed rites of the Catholic Church (fig. 95).

The key ingredient for the success in this project was the cooperation between the city government and the Church. The long-term relationship between the city officials and the pastoral leaders of the archdiocese and cathedral parish proved to be invaluable. Further, the professional design team worked diligently to carry out the project in full cooperation with all preservationist organizations.

When a specific area, artifact, architectural element or work of art inside the building has been designated a landmark, (e.g., stained glass windows) the local landmarks commission will require that the interior feature in question be restored or preserved and not removed or altered in such a way that it is no longer what it was intended to be. In the case of a place of worship owners seeking to alter the designated object or space would have to establish why the interior or exterior of a landmarked building hinders the requirements of current liturgical ritual books. Many adaptive reuse projects provide evidence that liturgical enhancements can be achieved successfully in older church or cathedral buildings without destroying the innate architectural or artistic significance of those buildings (whether or not they are landmarked).

Responsibilities of the Owners. Pastoral leaders at landmarked or historically significant churches and cathedrals have a threefold responsibility. (1) To care for the congregation and the neighbors served by that congregation. (2) To celebrate the sacramental rituals according to the current rites of the Church. (3) To care for the property.

The primary mission of every faith community is living out the gospel. This would clearly mean seeing to the true good of the congregation as well as those living in the immediate neighborhood. This mission has more to do with affordable housing, food, clothing and counseling services. The church building may be considered a low priority in these cases. In some cities church buildings actually serve as places where people can get a hot meal and a shower. Some churches and cathedrals are used as shelters.[13] Food for the human spirit is also important. All people should have an opportunity to enjoy the performing arts. Often a church or cathedral will sponsor elite events to raise money. The right thing to do would be to give complimentary

---

[13] The Cathedral of Saint John in Milwaukee provides food and shower facilities for homeless men. They also operate a shelter for women. These spaces are part of the cathedral block.

tickets to the people who frequent the soup kitchens and shelters in the neighborhoods. These inspirational and uplifting musical and artistic events should always be available to those who cannot afford a ticket to a museum or concert hall.

The second responsibility has to do with worship. Making liturgical changes to an older building that is known as an artistic treasure is extremely hard to do without experienced professionals. Because of the emotions surrounding such a building, most pastoral leaders will leave everything "just the way it is." The word "renovation" thus has come to mean a new coat of paint and new gold leafing. Is the architectural style of the building or the art inside still more important than the primary purpose of the worship space? Experience has shown that many architectural treasures among the churches in North America have been adapted to suit the liturgical life of the church today.

The third responsibility—to care for the property—can be guided by the many helpful agencies and their publications. For example, the Preservation League of New York State has a pamphlet called *How to Care for Religious Properties*.[14] Preservation agencies in other states may have similar publications.

---

[14] Michael J. Lynch, *How to Care for Religious Properties* (The Preservation League of New York State, Albany, New York, 1982). Go to http://www.preservenys.org/.

Chapter 27

Inculturation in Our Places of Worship

IT IS NO NEWS that the migration paths to North America have shifted. This situation has already affected the Church. Congregations that were formerly all white and defined by the homeland of their ancestors are much more diversified. Now they are characterized by different racial groups as well as by ethnicity. Consider that the Hispanic population in the United States is the largest minority group in the country and that people from the Pacific Islands and Asia are migrating in larger numbers than ever before. These statistics have already affected congregations that were once made up of second, third and fourth generation descendents of European families. How do our church buildings reflect the diverse cultures that now comprise these changing congregations? Further, how do these spaces resonate with the emerging cultural patterns of Generations X, Y and Z within diverse groups of people?

New members are joining the faith community where I worship. Most of them are young healthcare professionals who have moved into the area to work in local hospitals. They are Filipinos. For some of them English is a second language. Many of them speak either Filipino (Pilipino) or Tagalog. They have begun to marry and raise families. They usually come to the early liturgy on Sunday and I have noticed that they like to sit together. They have introduced me to the salutation of the Mano whereby respect is shown for elders . . . and clergy. (They bow slightly as they take the elder's hand and respectfully place it to their own foreheads.) Slowly, they are now becoming more involved in the ministerial life of this active parish. As I listen to our music and songs and look at the art in our church, I find that, so far, there is really nothing that speaks of the Filipino Catholic culture, nothing that might make these new members feel at home. Something needs to be done to acknowledge their traditions. It would be unfair to them to ask them to assimilate into the community without also expecting to learn something from them about their symbols and rituals. Such a mixing and blending of different traditions can only enrich the Church.

I remember visiting the Catholic Cathedral of the Immaculate Conception of Our Lady in Beijing in 1987. I noticed the faces on the Stations of the Cross were modeled after fair-haired Caucasians—the same as one would find in a European church. I wondered then if Catholicism is to be understood as a package deal—that the art, music, prayers and places of worship were all the same no matter where you were. The only indigenous element in the cathedral that day was the language used in the people's parts of the liturgy. It was Mandarin. The Eucharistic Prayer was said in Latin.

The great strides that have been made in the Church since the 1960s happened because of a willingness to understand and enact liturgy in a new way that is yet rooted in our traditions. This was risky business because it challenged the easy assumption that religion is something that, by its nature, does not change. The council's document on the liturgy called for a radical adaptation of the rites and stated that even in the liturgy the Church has no desire to impose a rigid uniformity in matters that do not affect the faith.[1] New customs have already begun to give the liturgy in North America a distinctive character that celebrates the diversity of the Church's membership.[2] Further, scholarly and pastoral contributions to these efforts are innumerable and have served to encourage and sustain the process of inculturation.[3] Good examples of responsible adaptation to the mixture of diverse cultural groups have been found in language, music, songs, postures, gestures, vesture and vessels. However, the tone of recent instructions for the right implementation of the liturgy is cause for concern among those working to adapt worship for an increasingly diverse church membership.[4]

[1] Constitution on the Sacred Liturgy, nos. 37–40.

[2] See Joseph P. Swain, "Inculturating Liturgical Music," in *America*, September 13, 2004, 14, for an example of the place of music in a diverse church.

[3] For example, Virgilio P. Elizondo and Timothy M. Matovina, *Mestizo Worship: A Pastoral Approach to Liturgical Ministry* (Collegeville: Liturgical Press, 1998); Mark Francis, *Multicultural Celebrations/Celebraciones Multiculturales: A Guide/Una Guía* (Oregon: OCP Publications, 2004); Anscar J. Chupungco, *Liturgical Inculturation: Sacramentals, Religiosity, and Catechesis* (Collegeville: Liturgical Press, 1992).

[4] "Varietates Legitimae," The Congregation for Divine Worship and the Discipline of the Sacraments, Vatican City, March 29, 1994; "Liturgiam Authenticam," The Congregation for Divine Worship and the Discipline of the Sacraments, Vatican City, May 7, 2001; "Redemptionis Sacramentum," The Congregation for Divine Worship and the Discipline of the Sacraments, Vatican City, April 23, 2004.

As a counterpoint Nathan Mitchell argues, "The religious imagination and its symbols . . . are inescapably connected not only to our bodies but culture activity itself." He writes, "We have to admit that the liturgical future belongs neither to academics, nor to the dwindling ranks of the ordained, nor to a coterie of authorities issuing edicts from a Vatican dicastery. The liturgical future belongs precisely to those people—of Generations X, Y, Z, and their heirs—who think, feel, imagine, dance, speak, and sing the world in ways quite different from those favored by folks who have been promoting (or lamenting) liturgical reform and renewal for the last forty years."[5]

Imaginative non-denominational congregations are responding to multi-culturalism and the needs of different age groups in creative ways. For example, Gerardo Marti writes about Mosaic, one of the largest multi-ethnic churches in North America.[6] Mosaic does not target ethnic groups but provides "havens of inclusion and commonality that render ethnic differences moot. These havens are arenas for multi-ethnic companionship, cooperation, and camaraderie that arise out of a union of creative volunteer resources and the ambitious global mission of the church. The congregation aims to reconstruct evangelical theology, personal identity, member involvement, and church governance in an attempt to create an institution with greater relevance to the social reality of a new generation."[7]

Imagination and creativity can be used to identify emerging and diverse cultures in religions like Catholicism where homogeneity was once an identifying, unifying factor. The term "inculturation" cannot be limited only to issues of liturgical practice. The cultural cues that are evolving because of age or race or ethnicity must be identified and acknowledged if the liturgy of the community and its worship environment are to be effective.

What can be done in a church building to reflect the collective customs and traditions of an emerging cultural mix especially when two or more diverse groups of people are coming together?

The first step for a congregation experiencing changes within its identity is to formally redefine itself. This can occur through a process of self-evaluation and strategic planning. When the group has a vision for itself it will be in a better position to find ways to celebrate its new identity and to express itself to the neighborhood. The first question,

[5] Nathan Mitchell, "Finding the 'Cult' in Culture—Whose Future" in *Worship*, January 2005, vol. 79, no. 1, 73, 75.

[6] Gerardo Marti, *A Mosaic of Believers: Diversity and Innovation in a Multiethnic Church* (Bloomington, IN: Indiana University Press, 2004).

[7] Taken from an online description of the book. See http://www.amazon.com.

therefore, is less about art, furnishings and interior design. It is about mission. The community should ask two hard questions of itself in this discernment process: (1) who are we and (2) what good are we doing here? The answers to these questions might be surprising.

The mission of the congregation will change as the community changes. For example, if a church that was once used by a wealthy congregation were to become home to families living at the poverty level, the first need would be an outreach center. If there is no space to house the social programs the church itself may become the community center. The people would not only worship in the church but also go there for meals, clothing, language classes, job searches, daycare. The basic challenge to the notion of a church as a place of refuge will continue to be the economy. Can the congregation support itself and its programs or will it have to seek welfare from other sources?

As the congregation goes through a period of transformation in terms of identity and mission, so too will its worship change. Soon, the question must be asked (as it must in all congregations) "does our worship environment help or hinder our liturgical practice?" Perhaps the seating plan in the church does not allow full participation of the assembly. Maybe the interior décor (colors and ornamentation) of the space clashes with the cultural nuances of the community. Possibly the artifacts, appointments and furnishings used for worship do not reflect the tastes of the congregation.

When new members are moving into an established and stable congregation it is a matter of assimilation and incorporation. As the new members get adjusted the rest of the community is obliged to include them by adapting to new music, art, language and ritual practice. In some cases, where different congregations are merging into one and the previous church properties still exist, it will be important to decide which buildings will serve them best of all in the future. Also, it will be important to have a plan for combining liturgical and artistic assets. In some situations it may be economically advantageous to close down all of the old church buildings and construct a new one.

Even though works of art, music and preaching can nourish people a church building dedicated to the underprivileged may evolve into a different place of sustenance, one that is designed and decorated in a very simple manner. And, there may not be the luxury of replacing existing art and furnishings with new things that are more reflective of the cultural background of the membership. If there is absolutely no money, the people will most likely learn to accept what is present in the church. Or, they themselves will arrange and decorate their church in ways that are pleasing to their eyes. However, if the congregation is disposed to making modifications, and has the resources to do so, then it will be wise to create a master plan for spatial modifications, art, furnishings and decorative work. This would be a written program describing what will be done in the church, who will do it, how much it will cost and how long it will take to complete the modifications. In every situation the very best design professionals should be retained to guide the process. The strength of a long-term master plan is that it can be phased according to resources. It will also guard against tacking ersatz images on the wall or incorporating something that bears no resemblance to the cultural foundations of the congregation.

Buildings reflect communities. Along with the art and artifacts they are the narratives that sustain and challenge the membership in mission and worship. As the radical adaptation of the liturgy continues thought must be given to the ways in which church buildings reflect the emerging multi-cultural character of the Church.

Chapter 28

The Architectural Style
of Church Buildings

RUSTICHELLO WROTE *The Book of Travels* with Marco Polo to record Polo's excursions to the Orient. Christopher Columbus and other explorers who read this travelogue thought the ocean east of China and India was the same body of water west of Europe. Columbus sailed west and so did Christianity. Far fetched as it may be, imagine if Catholicism found its way to the Americas by way of the Middle and Far Eastern world and the Pacific Ocean? The familiar rituals, customs, music, art, language, gestures, postures and governance of the Church might be considerably different, as would church buildings. The classical style of the Greeks and Romans, the Byzantine forms of the East, the Romanesque, Gothic, Renaissance, and later Baroque and neo-classical styles perhaps would not have served as the only models for Christian places of worship. Instead, the ziggurats and temples of the Mesopotamian plains, the pyramids of the Nile, the mosques of Iran and Iraq, the temples and stupas of India and Burma, the pagodas of China and the shrines of Japan would have provided much different foundations for Christianity to build on.

Further, imagine if the indigenous peoples of the South and Central Americas had been encouraged to build places of Christian worship using their own models? Perhaps the churches in those countries and later in the Southwestern regions of the United States would look less like the Baroque buildings of the Iberian Peninsula and more like the pyramids and temples of the Mayans, the Aztecs and the Incas.

And whatever did happen to the humble house, the original model for Christian places of worship? What if all churches were modeled not after imperialistic temples but people's homes? What if the Roman Empire were not so dominant during paleo-Christian times? What if Constantine lost that battle at the Milvian Bridge on October 28, 312?

194

Fig. 96 *Saint Francis de Sales Church, Morgantown, WV.*
Architect, Rafferty Rafferty Tollefson. Consultant, James Moudry.
Photograph by Steve Bergerson.

From a liturgical point of view, a new church does not have to emulate a particular contemporary style nor does it have to be reminiscent of another period of ecclesiastical history in order to be defined as a Catholic house of prayer. Certainly Notre Dame du Haut in Ronchamp is an important Catholic place of worship even though, for some critics, it does not "look like a Catholic church!" Every new church should, first of all, reflect the people of the faith community. The next important thing is how the whole place functions for liturgy. The design for every church then begins with the interior and how it accommodates the ritual life of the congregation. The exterior form should follow that function."[1] Better yet, as Frank Lloyd Wright would understand it, "form and function are one."[2] What the building actually looks like on the outside could depend on the land or the neighborhood architectural genre if there is one. The challenge for designers is to create original buildings where the interior and exterior harmonize. There is really no need to copy a style from another age or foreign land.

Under normal circumstances the sensitive and creative use of simple and natural materials indigenous to a region should result in the construction of a time-honored and worthy church complex. Thus, the simple, older architectural structures found in any region might very well serve as appropriate models for the style of a church. The new Saint Francis de Sales Church in Morgantown, West Virginia, was constructed on a one hundred year old dairy farm. Five new structures

[1] This well-known axiom is attributed to architect Louis H. Sullivan.
[2] John Lloyd Wright, *My Father Frank Lloyd Wright* (New York: Dover Publications, 1992) 120. Frank Lloyd Wright was a student of Louis Sullivan.

195

Fig. 97 *Richard B. Fisher Center.* Bard College, Annandale-on-Hudson, NY.
Architect, Frank Gehry.

surround the original barn (fig. 96). The interior was in keeping with the styles native to the region. It would not have been appropriate to put up a neo-Gothic or neo-classic structure in the middle of the field.

Another opinion, however, suggests that churches do not have to look like every other building in the neighborhood or the region. Certainly, in the world of public architecture, no one appears to be protective of a regional style. Consider the Richard B. Fisher Center for the Performing Arts on the campus of Bard College north of New York City. Frank Gehry's building introduced a bold dynamic into the Hudson River region. One wonders what Thomas Cole (1801–1848) the founder of the Hudson River School of Art would have to say about the titanium-clad center that appears to have been dropped into place with little reference to the natural environment (fig. 97).

Again, the cathedral in Los Angeles and the church in Tor Tre Est suggest that when a downtown neighborhood or suburban development lacks architectural distinction, a church building sometimes can serve as a counterpoint to what is already there. In Los Angeles the new cathedral sits among tired old government buildings. In Rome the new church is in a working-class neighborhood lined with high-rise apartments. In such situations the architectural style of the religious edifice may indeed be strikingly different from its surroundings. I suppose someone might even argue that a Gothic- or classical-style building might also be appropriate in these situations.

196

But the neighborhood is not the only reference for architectural style. In earlier chapters I indicated that ethnic pride was also important. In his work *Houses of God,* Peter Williams examines the built environment of religion in the United States, "its architecture, landscape, and other dimensions of its public physical aspect—with special attention to the importance of geographical and cultural region in shaping that expression."[3] Williams gives an example of the "Polish cathedral" style that emerged in Detroit and Chicago at the end of the nineteenth century. "Where most Catholic churches were built in grander or humbler variations on the Gothic and Romanesque themes popular across the country, the ambitious prelates and their loyal congregations in the Great Lakes Polonias often chose instead to make monumental statements in the Renaissance style of the mother country."[4]

Ornamentation. Architects like Mies van der Rohe and Buckminster Fuller employed the axiom "less is more" in their work.[5] But other architects argue the opposite. In the controversial book *Learning from Las Vegas,* architect Robert Venturi said that ornamentation, form and decoration should be a priority in design. He did not emphasize issues like internal layout, function or usability. Disagreeing with modernism, he said that less was not more and coined the expression, "less was a bore." The Las Vegas Strip for Venturi and his colleagues thus became a model for design brilliance.[6] Some Catholics continue to be dismayed over the lack of ornamentation or decoration in new or renovated church buildings. Part of the feeling is connected to the style employed in older churches. But ornamentation reaches beyond the world of religious architecture. In the history of humankind it would be hard to identify a group of people for whom ornamentation was not important. Ornamentation may be found in body art, clothing, paintings and buildings and is most often expressive of the trends, tastes and styles of the people of each age and region of the world. It would be most

---

[3] Peter Williams, *Houses of God: Region, Religion, and Architecture in the United States* (Chicago, IL: University of Illinois Press, 1997) xi.

[4] Ibid., 179.

[5] The saying is probably taken from Robert Browning (1812–1889) who used the expression in a poem about the painter Andrea del Sarto who addressed his wife Lucrezia, "Yet do much less, so much less, Someone says, (I know his name, no matter)—so much less. Well, less is more, Lucrezia: I am judged."

[6] Robert Venturi, Steven Izenour, Denise Scott Brown, *Learning from Las Vegas—Revised Edition: The Forgotten Symbolism of Architectural Form* (Cambridge, MA: MIT Press, 1977).

difficult to list the variation in styles of ornamentation used throughout the history of architecture.[7]

On the other hand, it is also important to discern when ornamentation is natural to a church and when it is not. Louis Sullivan often applied terra cotta designs to masonry walls. But he would insist that the ornamentation be derived from nature and that classical references be avoided.[8] History reminds us that two- and three-dimensional ornamentation varied in church buildings from region to region, age to age. It was also absent in others. Would it be right to replicate ornamentation indigenous to a particular building type from another era or region for use in a contemporary building totally different in architectural style? For example, would it be appropriate to copy a decoration from the Celtic High Crosses and incorporate it in a modern church in the midwestern region of the United States just to add ornamentation? Perhaps, yes, especially if the church serves a community with strong Irish roots. But would a stylized floral or circular motif taken from a Prairie-style home (designed to blend with the flat prairie terrain) in Wisconsin look right in a church along the Appalachian Trail? Or, should the designer find a way to decorate the construction in a more indigenous manner?

Further, does ornamentation have to be only a geometric pattern with correct proportions and colors? Can ornamentation contribute to the narrative of a faith community? Consider the decoration of some adobe churches in the southwest regions of the United States. The paintings on the walls of San José de Laguna Church in the Laguna Pueblo in New Mexico depict colorful birds resting on tombs. The birds symbolize the souls of deceased persons buried beneath the trampled earthen floor.[9] If ornamentation is to be employed in a place of worship, like the building itself, it should have something to do with the people of the community. Ornamentation (whether on walls, floors, ceilings, along friezes or in the capitals on columns) just for the sake of ornamentation would not be appropriate.

It was the correct thing to do—to add ornamentation in the renovation of the Cathedral of Christ the King in Superior, Wisconsin. The building, designed in the Romanesque style, was barren inside. Early post-conciliar renovations removed the paintings that were in the apse

[7] Read Owen Jones, *The Grammar of Ornament* (New York: Dorling Kindersley, 2001) for a review of 2,500 patterns.

[8] See http://architecture.about.com/library/bl-sullivan.htm.

[9] Thomas Drain, David Wakely, *A Sense of Mission: Historic Churches of the Southwest* (San Francisco: Chronicle Books, 1994) 40.

and transepts. The cathedral is now enhanced with mosaics depicting the Pantocrator, the Theotokos and the patron of the diocese, Saint Augustine of Hippo (fig. 98). Angels are painted on six spandrel spaces while decorative elements were added to the capitals and in the ceiling. At the same time, however, significant liturgical changes were also accomplished to accommodate the post-conciliar ritual books.

To say that ornamentation is essential in every place of Catholic worship is to misunderstand the fundamental purpose of the church or the nature of ornamentation. Further the application of ornamentation into a building that, by its very nature should not be decorated, would be inappropriate. When the Constitution on the Sacred Liturgy called for noble simplicity rather than sumptuous display it was referring to excessive decoration and the unnecessary duplication of statuary. This pastoral principle did not suggest that the great churches and cathedrals of the world be stripped of all ornamentation and decoration. It was, however, calling for moderation especially in the design of newer churches. Bernard of Clairvaux wrote about excessive decoration in church buildings in the twelfth century as did Thomas Merton in the twentieth century.[10]

Fig. 98 *Saint Augustine of Hippo.*
Christ the King Cathedral, Superior, WI.
Artisans, Conrad Schmitt Studios and Miotto Mosaics.

[10] From Bernard of Clairvaux. *Apologia to Abbot William*. As reproduced in *The Works of Bernard of Clairvaux*, Cistercian Fathers Series IA, trans. Michael Casey, O.S.C.O. (Kalamazoo, MI: Cistercian Publications, 1970) 63–66; Thomas Merton, "Absurdity in Sacred Decoration," in *Disputed Questions* (New York: Harcourt Brace & Co., 1960).

Catholic Liturgy and Architecture. What is the connection between liturgy and architectural style? In the first part of this book I offered a way of approaching the task of building or renovating a place of worship that did not begin with discussions about what the edifice should look like. Instead I suggested that other building blocks were more important and that faith communities need to wrestle with deeper issues of identity and theology before deciding on what their church should look like or how it should be laid out. Of course, all of the factors are interconnected. And, that is the main point. The whole question of what a church should look like is not only about the architectural style. It is about what the people of God look like, what they believe, and what they do.

Some will contend that there is such a thing as a Catholic type of church building, that certain building styles and interiors are more characteristic of the Catholic genre than others. It is important to recall that no one particular style of architecture was ever developed specifically to house Christian worship. Nor has the Church ever endorsed one particular style of architecture to house its worship. In fact, the history of architectural styles in North American religious buildings reveals that diversity is actually the norm and that shifts in styles over the centuries is commonplace.[11]

[11] See Jeffrey Howe, *House of Worship: An Identification Guide to the History and Styles of American Religious Architecture* (San Diego: Thunder Bay Press, 2003) and Marilyn J. Chiat, *America's Religious Architecture: Sacred Places for Every Community* (New York: John Wiley & Sons, 1997) for two well-researched sources that trace the history of religious architecture in North America.

Chapter 29

Megachurch Models

THERE IS a diocese in the Northeast where the bishop, in the 1970s, requested that every new church have a seating capacity of no more than five hundred. The bishop's thinking was based on solid liturgical principles. The Council teachings invoked full, conscious and active participation as the norm during worship. Every attempt was to be made to create environments where all worshipers could see and hear everything that occurred during the Mass. Good sight lines and excellent acoustics in the space were extremely important. The font, altar table and ambo were to be located in the space so that everyone could engage in the ritual actions without hindrance. Great distances from the ritual actions would work against the principle that proclaimed liturgy as the work of the people and would foster passivity and spectatorship.

Now these church buildings are considered inadequate not because they do not function well for the liturgy but because they are too small.[1] As great numbers of people move farther away from cities more demands are placed on sleepy farmland communities. The exodus not only affects utilities and the land (water, gas, electric, green space, roadways) but also the size of church buildings. The second reason has to do with the dwindling number of priests who are available to worship with these growing communities. Larger congregations who have small churches require several liturgies on the weekend to accommodate everyone. Some parishes have to schedule simultaneous liturgies—one in the church and another in the gym (if there is a gym and a second priest).

---

[1] Size is a relative issue. In many rural communities where the population is stable, a seating capacity of five hundred would be more than adequate.

Further, people's expectations of their worship environments are more demanding. Ample parking spaces, barrier-free accessibility, welcoming lobbies, convenient toilet facilities, childcare rooms, comfortable seats, good sight lines, good acoustics and even a cup of coffee afterward are now considered essential amenities in places of worship. Although all church buildings, large and small, should be designed or retrofitted to accommodate these expectations, some older churches are not.

As the Catholic population continues to grow and migrate to exurbia and as the number of clergy continues to decline some believe that building bigger churches in some regions is inevitable. But, are larger church buildings the answer? How big can a Catholic church be before it looks and feels like another auditorium? Will immense worship environments affect the manner in which Catholic liturgy is enacted?

What can we learn from the megachurch model? I once visited a megachurch on the outskirts of Rio de Janeiro which had a seating capacity of twelve thousand and it was filled three times each weekend! This is a country that once was 95 percent Catholic. That number is now about 80 percent as evangelical religions have managed to preach a more attractive and realistic message to the people. There are megachurches in the United States. The most famous ones are Willow Creek in South Barrington, Illinois, and Saddleback Church in Lake Forest, California. One of the largest ones is Southeast Christian Church in Louisville, which seats ten thousand in the worship center (fig. 99). The emphasis is on hospitality and ministry in these nondenominational churches. From the moment you enter the grounds you are given the feeling that someone wants you to be there. Parking attendants greet you and guide first-time visitors to convenient reserved spaces. When you enter the church building at Willow Creek, more greeters extend a welcome and are ready to answer any question and escort you to wherever you want to go.

The buildings themselves are modern, clean and unadorned. Saddleback, south of Los Angeles, takes advantage of the warm climate and much of the social activity occurs on the plaza. There are no religious symbols on or near these buildings. Signage shows you the way everywhere. The main lobby at Willow Creek is more like an atrium in a mall than a narthex in a church. Full of abundant natural light this space is a hub from which you can go to the worship center, the bookstore or the family café. The Willow Creek church also features Promiseland, which is designed for children from birth through the fifth grade. It is a safe and secure environment where the youngsters are taught Bible lessons and how to play with one another.

Fig. 99 *Southeast Christian Church, Louisville, KY.* Architect, David E. Miller, AIA.

The feel-good atmosphere prevails throughout the church building as you find your way to the amphitheatre worship center. There are no religious symbols or ritual furnishings here either. In Saddleback a large baptismal font is located outdoors. When I was there, the lines for baptism were very long. Inside, the focus is on the stage where there is a large orchestra and a single podium for the preacher. Each seat is comfortable, comparable to what you would find in a theatre. In these churches the seating capacity is in the thousands. The worship service centers on the sermon, which is often complemented by one-act plays to give the biblical texts a contemporary twist. The music and singing are reviving. The sermon is vigorous. The lack of any religious imagery does not seem to be an issue for the several thousand worshipers who attend these services. They came to hear inspirational preaching and singing. The bottom line is: Does the message connect with the worshiper on a personal level?

The second noteworthy component in the megachurch is the use of projected media, light and sound. Video monitors and acoustical speakers are mounted on walls and columns throughout the facility.

Even if you are not actually in the worship center, you can see and hear the singing and the sermon. I remember seeing a mother in a rocking chair feeding her child while watching the service on a nearby monitor. Inside, huge screens are used to project larger-than-life images of the different ministers participating in the service. The sight lines and acoustics are excellent. Some argue that the worship experience is a passive one and borders on entertainment. Although you could call the service "made for TV," the overriding and simple message is perfectly clear. Robert Hovda once wrote that homilies should be accessible and intelligible. The megachurch certainly works hard at doing just that by utilizing sophisticated communications technology.

History will tell us whether the megachurch phenomenon endures. Some studies indicate that already the children of those boomers that flocked to the megachurch as seekers are now turned off by the big box, big church service and are looking for much smaller, more intimate and personal worship experiences. These groups are now gathering in coffee houses and even taverns. Ironically, the house-church model of the early Church has now found favor with many new religions while others of us, with fewer clergy and more Catholics, are now required to build megachurches for worship.

Is there an alternative to the big box church? I use the term "big box" in describing these large buildings because, in part, architects seem to be artistically challenged when it comes to designing structures to house congregations of two to five thousand persons without making the place look like a conference hall in a convention center. From the outside the buildings with their expansive roofs appear to be characterless. Value engineering has resulted in cost-saving solutions to building design but the beauty of the place suffers. Roof lines, glazing and materials tend to be more efficient than architecturally pleasing. Mathew Comfort writes: "The most common design form (for megachurches) seems to be the adaptation of blending function over form in direct proportion to a church's budget. The economic advantages of Modernist architectural design and advanced building materials are understandably appealing."[2]

No doubt the Catholic Church could learn more about using advanced technology and the ministry of hospitality to spread the gospel message. And, it can do so without eschewing the symbol system that is essential in the celebration of the sacraments. It does not have to

[2] Mathew Comfort, "A 'New' Way of Thinking," in *Church Business,* September 2002, 26. Go to www.churchbusiness.com.

resort to the megachurch model that fosters passivity during worship. What are some options?

1. The first obvious solution is not an architectural one. The celebration of Eucharist is necessary for the survival of the Church. The population of the Catholic Church continues to grow.[3] The number of priests continues to dwindle at record rates.[4] In terms of church buildings, the leadership currently is focused on two solutions to this problem: One is to close or merge parishes in areas where the congregation is moving out or cannot maintain the property. The other is to build much larger churches where the population is growing. This seems to be a logical way to deal with the problems of clergy shortage and shifting, growing populations.

2. Another alternative would be to build smaller churches to house the day-to-day needs of the community and then *rent* larger spaces for weekends and liturgies during Christmas and the Triduum. This practice is already common in many dioceses where the cathedral is not adequate for such gatherings as synods, ordinations and marriage anniversary liturgies. This practice has become popular with Jewish congregations. At one time the idea was to build a sanctuary that would accommodate the small congregations that gather for Shabbat services and other life-cycle events. Such a sanctuary would then expand by opening to other spaces, usually a banquet hall, which would provide additional seating for the high holy days. Now, instead of such large buildings, the trend is to provide adequate spaces for the regular worshipers but then rent a large place for the high holy days. Although the ambience can never be the same as that found in the synagogue, the application of imagination and creativity can often result in beautiful environments.

3. The final alternative here is to concentrate on building bigger churches that will house a desired number of worshipers but also maximize the full engagement of the assembly. These two objectives will not be easily achieved. The challenge is to design churches that will spatially draw all people close to the ritual furnishings in a way that both clergy and laity can carry out their rightful liturgical roles. Good acoustics, ample lighting, varied color palettes and appropriate

[3] *The CARA Report*, ibid. (vol. 10, no. 1, Summer 2004) reports that the 2004 Catholic population in the United States is 63.3 million or 23 percent of the total population.

[4] Ibid. There were 35,925 diocesan priests in the United States in 1965. There are 28,967 in 2004.

use of the media arts are essential in this regard. However, it also means that the entire assembly will have to be arranged in concentric circles around the altar table so the distances between clergy, laity and ritual furnishings are reduced significantly. Inevitably this means that new churches will have to be more sociopetal in plan than sociofugal. The truly centralized plan, which I discussed earlier, is a good design solution when the church seating capacity has to be very large. By its very nature a sociopetal plan can draw large numbers of people into the liturgical action. Even if the capacity requirements are such that the circular plan has to include a second level (a mezzanine directly accessible to and from the main level), this would be a far better solution for engaging maximum numbers of people in worship than stretching out a structurally rectilinear processional plan.

In the end it must said that the megachurch model is not a good one for the Catholic Church. No matter how hard liturgy planners will try to effectively carry out the rituals in such vast spaces the symbol system will suffer and passivity will reign. Such is the nature of gathering in a big arena for any event.

Since the beginning of Christianity, the Eucharist has sustained the baptized faithful. Even when there were no church buildings as we know them Christians kept gathering in their homes and elsewhere. In fact, they survived terrible persecutions for close to three hundred years without church buildings or large properties. Perhaps the solution today is to re-imagine possibilities for the Church rather than focus on church buildings. Maybe there is some way to tap into the Spirit of God to find directions for the future.

Chapter 30

Cathedral Models

WHAT WOULD the state of church art and architecture be in the post-conciliar era if temporary arrangements in all cathedrals were to be given a final form? "Some of the provisionary solutions still in use are liturgically and artistically unsatisfactory and render difficult the worthy celebration of the Mass."[1] There are few studies regarding the state of cathedral architecture in the United States.[2] Over the past forty years many cathedrals have been modified to suit the liturgy but it appears that most of them have only been redecorated.[3] This unfinished business has contributed to some of the confusion surrounding art and architecture for worship today. How does one explain to a local congregation the importance of transforming their place for worship when the cathedral in the diocese has not been so transformed?

Is there a way to re-imagine cathedrals as models in their dioceses? There are various answers. One could measure the value of the cathedral simply because it is there and symbolizes the unity in the diocesan community as it gathers about the bishop. Another assessment could

---

[1] *The Third Instruction on the Correct Implementation of the Constitution on the Sacred Liturgy*, Congregation for Divine Worship and the Discipline of the Sacraments (Vatican City, September 5, 1979, no. 10).

[2] Bryan T. Froehle, *National Cathedral Profile, Summary Report*, December 1997, is summarized as "Study Profiles the Nation's Cathedrals" (Georgetown University, Center for Applied Research in the Apostolate, vol. 3, no. 3, Winter 1998). See also the compendium by David A. Kavelage, *Cathedrals of the Episcopal Church in the U.S.A.* (Cincinnati: Forward Movement Publications, 1993).

[3] Only four new Catholic cathedrals have been built in the United States since the Council: Saint Mary's, San Francisco (1971), Immaculate Conception, Burlington, Vermont (1977), Our Lady of Guadalupe, Dodge City, Kansas (2001) and Our Lady of the Angels, Los Angeles (2002). As of this writing, new cathedrals for the dioceses of Houston, Oakland and Orange are being planned.

be made in light of the good work that the cathedral community is doing regardless of the structural, liturgical or aesthetic condition of the building. Many congregations are proactive for social justice in their urban neighborhoods. If the cathedral is the model for all other churches, should the mission of the cathedral's faith community be a model for all parishes in the diocese?[4] The commitment to the arts is a third touchstone. Cathedrals have traditionally been places for the performing arts. Often this means that the building has an exceptional pipe organ that is used for worship as well as concerts.

Outreach and education are vitally important in cathedral communities. But what of the space and the liturgy? Is the cathedral a model? I will select a single feature found in various cathedrals in an effort to create a medley of ideas that collectively might create a good example for others. This is not to say that each of these cathedrals is perfect or that others are not noteworthy. Each project should be carried out in a unique way to reflect the local church.

The enhancements realized in some cathedrals have been more dramatic than in others. However, in every case, the liturgical implications are significant. The re-formation that has occurred in each of these buildings points to the transformations that are taking place in the respective congregations. I will draw largely from projects I have had the privilege of working on because I am most familiar with them.

Gathering Places. In many countries cathedrals are located on a large public plaza in the center of a city. San Francisco in LaPaz and San Marco in Venice are fine examples. The grid layout of most North American cities creates a different sense of place.[5] It is rare to find a cathedral located on a prominent square or plaza in the United States. Saint John's in Milwaukee, Saint Louis in New Orleans and San Fernando in San Antonio are notable exceptions. Most cathedrals are built along city streets with little or no space for an outdoor plaza or gathering areas of any sort. While some streets are grand (e.g., Saint Patrick's on Fifth Avenue), others are quite unremarkable.[6]

San Fernando Cathedral is located on the main plaza of San Antonio. The popular River Walk now has a landing near the plaza

[4] *Ceremonial of Bishops,* Congregation for Divine Worship and the Discipline of the Sacraments, Vatican City, September 14, 1984, no. 46.

[5] For more insights on city planning see Witold Rybczynski, *City Life* (New York: Touchstone, 1995) and Joseph Rykwert, *The Seduction of Place: The History and Future of the City* (New York: Vintage Books, 2002).

[6] *Ceremonial of Bishops,* ibid., no. 54 calls for a "gathering place of people." This could be a suitable hall or square.

Fig. 100 *Courtyard.* San Fernando Cathedral.
Architects, Rafferty Rafferty Tollefson and Fisher Heck.
Consultant, Richard Vosko. Photograph by Chris Cooper Photography.

Fig. 101 *Plaza.*
Cathedral of Our Lady of the Angels, Los Angeles.
Architect, Rafael Moneo and Leo A. Daly.
Photograph by
Julius Schulman and David Glomb.

giving the cathedral even more exposure to tourists. The cathedral community takes advantage of the plaza and the surrounding city streets especially for the Holy Week services. The planning program for the restoration of the cathedral included razing the existing residence and office building to make room for a Cathedral Center and an intimate courtyard (fig. 100). The center now includes a gift shop, a museum, various meeting rooms and the sacristies. As the cathedral continues to take advantage of the public spaces, it also invites everyone into the inner courtyard.

Our Lady of the Angels Cathedral in Los Angeles is situated on a 2.5-acre landscaped plaza that is complete with a children's garden, an Easter Fire hearth, various works of public art, a shrine in honor of Our Lady of Guadalupe and a Native American memorial (fig. 101).

Fig. 102 *Commons.* Saint John the Evangelist Cathedral, Milwaukee, WI. Photograph by KOROM.COM.

The café, gift shop and cathedral offices are located in the Conference Center, which is part of the complex. The plaza, which can accommodate up to six thousand people, is used for liturgies, concerts and dinners. The climate in both of these cities makes it possible to use these outdoor spaces for socializing as well as liturgical events.

Rochester, New York, is a different story. The climate is not conducive to year-round outdoor gatherings. The planning program for the Sacred Heart Cathedral included linking the adjacent residence with the cathedral to create a large narthex or commons that has ample space for various social gatherings and liturgical processions. It also includes a suite of offices. The front steps of the cathedral were expanded to create a large terrace to facilitate ease of movement in and out of the building. Likewise the plan for Saint John's Cathedral in Milwaukee links it with other rehabilitated structures on the block to create a complete center offering outreach programs, pastoral counseling, educational opportunities as well as prayer and worship (fig. 102).

Baptismal Font. By now most renovated cathedrals should have baptismal fonts that allow for the options contained in the current ritual books.[7] The fonts in the cathedrals in San Antonio, Memphis, Seattle, Louisville and Milwaukee incorporate older historic pedestal

---

[7] Ibid., no. 52 indicates that the cathedral should have a baptistery that is designed and equipped "in keeping with the provisions of the Roman Ritual." This reference implies that the font should allow for baptism by immersion.

Fig. 103 *Old with new font.*
Saint John the Evangelist Cathedral, Milwaukee, WI.
Designer, James Shields. Consultant, Richard Vosko.
Photograph by KOROM.COM.

Fig. 104 *New font.*
Sacred Heart Cathedral, Rochester, NY.
Architect, Williamson Pounders, Inc. and
LaBella Assoc. Consultant, Richard Vosko.
Photograph by © 2005 Tim Wilkes/www.timwilkes.com.

fonts into the design of larger pools that allow for baptism by immersion (fig. 103). The pedestal font in San Antonio was a 1759 gift from Charles III, King of Spain. The cathedrals in Los Angeles, Colorado Springs, Dodge City, Superior and Rochester have brand new fonts (fig. 104). In these cases a single large font was designed to accommodate both infant and adult baptism by immersion. The fonts in all these cathedrals are located in or near the main entrance to the worship space, the best location in terms of history, symbolism and function.

Altar Table. The most significant decision of any cathedral or church project has to do with the location of the altar table. This ritual furnishing is the symbol of Jesus Christ.[8] A good way to express this Christo-centric symbolism is to place the table as far as possible into the midst of the assembly. Saint James Cathedral in Seattle was the first post-conciliar cathedral renovation in the United States to place

---

[8] *Dedication of a Church and an Altar* (Congregation for Divine Worship and the Discipline of the Sacraments, Vatican State, May 29, 1977) no. 16.

Fig. 105 *Plan before renovation.*
Saint James Cathedral, Seattle, WA.

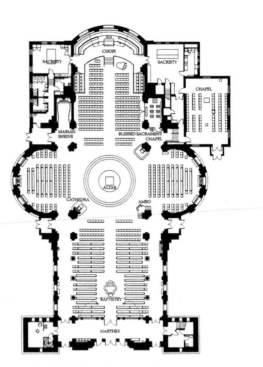

Fig. 106 *Plan after renovation.*
Saint James Cathedral, Seattle, WA.
Architect, Bumgardner Architects.
Consultant, Richard Vosko.

the altar table exactly in the center of the room (figs. 105 and 106). In this case, the altar table now rests directly beneath the cupola of the cruciform cathedral. The building expresses quite clearly that every worshiper is called to participate in the offering of the Eucharist. This project shows clearly that older cathedrals and churches can be adapted to honor the liturgical reforms in creative and imaginative ways without ignoring the architectural aesthetics or symmetry of the building (fig. 107).

Since then other cathedrals have been effectively adapted for worship by moving the altar table into the center of the faith community. The Cathedral of Saint John in Milwaukee was reordered to comply with the spirit of Vatican II. In the original plan the congregation was quite removed from the altar. The first pew was about forty feet away from the altar table. The principles of the sociopetal setting discussed earlier were applied during the renovation. The table was moved into the assembly area to achieve better sight lines. The fixed pews were replaced with movable chairs for increased flexibility. As in every renovation project improved lighting and acoustics helped to create a worship space that would foster more participation in the rites.

Fig. 107 *Sacred Heart Cathedral, Rochester, NY.*
Architect, Williamson Pounders, Inc. and LaBella Associates.
Consultant, Richard Vosko.

Cathedra. There are imaginative ways to reflect the hierarchical nature of the Catholic Church without separating the clergy from the laity or positioning the clerics in places of honor that appear regal or majestic. Although there are different ministries and offices in the Church,[9] the assembly is the primary symbol of the Body of Christ. Even as clergy have specific responsibilities to preside at the liturgy there is no reason why they could not take their places with the assembly. The practical task is to provide good sight lines so that all liturgical ministers, presiders included, can be seen and heard. The bishop's chair can be placed with the assembly as a symbol of service and leadership.[10] The traditional location for the cathedra was derived from the basilican plan where the chair for the emperor or regional administrator was placed at the far end of the apse. The liturgical reforms have prompted a different approach: the plan of a church should reflect harmony in the Church where clergy and laity are perceived as a sacrament of unity.

The Milwaukee cathedral makes a most important statement about the distinctions between the clergy and laity. Before the renovation the

[9] Constitution on the Sacred Liturgy, no. 26.
[10] *Ceremonial of Bishops*, nos. 42, 47.

213

Fig. 108 *Cathedra*. Saint John the Evangelist Cathedral, Milwaukee. Photograph by KOROM.COM.

archbishop sat in a stately throne that was remote from the assembly. Now the *cathedra* is part of the circular layout where the archbishop sits "first among equals" (fig. 108). Such an equitable seating plan does not diminish the importance of the bishop or priest presiding at worship. The design of the chair *is* quite distinct from the assembly seats, but this proximate location creates an environment that expresses solidarity among all worshipers and states quite clearly that liturgy is not something performed or delivered to the congregation by clergy.

Blessed Sacrament Chapel. The location of the tabernacle was reviewed in a previous section. Guidelines for the location of the tabernacle are evident and clear. The question is how well do cathedrals serve as models for the placement of the tabernacle. A distinct chapel is preferred, especially in those cathedrals or churches that are frequently

214

Fig. 109 *Chapel of Eucharistic Reservation.* San Fernando Cathedral, San Antonio, TX.
Architects, Rafferty Rafferty Tollefson and Fisher Heck.
Consultant, Richard Vosko. Artisan, Leonardo Soto Recendiz.
Photograph by Chris Cooper Photography.

visited by pilgrims or used for the performing sacred arts.[11] Here are
two cathedrals that provide worthy examples for placing the taber-
nacles in one of the two places now listed in current legislation.[12] There
are other good models as well.

San Fernando Cathedral in San Antonio is a French Gothic building (1868) that was attached to the colonial church (1738–1750). The
altar table is now in the midst of the nave in the newer section. The
colonial section is cruciform in shape and serves as a place for private
devotion as well as overflow seating. The planning program indicated
it was time to complete the apse and transepts with three new *retablos.*
The central one, crafted by artisans from Mexico City, is now the
fitting place for the tabernacle (fig. 109).

    [11] Ibid., no. 49 and *Holy Communion and Worship of the Eucharist Outside of Mass*
(Congregation for Divine Worship and the Discipline of the Sacraments, Vatican
State, June 21, 1973) no. 9.
    [12] *General Instruction of the Roman Missal* (Congregation for Divine Worship and
the Discipline of the Sacraments, Vatican State, March 17, 2003) no. 315. See also
Built of Living Stones (Washington, DC: United States Catholic Conference of Bish-
ops, November 16, 2000) nos. 74–80, and *Our Place of Worship* (Ottawa: Canadian
Conference of Catholic Bishops, 1999) 35.

Fig. 110 *Chapel of Eucharistic Reservation.*
Sacred Heart Cathedral, Rochester, NY.
Artisans, Conrad Schmitt Studios.

This cathedral is a good model for locating the tabernacle behind the altar table in an area where Mass is not celebrated. In each example the tabernacle is far enough away from the altar table and the space itself is conducive to private adoration of the sacrament.

In the Sacred Heart Cathedral in Rochester, the tabernacle was relocated to an unused baptistery where three glorious stained glass windows were hidden from full view of the assembly. Walls were taken down and the ceiling was reconstructed to create a spacious, barrier-free and well-lighted chapel for the reserved Sacrament that is visible from the assembly. The canopy over the tabernacle was once over the *cathedra* (fig. 110).

In the Los Angeles cathedral the chapel for the reserved Eucharist is distinct from the cathedral proper and cannot be seen from the assembly at all. However, there is no doubt about the location of the chapel, which is easily reached from the main ambulatory or the assembly area. The tabernacle is a ten-foot tall obelisk. Two doors swing open wide to reveal the sacrament in its container. Again, angels are carved into the inside panels of these doors like sentinels. Light from the alabaster windows inside the chapel embraces the visitor in a place of quiet prayer and adoration (fig. 111).

Unlike most churches, cathedrals can be used for a variety of activities some of which are quite civic in nature. It makes good sense to reserve the sacrament in distinct chapels in these places in accordance with time-honored traditions.

216

Flexibility. Flexibility is not a common household word in North American cathedrals. There are some notable exceptions like Saints Peter and Paul in Indianapolis, Saint John the Evangelist in Milwaukee and Sacred Heart in Rochester. However, there seems to be an aversion to the practice of regularly re-arranging the worship space. This is an unusual attitude in a church where flexibility was the norm for most of its history. Architect Edward A. Sövik would often remark how odd it was for a pilgrim church to fix its seats to the ground! The best examples of flexibility in worship places today are found in Episcopalian cathedrals. Here are two examples.

Both the Christ Church Episcopal Cathedral in Saint Louis and the Cathedral Church of the Saviour in Philadelphia have been re-ordered with maximum flexibility in mind. Both buildings are located in urban settings and have struggled to stay open and alive. I discussed the Christ Church Cathedral in an earlier chapter. The cathedral in Philadelphia also has all movable seats and ritual furnishings. Only the baptismal font (which accommodates baptism by immersion) and the *cathedra* (which is part of a curved stone bench in the apse) are fixed to the floor. New lighting and acoustical systems also complement the array of liturgical rituals and performing arts events now held in this cathedral.

People marvel at the great cathedrals of the world mostly because of their impressive architecture grandeur and artistic details. Many of them are also home to incredible collections of art. However, these are secondary considerations. How many cathedrals have been carefully transformed to resonate with the liturgical reforms of our time?

Fig. 111 *Tabernacle.*
Cathedral of Our Lady of the Angels, Los Angeles, CA.
Photograph by Julius Schulman and David Glomb.
Sculptor, Max DeMoss.

217

Chapter 31

Stewardship

WHY SPEND money on church buildings when it could be given to poor people? The answer is usually couched in scriptural terms about stewardship and the most often cited passage is the one about Mary using fragrant oils to anoint the feet of Jesus (Mark 14:3; Matt 26:7 and John 11:55). Some complained that the money should have been given to the poor. Jesus answered by saying the "poor will always be with you, but I will not." Certainly injustice will always be with us. We hope for peace. We do works of justice to bring some peace to those who are powerless. Is the construction and decoration of a place of worship an act that has any merit in terms of serving homeless, hungry, oppressed people? Should there be a moratorium on all church building and renovation projects until there is not one single homeless or hungry person in the community? Is there a way to provide houses for worship that are consistent with the gospel? Mother Teresa was once asked if the Vatican Museum should sell its artistic treasures. After some contemplation her reply indicated that all people need beauty. Not to have it would create a "different kind of poverty."[1]

The Mission of the Church. There are different ways to address the concern about spending money on churches. The first has to do with the mission of the congregation. It is true that Jesus never gave instructions to build temples for the worship of God. Everything he said and did implied that the way to salvation was to love God and neighbor. No doubt the primary concern of the early Christians was to live out what Jesus taught them by ministering to those in need. They were not concerned about building places of worship. They were worried

---

[1] A story told about Mother Teresa when she visited an exhibition of art from the Vatican collection at the Forty-first International Eucharistic Congress held in Philadelphia in 1976.

about surviving. To follow the earliest Christian tradition, then, would be to feed the hungry, provide housing for the homeless, and help the sick before all else. Building a church would not be a top priority.

Today, before deciding to build or renovate a church it should be determined whether or not the faith community is seriously committed to doing good work. The work of the Gospel is something that the Church should be doing no matter where it worships. Should the congregation then decide to build or renovate a church, that mission, whatever it is, should not be compromised. This is why I ask the questions at the start of every project, "Who are you and what good are you doing?" The rationale for building a church is deeply connected with the mission of the Church. Where we pray shapes our prayer and how we pray shapes the way we live. Good stewardship in any project begins in the early planning meetings where one of the first questions that should be asked has to do with how the place of worship fits into the overall mission of the Church.

The Rationale for Building a Church. It may be easy to justify constructing places that are used all week long like a school or office building. But why spend money on a church that may be used only four or five hours a week? Couldn't we read the Scriptures by ourselves or in small groups? Couldn't we share the bread of life and cup of eternal blessing anywhere we gather? Couldn't we praise and give glory to God anytime, anywhere, alone or with others? What is the relationship between buildings and mission? New evangelical churches are now open 24/7 in order to serve their congregations. Brad Eisenmann writes, "Going to church has become far more than a Sundays-only priority. Increasingly, churches are humming with activity that's intended to address the needs of a broad demographic, twenty-four hours a day, seven days a week. It's no longer uncommon to find an Internet café or a commuter station attached to a church and, of course, childcare has been based at many churches for a number of years. In addition, there may be events scheduled nearly every night of the week, which can include meetings, seminars and ministry gatherings sponsored by the church as well as those sponsored by outside organizations using the church's space."[2]

As Christians, we develop properties to house those programs that are designed to serve people. Here are some examples. We build schools to house educational programs. We build hospitals to provide health care. We build offices that are equipped to accommodate differ-

---

[2] See Brad Eisenmann, "24/7 Congregations Have Changed the Nature of Church Construction," in *Church Business* (September 2003).

ent ministries. We build housing for persons who are homeless or abused or elderly. And we build places of prayer so we can gather as a faith community to worship the God who calls us to do good work on this planet. Human beings function best in groups. The Church is a collective of persons called by God to do good work on earth, to help humanity realize the gracious presence of God. Human beings require shelter to live, work, study, play and pray. No matter what part of the world we live in, shelter is something we cannot do without. So, the practical reason for building a church is to provide shelter for whatever it is we must do as faithful sojourners—including public prayer.

The less practical rationale has to do with inspiration. The beauty that can be inherent in a work of art, a piece of music or an architectural place can energize people. Traditionally, churches, like synagogues and mosques, are architectural and artistic places that can inspire good works just as good homilies and music can. Imagine a society without works of architecture, art or music. Imagine if there were no museums, concert halls or religious buildings. This concern for interacting with beauty as a way of being nurtured must not be overlooked when building or renovating a place of worship. Some will protest the construction or renovation of a church or cathedral. In these cases leaders should be certain that no one in the community suffers because of the cost of the project. In turn, while it is not expected that the church building will provide a financial windfall, there is hope that it will inspire the faith community to excel in good works. Creating and sustaining church buildings that are beautiful to behold is one issue. Building and renovating churches to accommodate the reformed liturgy is another. One must question the use of money used to redecorate a church without also making modifications to facilitate the celebration of the sacraments according to the reformed liturgical books.

What to Spend on Shelter. But does the need for shelter even while worshiping justify spending money on elaborate churches? Buildings designed to last a long time are not cheap. The cost of materials and labor today can consume even the most carefully made budgets. Responsible stewardship begins here. It is not wise to construct something that will not last. Even the simplest structures have to be designed according to certain standards. Measuring up to present-day codes can consume a lot of the budget. Constructing a church that is environmentally sensitive and energy efficient is very costly. To remove asbestos or retrofit a church according to current seismic codes is time consuming and expensive. Preserving or restoring buildings or works of art requires enormous funding. Millions of dollars have been spent just to make sure they are stabilized. When the basics are taken care of, there is not a lot of money left over to spend on art, ritual furnishings, ornamentation and decoration.

How does a congregation figure out how much to spend? Typically the answers depend on whether there are any savings, if there is property to be sold, if a donor has made a generous gift and how successful the fund-raising campaign is. The community has to decide on the size of the project and the quality of materials to be used and how much they can afford to do. Once again, the owner can only choose two of three factors: scope of the work, quality of the materials and the size of the budget. The architect chooses the third. For example, if the congregation wants a lot of building constructed with the best materials, the architect will determine the budget.[3]

There is a caveat that cannot be overlooked when trying to save money on a church project. Many denominations today shop around for the least expensive way to build a new church. They are attracted to the "all-in-one" church building companies that provide complete design-and-build services including fund raising for a guaranteed maximum price. How can these companies afford to do this? They standardize the product to bring the cost down. One company, for example, will provide plans for a church to fit any size and any budget.[4] This approach can be a real threat to the process of building a place of worship that uniquely reflects the faith community. Further, all of the concern over art and ornamentation and architectural style is for naught.

Collaborative Projects. There are some ways to approach the expenditure of monies for the construction or renovation of a church without compromising the mission of the congregation. One approach is to network with other congregations in the neighborhood regardless of denomination or faith tradition. Perhaps some programs are similar. There would be no need to duplicate properties to house these programs. For example, why should three or four congregations sponsor day-care programs in their own facilities when they could consolidate funds, personnel and budgets to provide one good program? Similarly, why does every single Catholic congregation have to provide religious studies programs for their members? Wouldn't it be more

[3] I first heard this equation from Herman Hassinger, FAIA, a prolific church builder.

[4] See Mathew Comfort, *Megachurches*, op. cit., 170.

221

efficient to coordinate teachers and learning spaces rather than duplicate? It may be more difficult when trying to share worship centers.
Nevertheless, such consolidation efforts, even though unpopular, are
already going on in some Catholic dioceses.

Creating a Sense of Stewardship. This term has been used a lot lately
in different churches in an effort to encourage members to commit a
portion of their resources to support the mission of their Church. This
commitment is designed as an alternative to the weekly "drop a dollar
in the basket" habit. The foundation is scriptural. The Hebrew Bible
indicates that giving a tenth of one's resources was obligatory and
may have been connected to worship. The tithes consisted of animals
and fruits of the earth (Gen 14:20; 28:20; Exod 23:19; 34:26; Lev 2:14).
The New Testament indicates that Jesus spoke about tithing (Luke
18:12 and Matt 23:23). Paul uses the word "generosity" in appealing to
the Corinthians to make sacrifices willingly for the common good.

Most capital campaigns designed to raise money for renovation or
building churches use the stewardship model. The basic idea is to
create a larger context for the project that has to do with the overall
mission of the congregation. Thus, a contribution to a new or renovated church building project is seen as an ongoing commitment to
supporting the good work of the community and not just a one-time
pledge or donation. This model has worked well in some cathedral
projects that are funded as part of a diocesan-wide capital campaign
where a portion of the monies is set aside for the cathedral building,
one of many projects subsidized by the campaign.

Partnering with a Habitat for Humanity Project. I have often recommended to a congregation that, while they are building or renovating
their church, they commit to building a new house as partners with
Habitat for Humanity or some other organization dedicated to building homes for families living at or below the poverty level. Habitat for
Humanity[5] is a non-profit, non-denominational Christian housing
organization. Houses are sold at no profit, with no interest charged on
the mortgage. Homeowners and volunteers build the houses under
trained supervision. Individuals, corporations, faith groups and others
provide financial support in addition to actually working on the house.
There is a sense of goodwill when a congregation finishes building
a new home for a needy family and at the same time dedicates or
re-dedicates its church. In Albany, for example, it now costs about
$65,000.00 to build a new home for a family of four with Habitat for

[5] For more information go to http://www.habitat.org.

Humanity. This is 1 percent of what it would cost to build a new church to seat fifteen hundred people in some parts of the United States.

An alternative gesture would be to increase the building budget in order to make a substantial gift to a local charity or peace and justice organization. The Saint Vincent de Paul Society or Social Action committee in the congregation could organize this campaign within a campaign.

Twinning with a Community in a Developing Country. "Twinning" is a word that is now used across the globe to describe the relationships between communities in First World countries and those in developing nations. There are no statistics of the numbers of congregations in North America that are already sharing resources with a parish, school or hospital in the Third World countries. In some cases an entire diocese will select a country. For example, the Diocese of Richmond twins with churches in Haiti. The objectives are listed on the diocesan website.[6]

- To develop a sense of solidarity for both our sisters and brothers in Haiti and the members of our diocesan communities

- To provide a sense of the universality of Christian community for both partners

- To discover ways in which members of our Virginia communities can share their time and talent with the people of our Haitian twins, and to facilitate that sharing

- To discover ways in which members of our Haitian twins can share their faith and hope with people of Virginia, and to facilitate that sharing

- To be an advocate for the people of Haiti in the U.S. and to support the actions of the U.S. that will improve the quality of life for Haitians

- To provide sharing of the material wealth of our Virginia twins with our Haitian twins, as we listen to their needs and desires

Once again, a congregation that is not parochial about its mission will find a way to serve other countries. If a faith community can afford to spend millions to build a new church or to fix up an older one then surely it must have the resources to help others in distant lands, not to mention the poor in local communities.

[6] See http://www.richmonddiocese.org/haiti/hat122.htm for more information on this diocese's program.

Other commitments can be made to help balance out the money being spent on building and renovation projects: fixing up the local neighborhood, adapting a highway to keep clean, transporting inner-city youths to play on spacious grounds of a wealthy suburban parish, opening a food pantry or a used clothing outlet, staffing soup kitchens, inviting street people to classy cathedral concerts.

Chapter 32

Environmental Stewardship:
An Ethical Concern

LIVING CLOSELY together on this globe as it twirls through space demands responsibility not only for keeping peace among humans but
also for being stewards of God's creation. But the distractions on earth
are confusing. Susan Henshaw Jones wrote that the United States is
experiencing "intense growth in and around cities and unfortunately,
the development that such growth entails is often at odds with the
natural environment."[1] This concern is one that should be shared by
the Church as it continues to build and renovate churches both in the
suburbs and cities. The Catholic bishops began to address this issue
with their Environmental Justice Program in 1993. This program "calls
Catholics to a deeper respect for God's creation, and to engage parishes
and dioceses in activities aimed at dealing with environmental problems, particularly as they affect the poor."[2] The impact of this program
as it relates to church construction and renovation projects remains to
be seen.

Many non-religious national and international groups are also
dedicated to addressing ecological and environmental concerns. There
are wonderful opportunities for religious organizations to partner with
these pro-active movements to protect the environment from abuse.
This responsibility is an important component of the stewardship
issues discussed previously. How this task translates into the building
or renovation of a worship space is the concern in this section.

---

[1] Susan Henshaw Jones, "Foreword," in *Big and Green: Toward Sustainable Architecture in the 21st Century*, ed. David Gissen (New York: Princeton Architectural
Press, 2003) 6.

[2] See http://www.nccbuscc.org/sdwp/ejp/.

Principles of Sustainability. Sustainability is a key word in the world of architecture. Nicholas Roberts writes that spaces for worship affect and are affected by three components. (1) The social aspect addresses how people can sustain one another. (2) The economic part questions whether people have enough money to survive. (3) The third facet deals with the environment. Roberts suggests that solutions occur within the intersection of all three.[3] Gary Gardner writes in the Worldwatch Paper 164, "The effort to build a sustainable world could advance dramatically if religious people and institutions and environmentalists and advocates of sustainable development were to embrace each other's central concerns."[4] He claims that religion has the power, the people, the money and the interest in serving the larger community to make a difference.

In 1993 the non-profit, non-governmental United States Green Building Council (USGBC) was founded. "It was created by a coalition of building industry and professional interests with the goal of promoting high performance design in the national built environment marketplace."[5] The most significant accomplishment of the USGBC was the development of the Leadership in Energy and Environmental Design (LEED) Green Building Rating System in 1998. It is a voluntary, consensus-based national standard for developing sustainable buildings. The council represents all segments of the building industry. LEED standards are currently available for new construction and major renovation projects and existing building operations. LEED was created to define "green building" by establishing a common standard of measurement, to promote integrated, whole-building design practices, to recognize environmental leadership in the building industry, to stimulate green competition, to raise consumer awareness of green building benefits and to transform the building market.[6]

But what is green building? "Environmentally responsible" seems to be the consensus when it comes to defining a green building. When LEED evaluates a building, it numerically gauges how well a building performs in five categories: site sustainability, water efficiency, energy efficiency, content of materials and resources, indoor environmental

---

[3] Nicholas W. Roberts, *Building Type Basics For Places of Worship,* series ed. Stephen A. Kliment (New York: John Wiley & Sons, Inc., 2004) 97.

[4] Gary Gardner, *Invoking the Spirit: Religion and Spirituality in the Quest for a Sustainable World,* ed. Jane Peterson (Wordwatch Paper 164, December 2002) 5.

[5] From notes by architect Bill Beard, Colorado Springs, CO.

[6] Go to the United States Green Building Council website for more information http://www.usgbc.org.

quality and innovative design.[7] Specific green building ideas that could be applied in any church building or renovation project include the following:

1. Choose a building site with access to natural light and shade.

2. Implement day lighting, sloped ceilings, inner windows/atriums and other passive solar techniques.

3. Use recycled content products.

4. Reduce dependence on air conditioning and heating systems by using natural light and shade as well as building features to store heat and cold.

5. Avoid building materials with volatile organic compounds.

6. Pay attention to the culture and history of the community as well as past uses of the building (if it is a renovation).

7. Research financial incentives and regulations that facilitate green design.[8]

Where is there information on how to go about achieving some of these ideas? The *Field Guide for Sustainable Construction* contains very thorough chapters dealing with the site, material selection, waste prevention, recycling, energy conservation, building and material reuse, construction technologies, health and safety and indoor environmental quality. This guide could be adapted for use for almost any building project including places of worship.[9]

What are the costs related to green building? Does the owner save any money in the long term? Constructing a better long-term building will undoubtedly cost more up front. How much will it cost and how long will it be before those costs are recuperated? These questions are difficult to answer because of regional factors such as cost of labor and materials and how many of the five criteria have actually been carried out in the project. Architect Maggie McInnis points out, "An energy efficient church can also reduce operation costs. Thus, potentially it could cost less than a church built using current conventional designs."[10]

[7] Ibid.

[8] See http://www.greenbiz.com.

[9] *Field Guide For Sustainable Construction*, The Partnership for Achieving Construction Excellence, Pennsylvania State University, 2004.

[10] From notes by architect Maggie McInnis, Ann Arbor, MI.

Obstacles. Paul Hawken wrote that sustainable architecture is about re-imagining the relationship between human beings and living systems.[11] He added that architects must learn to work with systems, that they must design new ways of living and working in which buildings play a key role. However, according to Bill Beard, sustainability comes from the client-owner's value system more than that of the architects. Also, certain obstacles have to be dealt with before sustainability becomes a household word in the church. They include: unfamiliarity with the principles and rules of sustainability, fear of taking on a green church building project and the lack of leadership. Beard suggests that certain strategies will help eradicate the obstacles. First, he says, there must be a reverence for creation that will lead to "life-centered" behavior in the lives of church members. Then, it will be important to envision how places of worship can support such a life-centered attitude, and vice versa. He acknowledges that to create such a church building will require a very different process involving major transformations in the way people think about their lives and their houses of prayer. Finally, Beard believes that the impetus for change will occur from the bottom up, one community and one place at a time. The degree of difficulty for visionaries will be great, but the rewards will be greater.[12]

"Sustainability will not happen," writes Larry L. Rasmussen, "nor itself be sustained, if no living inner world roughly accords with the outer world we seek. Moral, spiritual, and cultural dimensions are as crucial as technical ones." He continues, "Broadly speaking, what is untenable for sustainability is a moral universe that circles human creatures only and does not regard other creatures and earth as a whole as imposing moral claims we need worry over."[13] This compelling statement suggests that a whole new understanding of church architecture is required in order to harmonize building systems with life systems and that the worshipers meeting in those churches need also to ponder how responsible they are for their own lives and as stewards of the planet created by the very God they are praising. McInnis adds, "Because the church building is a focal point in the community it could influence the neighborhood. The Church's leadership in sustainable architecture could eventually transform outlying areas as well."[14]

[11] Paul Hawken, "Preface," in *Sustainable Architecture* (New York: Earthpledge Foundation, 2000) xi–xii.

[12] Bill Beard, ibid.

[13] Larry L. Rasmussen, *Earth Community Earth Ethics* (Maryknoll: Orbis Books, 2000) 344.

[14] McInnis, ibid.

Toward Solutions. There are different ways to create green places of worship. One is to retain design professionals who are LEED accredited or sensitive to the issues of sustainability. Some congregations are already doing it. In one example, architect David Arkin designed Mary, Star of the Sea Church in Gualala Point, California, by taking advantage of the site and the atmosphere. The church, built of Douglas fir, "fuses climate, atmosphere and site." It is perched on a crest and fits neatly into a niche in the rock formations to blend in with the environment. The building has features that take advantage of the prevailing winds to cool the structure in the summer. In the winter, the concrete floor retains heat from the sun to warm the space. "Green technology was used to connect the terrestrial with the transcendental."[15] Choice of materials is another way toward green building. Bill Beard served as architect for the eighty-seat Pax Christi Chapel in Highland Ranch, Colorado, which was constructed of straw bale and plaster in 1997. It has a stucco exterior, plaster interior and a concrete floor with radiant heat. There is no air conditioning. These materials have been used for over a century in the construction of pioneer homes in places where there were no trees. With a good foundation and roof, a plaster finish, straw-bale building could last indefinitely. This energy efficient and non-toxic material is known for its breathability and acoustical quality. While not appropriate for every church project, straw bale is one example of a material that is environmentally friendly.[16]

Networking. Another way to approach a project with sensitivity to the environment and the incorporation of energy-efficient designs and materials is to join an organization to raise the consciousness of the congregation. The Maine Council of Churches' Environmental Justice Program works in partnership with the Maine Interfaith Power & Light Company to "advocate green electricity from renewal sources."[17] This group is part of the National Religious Partnership for the Environment. The founding members of this organization include the U.S.

[15] James Wines, *Green Architecture* (New York: Taschen, 2000) 121–22.

[16] Straw-bale construction uses baled straw from wheat, oats, barley, rye and rice in walls covered by stucco. Straw bales are traditionally a waste product, which farmers do not till under the soil, but do sell as animal bedding or landscape supply due to their durable nature. In many areas of the country, it is also burned, causing severe air quality problems. It is important to recognize that straw is the dry plant material or stalk left in the field after a plant has matured, been harvested for seed, and is no longer alive. See http://www.greenbuilder.com/sourcebook/strawbale/html.

[17] "Maine Churches Add Environmentalism to Ministries," in the *New York Times*, July 17, 2004, B6.

Conference of Catholic Bishops, the National Council of Churches of Christ, the Coalition on the Environment and Jewish Life, and the Evangelical Environmental Network. The objective is to "integrate care for God's creation throughout religious life: theology, worship, social teaching, education, congregational life, and public policy initiative. We seek to provide inspiration, moral vision, and commitment to social justice for all efforts to protect the natural world and human well being within it."[18] Anne Burt, the director of the council, indicated "people are beginning to see saving the planet through a faith journey."[19]

Funding. One of the concerns about sustainable architecture is the up front cost of incorporating LEED standards into a building or renovation project. Funding sources if they exist will vary. The New York State Energy Research and Development Authority (NYSERDA) is one good example.[20] Not-for-profits and private institutions including churches, synagogues and mosques are eligible. The only requirement is that applicants must be building owners served by electric utilities participating in the New York Energy $mart programs. NYSERDA offers technical assistance to evaluate and design energy saving options. It gives cash back for installation of cost-effective electric efficiency measures in new or renovated buildings. It also provides additional incentives for green buildings and solar technologies.[21] Similar programs may exist in other communities.

Many congregations may not see the immediate benefits of creating green places of worship and will continue to ignore environmental and energy related issues when building or renovating a church. The larger religious or spiritual understanding of creation may help. Church buildings are constructed to house the programs designed to serve people. Worship is one of those activities. The church building then should be designed to reflect the mission of the congregation. It must function so the people can carry out that mission. Caring for all of creation is part of caring for human beings. Constructing or renovating a church building without paying attention to the guidelines and standards presented by agencies concerned with sustainable architecture is a grave error.

[18] See the website for the National Religious Partnership for the Environment at http://www.nrpe.org.

[19] "Maine Churches Add Environmentalism to Ministries," ibid.

[20] For more information go to the New York State Energy Research and Development Authority website http://www.nyserda.org.

[21] New York State Energy Research and Development Authority, "New Construction Program Handout."

Afterword

Arnold Toynbee studied the rise and fall of different primitive and higher societies.[1] Writing about the characteristics each group held in common during periods of growth, transition and decline he cautioned, "What is past is prologue." By this he urged that history can and often does repeat itself and that the wise student today will learn from this pattern. In doing so measures can be taken to avoid mistakes made in the past. In these situations, according to Toynbee, imagination and creativity are essential but often missing.

Similarly, the Church has grown into a powerful institution. Now it is going through a challenging time of transition. The old paradigms are changing. The future of the Church will depend not only on respecting tradition but also using the imagination. The objective is to build upon foundations in order to rise to new heights. This is why all matters pertaining to worship are important. We have learned that the liturgical life of the Church is both a source and a summit. The roots are well known but the destination is not. The quest just might be found in the journey.

The primary purpose of a church is clearly that of a meeting house, a home for the assembly. It is a center for public prayer and human sustenance. In this sense God's house is our house. Robert Hovda wrote, "Each Church gathers regularly to praise and thank God, to remember and make present God's great deeds, to offer common prayer, to realize and celebrate the kingdom of peace and justice. That action of the Christian assembly is liturgy."[2]

It is my hope that this book will help those working in the disciplines of liturgy, architecture and the arts to re-imagine the environment for worship.

---

[1] Arnold Toynbee, *A Study of History*, abridgement by D. C. Somervell (London: Oxford University Press, 1947 and 1957).

[2] *Environment and Art in Catholic Worship*, op. cit., 9.

Glossary

Ambo—a reading desk. Once referred to as the pulpit. Often called a lectern.

Apse—a domed or vaulted end of the church in the shape of a circle or polygon traditionally located at the east end of the building.

Cathedra—the bishop's chair in the cathedral.

Champlevé—refers to the etched area on metal that is filled with enamel.

Chancel—that part of the church between the nave and the apse end.

Charrette—a term used to describe a session when an intense effort is made to finish developing a design.

Clerestory—the upper section of a church above the aisle roof. Windows at this level allow light into the church.

Fibonacci Sequence—a series of numbers where each number is equal to the previous two numbers, (e.g., 1, 1, 2, 3, 5, 8, 13, 21). The sequence is noticed in many parts of nature.

Fresco—a method of painting on either dry or wet plaster.

Iconostasis—in Eastern churches a screen separating the sanctuary and nave. It contains doors and images of holy men and women.

Intaglio—a term used to describe the process of making prints from incised metal plates that have ink in the grooves.

Intrado—that building part that is beneath an arch or vault.

Mosaic—a decorative image made of small pieces (tesserae) of stone, glass or tile.

Narthex—a porch or lobby in a church.

Nave—that part of the church reserved for the congregation. Distinguished from the sanctuary or presbyterium reserved for the clergy. In a centralized plan these spaces are merged.

Pendentive—a spherical triangle between a circular dome and a square base upon which rests the dome.

Presbyterium—in the Catholic Church a term used to define the area in a church reserved for the clergy.

Program—a document describing the needs and expectations of the congregation pertaining to the church building.

Proxemics—the study of the relationship of people to objects, furnishings and other people in the surrounding environment.

Reliquary—a container for keeping or displaying relics.

Repoussé—a method of making a metal relief by hammering a sheet of metal from the backside.

Reredos—traditionally a decorative screen or backdrop behind the altar table.

Retablo—the Spanish word for retable, the structural and decorative elements of a *reredos*.

Rood screen—a decorative screen beneath the rood (cross) at the intersection of the nave, transepts and choir. Separates the nave from the chancel or choir area of the church.

Sanctuary—traditionally that part of the church where the altar table is located.

Santero—an artist who creates *santos*.

Santos—simply painted wooden sculptures of holy people.

Sociofugal—the term used in the study of proxemics to describe a spatial arrangement where the rows of seats are all facing in one direction.

Sociopetal—the term used in the study of proxemics to describe a spatial arrangement where the seats are arranged in a circular pattern facing inward.

Stoup—a small dish for the holy water usually located near the doors. Today the baptismal font at the main entrance has replaced the stoups.

Tabernacle—the container used for the reservation of the holy Eucharist.

Tapestry—a textile whereby threads are woven into a warp (vertical threads at the top and bottom of a loom). The result is a colorful image.

Transepts—traditionally the north-south arms of a cruciform church that intersect with the nave and the chancel.

Documents and Instructions

Built of Living Stones; Art, Architecture and Worship. Washington, DC: United States Conference of Catholic Bishops.

Ceremonial of Bishops (Collegeville: Liturgical Press, 1989).

Constitution on the Sacred Liturgy, December 4, 1963.

Dedication of a Church and an Altar, Sacred Congregation for Worship and the Discipline of the Sacraments, May 29, 1977.

Dies Domini, Pope John Paul II, May 31, 1998.

Directory on Popular Piety and the Liturgy, Congregation for Divine Worship and the Discipline of the Sacraments, Vatican City, December 2001.

Directory for Sunday Celebrations in the Absence of a Priest, Congregation for Divine Worship and the Discipline of the Sacraments, June 2, 1988, no. 40.

Ecclesia De Eucharistia, Pope John Paul II, April 17, 2003.

Environment and Art for Catholic Worship (Washington, DC: United States Conference of Catholic Bishops, Publications Office, 1978) no. 29.

General Instruction of the Roman Missal (Washington, DC: United States Conference of Catholic Bishops, Publications Office, 2003).

Letter to Artists, Pope John Paul II (Chicago: Liturgy Training Publications, 1999).

"Liturgiam Authenticam," The Congregation for Divine Worship and the Discipline of the Sacraments, Vatican City, May 7, 2001.

Mane Nobiscum Domine, October 7, 2004 John Paul II.

Novo Millenio Ineunte, January 6, 2001, Pope John Paul II.

Redemptionis Sacramentum, Congregation of Divine Worship and the Discipline of the Sacraments, March 25, 2004.

Varietates Legitimae, The Congregation for Divine Worship and the Discipline of the Sacraments, Vatican City, March 29, 1994.

List of Illustrations and Credits

Every effort has been made to correctly identify images used in this book as well as photographers and other professionals who may have been involved in a project. All photographs were taken by me except where noted. Permission to use other works was obtained where necessary. However, errors are inevitable. I apologize for any oversights.

Chapter 2: *Imagination and Creativity*

1. *Cathedral of Our Lady of the Angels, Los Angeles, CA.* Architect, Rafael Moneo and Leo A. Daly. Photograph by Julius Schulman & David Glomb.
2. *Saint Francis Assisi, Taos, NM.*
3. *Dio Padre Misericordioso, Tor Tre Teste, Italy.* Architect, Richard Meier. Photograph: © Alan Karchmer/Esto. All rights reserved.

Chapter 8: *Later Movements in Church Architecture*

4. Plan. *San Stefano Rotundo, Rome.*
5. Plan. *St. Peter's Basilica, Rome.* After Etiene Dupérac's sketch of Michelangelo's plan.
6. Plan. *Sternkirche project, Berlin.* Architect, Otto Bartning.
7. Plan. *St. Joseph Church, Le Havre, France.* Architect, August Perret.
8. *Holy Intimacy.* Rudolf Schwarz.
9. *Holy Departure.* Rudolf Schwarz.
10. *St. Martin de Porres, Cleveland, OH.* Architect, Richard Fleischman.
11. *St. John's, Collegeville, MN.* Architect, Marcel Breuer. Consultant, Frank Kacmarcik.
12. *St. Louis Priory, St. Louis, MO.* Architect, Gyo Obata with Pier Luigi Nervi. Consultant, William Schickel. Photograph by J. Philip Horrigan.

Chapter 9: *Theology*

13. *Rectilinear hierarchical plan graphic.*
14. *Centralized relationship plan graphic.*

35. *Commons.* Hoversten Chapel, Augsburg College, Minneapolis, MN. Architect, SMSQ Architects.

Chapter 16: *The Church Baptizes*

36. *St. Jean Vianney Church, Baton Rouge.* Trahan Architects. Consultant, Marchita Mauck. Photograph by Timothy Hursley.
37. *St. Francis de Sales, Morgantown, NV.* Architect, Rafferty Rafferty Tollefson. Consultant, James Moudry. Photograph by Steve Bergerson.
38. *Font.* St. Charles Borromeo Church, Kettering, OH. Basin by Architectural Glass Art, Inc.
39. *Old font with new.* Christ the King Cathedral, Superior, WI. Architect, Architectural Resources, Inc. Artisan, St. Paul Fabricating & Decorating. Consultant, Richard Vosko.
40. *Ossuary.* Woodcarver, Jefferson Tortorelli. Photograph by Christopher Dow.
41. *Holy Oils Repository.* Christ the King Cathedral, Superior, WI. Artisan, St. Paul Fabricating & Decorating. Designer, Richard Vosko.

Chapter 17: *The Church Celebrates the Eucharist*

42. *Holy Thursday—Corpus Christi University Parish Church, Toledo, OH.* Architects, The Collaborative. Consultant, Richard Vosko. Photograph by Anne Spenny.
43. *Movable chancel modules.* Christ Church Episcopal Cathedral, St. Louis, MO. Architect, Kurt Landberg, AIA. Photograph by Kurt Landberg.
44. *Christ Church Episcopal Cathedral, St. Louis.* Photograph by Kurt Landberg.
45. *Christ Church Episcopal Cathedral, St. Louis.* Photograph by Kurt Landberg.
46. *Movable chairs.* St. Thomas More, Paducah, KY. Fabricators, New Holland Furniture.
47. *Pews.* Unkown.
48. *St. Catherine Church, DuBois, PA.* Architect, Edward Sövik, SMSQ. Consultant, Richard Vosko.
49. *Cathedra.* The Philadelphia Cathedral, Philadelphia, PA. Architect, George Yu. Consultant, Richard Giles.
50. *Chair.* Old St. Joseph Church, St. Norbert College, DePere, WI. Architect, James Shields, Hammel Green Abrahamson. Consultant, Richard Vosko.

Chapter 18: *Music Ministry, Instruments and Acoustics*

51. *Choir behind assembly.* St. John the Baptist, New Freedom, PA. Architect, Crabtree Rohrbach & Associates. Consultant, Richard Vosko.

52. *Choir in midst of assembly.* St. Benedict the African Church, Chicago, IL. Architect, Belli & Belli.
53. *Choir and Pipe Organ.* St. Hugo of the Hills, Bloomfield Hills, MI. Architect, Harley Ellington Pierce Yee & Associates. Consultant, Robert E. Rambusch.

Chapter 19: *The Role of Art in Worship*

54. *New stone altar.* Sacred Heart Cathedral, Rochester, NY. Architects, Williamson Pounders, Inc. and LaBella Associates. Consultant, Richard Vosko.
55. *Our Lady of Guadalupe and Jesus Christ Word and Sacrament Retablos.* San Fernando Cathedral, San Antonio, TX. Artisan, Leonardo Soto Recendiz. Photo by Chris Cooper Photography.
56. *Wooden altar.* Ss. Peter and Paul Cathedral, Indianapolis, IN. Architect, Edward A. Sövik, SMSQ Architects.
57. *Cross in Center.* Corpus Christi University Parish Church, Toledo, OH. Architects, The Collaborative. Consultant, Richard Vosko. Photo by Anne Spenny.
58. *Relics under table.* St. Benedict College Chapel, St. Joseph, MN. Architect, Hammel Green Abrahamson. Consultant, Frank Kacmarcik.
59. *Fixed ambo.* Sacred Heart Cathedral, Rochester, NY. Artisan, Brian DiBona, Oakwood Custom Woodworking.
60. *Movable ambo.* Old Saint Joseph Church, DePere, WI. Fabrication, Rick Findora. Designer, Richard Vosko.
61. *Accessible ambo.* St. Margaret of York Church, Loveland, OH. Architect, Cole + Russell Architects. Consultant, Joanne Kepes.
62. *Cross.* Otavalo, Ecuador
63. *El Cristo Negro and 18th century font,* San Fernando Cathedral, San Antonio, TX. Photo by Chris Cooper Photography.
64. *Crucifix.* Cathedral of Our Lady of the Angels, Los Angeles. Artist, Simon Toparovsky. Photograph by Julius Schulman & David Glomb.
65. *Processional crucifix.* Christ the King Cathedral, Superior, WI. Sculptor, Alexander Tylevich. Cross by St. Paul Fabricating & Decorating. Designer, Richard Vosko.
66. *Processional candlesticks.* Cathedral of Our Lady of the Angels, Los Angeles. Artist, Marirose Jelicich. Photograph by Julius Schulman & David Glomb.
67. *Dedication candle.* San Fernando Cathedral, San Antonio.
68. *Chasuble.* Designer, weaver, Katreen Bettencourt.
69. *Nylon canopy.* Grace Cathedral, San Francisco, CA. Textile artist, Nancy Chinn.
70. *Book repository.* Christ the King Cathedral, Superior, WI. Artisans, St. Paul Fabricating & Decorating. Designer, Richard Vosko.

71. *Retablo.* Santa Maria de la Paz, Santa Fe, NM. Altar screen by Marie Romero Cash, bulto of Santa Maria de la Paz by Félix López.

72. *Our Lady of Guadalupe.* Cathedral of Our Lady of the Angels, Los Angeles. Artist, Lalo Garcia.

73. *Mary the Teacher.* Corpus Christi University Parish Church, Toledo, OH. Sculptor, Steve Shields.

74. *Mary with Child.* Sacred Heart Cathedral, Rochester. Sculptor, Matteo Moroder.

75. *Communion of Saints tapestries.* Cathedral of Our Lady of the Angels, Los Angeles. Artist, John Nava. Photograph by John Nava.

76. *Communion of Saints tapestries.* Photograph by John Nava.

77. *Dancing Saints.* St. Gregory of Nyssa Church, San Francisco, CA. Artist, Mark Dukes.

78. *Kateri Tekakwitha.* Christ the King Cathedral, Superior, WI. Sculptor, Sister Margaret Beaudette, S.C., DePaul Sculpture Studio.

79. *Station of the Cross.* St. Joseph Church, East Millstone, NJ. Artist, Charles Wells.

80. *Station of the Cross.* Cathedral of Our Lady of the Angels, Los Angeles. Sculptor, Christopher Slatoff.

81. *Iconostasis.* Unknown.

Chapter 20: *Light and Color and Glass*

82. *Cathedral of Our Lady of the Angels, Los Angeles.* Photo by Julius Schulman & David Glomb.

83. *St. John Church, Hopkins, MN.* Architects, Rafferty Rafferty Tollefson. Consultant, Frank Kacmarcik.

84. *Rose window.* Neue Wallfahrtskirche Maria, Königin des Friedens, Neviges, Germany. Architect, Gottfried Böhm.

85. *Chapel Window.* United States Catholic Conference, Washington, DC. Artist, David Wilson.

Chapter 21: *Chapels*

86. *Interfaith Chapel.* Miami Valley Hospital Interfaith Chapel, Miami Valley, OH. Architect, Orin Group. Designer, William Schickel.

86a. *Oratory in Holy Rosary Church.* St. Amant, LA. Trahan Architects. Photo by Tim Hursley.

87. *Oratory tabernacle.* Old St. Joseph Church, DePere, WI. Architect, Hammel Green Abrahamson. Consultant, Richard Vosko.

88. *Chapel of Eucharistic Reservation.* Christ the King Cathedral, Superior, WI. Artisan, St. Paul Fabricating & Decorating. Metalwork, Rick Findora. Designer, Richard Vosko.

89. *Chapel of Eucharistic Reservation.* Mepkin Abbey, Moncks Corner, SC. Architects, Hammel Green & Abrahamson. Consultant, Bro. Frank Kacmarcik.
90. *Reconciliation chapel screen.* St. Thomas More, Paducah, KY. Designer, James F. Williamson. Consultant, Richard Vosko.

Chapter 22: *Memorial Places*

91. *Contemporary Saints.* Solanus Casey Center, Detroit, MI, Architect, Hammel Green Abrahamson. Sculpture by Karen Atta. Exhibition by DMCD. Consultant, Richard Vosko.
92. *Columbarium.* Metropolitan Community Church, Washington, DC. Architect, Suzane Reatig.
93. *Columbarium and Labyrinth.* St. Joseph Church, Richardson, TX. Architects for design, Landry and Landry, Architects & Planners and Architects of Record, Good, Fulton, and Farrell, Inc. Photograph by Donald L. Fischer.
94. *Memorial wall.* Corpus Christi University Parish Church, Toledo, OH. Architect, The Collaborative.

Chapter 26: *Preserving and Enhancing Older Churches and Cathedrals*

95. *San Fernando Cathedral, San Antonio, TX.* Architects, Rafferty Rafferty Tollefson and Fisher Heck. Photo by Chris Cooper Photography.

Chapter 28: *The Architectural Style of Church Buildings*

96. *St. Francis de Sales Church, Morgantown, WV.* Architect, Rafferty Rafferty Tollefson. Consultant, James Moudry. Photograph by Steve Bergerson.
97. *Richard B. Fisher Center, Bard College, Annandale-on-Hudson, NY.* Architect, Frank Gehry.
98. *St. Augustine of Hippo.* Christ the King Cathedral, Superior, WI. Artisans, Conrad Schmitt Studios, Miotto Mosaics.

Chapter 29: *Megachurch Models*

99. *Southeast Christian Church, Louisville, KY.* Architect, David E. Miller, AIA.

Chapter 30: *Cathedral Models*

100. *Courtyard.* San Fernando Cathedral. Architects, Rafferty Rafferty Tollefson and Fisher Heck. Consultant, Richard Vosko. Photo by Chris Cooper Photography.

101. *Plaza.* Cathedral of Our Lady of the Angels, Los Angeles. Photograph by Julius Schulman & David Glomb.
102. *Commons.* St. John the Evangelist Cathedral, Milwaukee, WI. Photograph by KOROM.COM.
103. *Old with new font.* St. John the Evangelist Cathedral, Milwaukee, WI. Designer, James Shields. Consultant, Richard Vosko. Photograph by KOROM.COM.
104. *New font.* Sacred Heart Cathedral, Rochester, NY. Architect, Williamson Pounders, Inc. and LaBella Assoc. Consultant, Richard Vosko. Photo by © 2005 Tim Wilkes / www.timwilkes.com.
105. Plan before renovation. *St. James Cathedral, Seattle, WA.*
106. Plan after renovation. *St. James Cathedral, Seattle, WA.* Architect, Bumgardner Architects. Consultant, Richard Vosko.
107. *Sacred Heart Cathedral, Rochester, NY.* Architect, Williamson Pounders, Inc. and LaBella Associates. Consultant, Richard Vosko.
108. *Cathedra.* St. John the Evangelist Cathedral, Milwaukee. Photograph by KOROM.COM.
109. *Chapel of Eucharistic Reservation.* San Fernando Cathedral. Architects, Rafferty Rafferty Tollefson and Fisher Heck. Consultant, Richard Vosko. Artisan, Leonardo Soto Recendiz. Photo by Chris Cooper Photography.
110. *Chapel of Eucharistic reservation.* Sacred Heart Cathedral, Rochester, NY. Artisans, Conrad Schmitt Studios.
111. *Tabernacle.* Cathedral of Our Lady of the Angels, Los Angeles, CA. Sculptor, Max DeMoss. Photograph by Julius Schulman & David Glomb.

Selected Resources

In addition to the references listed throughout the book, these sources may be helpful.

Books

Ackerman, Diane. *Deep Play.* New York: Random House, 1999.

Adams, William Seth. *Moving the Furniture: Liturgy, Theory, Practice and Environment.* New York: Church Publishing, 1999.

Artress, Lauren. *Walking the Sacred Path: Rediscovering the Labyrinth as a Spiritual Tool.* New York: Riverhead Books, 1995.

Bachelard, Gaston. *The Poetics of Space.* Trans. Maria Jolas. Boston: Beacon Press, 1958.

Barrie, Thomas. *Spiritual Path, Sacred Place.* Boston: Shambala, 1996.

Gans, Herbert J. *Popular Culture and High Culture: An Analysis and Evaluation of Taste.* New York: Harper Collins, 1974.

Giles, Richard. *Re-Pitching the Tent: Reordering the Church Building for Worship and Mission: Revised and Expanded Edition.* Collegeville: Liturgical Press, 2000.

Hayward, John F. *Through the Rose Window: Art, Myth and the Imagination.* Boston: Skinner House, 2002.

Jackson, John Brinckerhoff. *A Sense of Place, A Sense of Time.* New Haven: Yale University Press, 1994.

Kammen, Michael. *American Culture American Tastes.* New York: Alfred A. Knopf, 1999.

Kieckheffer, Richard. *Theology in Stone: Church Architecture from Byzantium to Berkeley.* New York: Oxford University Press, 2004.

Kostof, S. *A History of Architecture: Settings and Rituals.* New York: Oxford University Press, 1985.

Kunstler, J. H. *The Geography of Nowhere: The Rise and Decline of America's Man-Made Landscape.* New York: Simon & Schuster, 1993.

Leidy, Denise Patry, and Robert A. F. Thurman. *Mandala: The Architecture of Enlightenment.* Boston: Shambala, 1998.

Lundquist, John M. *The Temple: Meeting Place of Heaven and Earth.* New York: Thames and Hudson, 1993.

Mann, A. T. *Sacred Architecture.* Rockport, MA: Element Books, 1993.

Matthews, Thomas F. *The Clash of Gods: A Reinterpretation of Early Christian Art.* Princeton: Princeton University Press, 1993.

Mauck, Marchita. *Shaping a House for the Church.* Chicago: Liturgy Training Publications, 1990.

Miles, Margaret R. *Image as Insight: Visual Understanding in Western Christianity and Secular Culture.* Boston: Beacon Press, 1985.

Morrill, Bruce T., ed. *Bodies of Worship: Explorations in Theory and Practice.* Collegeville: Liturgical Press, 1999.

Pennick, Nigel. *Sacred Geometry: Symbolism and Purpose in Religious Structures.* New York: Harper & Row, 1980.

Postman, Neil. *Building a Bridge to the Eighteenth Century: How the Past Can Improve Our Future.* New York: Alfred A. Knopf, 1999.

Postrel, Virginia. *The Substance of Style: How the Rise of Aesthetic Value Is Remaking Commerce, Culture and Consciousness.* New York: Harper Collins Publishers, 2003.

Principles for Worship. Evangelical Church in America. Minneapolis: Augsburg Fortress, 2002.

Runkle, John Ander, ed. *Searching for Sacred Space: Essays on Architecture and Liturgical Design in the Episcopal Church.* New York: Church Publishing, 2002.

Santayana, George. *The Sense of Beauty.* New York: Dover Publications, 1955.

Schloeder, Steven J. *Architecture in Communion: Implementing the Second Vatican Council through Liturgy and Architecture.* San Francisco: Ignatius Press, 1998.

Seasoltz, Kevin. *Sense of the Sacred: Theological Foundations of Christian Art and Architecture.* New York: Continuum Books, 2005.

Sommer, Robert. *Tight Spaces: Hard Architectures and How to Humanize It.* Englewood Cliffs, NJ: Prentice-Hall, 1974.

Swan, James A. *Sacred Places: How the Living Earth Seeks Our Friendship.* Santa Fe: Bear & Co., 1990.

Tanizaki, Jun'ichiro. *In Praise of Shadows.* Trans., Thomas Harper and Edward Seidensticker. New Haven, CT: Leete's Island Books, 1977.

Vosko, Richard S. *Designing Future Worship Spaces.* The Meeting House Essays. Chicago: Liturgy Training Publications, no. 8, 1996.

Walton, Janet. *Art and Worship: A Vital Connection.* Collegeville: Liturgical Press, 1991.

West, Cornell. *Democracy Matters: Winning the Fight Against Imperialism.* New York: Penguin Press, 2004.

White, James F., and Susan J. White. *Church Architecture: Building and Renovating for Christian Worship.* Nashville: Abingdon Press, 1988.

White, Susan. *Art, Architecture and Liturgical Reform: The Liturgical Art Society (1928–1972).* New York: Pueblo Publishing, 1990.

Wolfe, Alan. *The Transformation of American Religion: How We Actually Live Our Faith.* New York: Free Press, 2003.

Wuthnow, Robert. *Creative Spirituality: The Way of the Artist.* Berkeley: University of California Press, 2001.

Videos

Churches for Common Prayer: Buildings for the Liturgical Assembly. Episcopal Church Building Fund, 812 Second Ave., New York, NY.

Lift Up Your Hearts. Chicago: Liturgy Training Publications, 1992.

Say Amen To What You Are. Chicago: Liturgy Training Publications, 1992.

Signs of Grace. New York Landmarks Conservancy, 141 Fifth Ave., New York, NY 10010, 1993.

Stauffer, S. A. *Re-examining Baptismal Fonts.* Collegeville: Liturgical Press, 1991.

This Is The Night. Chicago: Liturgy Training Publications, 1992.

The Roman Catholic Mass Today. Chicago: Liturgy Training Publications, 1992.

The Word of the Lord. Chicago: Liturgy Training Publications, 1992.

We Shall Go Up With Joy. Chicago: Liturgy Training Publications, 1992.

Gather Faithfully Together. Chicago: Liturgy Training Publications, 1992.

Soul of the City (Alma Del Pueblo). J. M. Communications, 1402 Banks St., Houston, TX 77006.

Index

A **BOLD** number indicates a photograph or a graphic.
The letter "C" indicates located in the color section of the book.

329